校企联合编写

MACROECONOMICS
宏观经济学讲义

英文版

刘 玲　蔡依平　戎如香　主　编
佟大木　彭争光　李安波　副主编

上海财经大学出版社
上海学术·经济学出版中心

图书在版编目(CIP)数据

宏观经济学讲义 = Macroeconomics：英文 / 刘玲，蔡依平，戎如香主编. -- 上海：上海财经大学出版社，2025.1. -- ISBN 978-7-5642-4514-6

Ⅰ.F015

中国国家版本馆CIP数据核字第2024ZK5524号

责任编辑：江　玉
封面设计：贺加贝

宏观经济学讲义
Macroeconomics
（英文版）

刘　玲　蔡依平　戎如香　主　编
佟大木　彭争光　李安波　副主编

上海财经大学出版社出版发行
（上海市中山北一路369号　邮编200083）
　　网　　址:http://www.sufep.com
　　电子邮箱:webmaster@sufep.com
全国新华书店经销
江苏凤凰数码印务有限公司印刷装订
2025年1月第1版　2025年1月第1次印刷

787mm×1092mm　1/16　18印张　352千字
定价:78.00元

CONTENTS

1 **GDP: Measuring Total Output and Total Income** / 001

　Learning Objective / 001

　Key Points and Exercises / 001

　1.1　What is macroeconomics? / 001

　1.2　Measurement of GDP / 002

　1.3　The three approaches to measuring GDP / 005

　1.4　Real GDP and nominal GDP / 013

　1.5　Other measures of total production and total income / 015

　1.6　The limitations of real GDP / 017

　Case Study / 019

　Terms and Concepts / 021

　Problems and Applications / 021

　Answers to Problems and Applications / 026

2 **Unemployment and Inflation** / 030

　Learning Objective / 030

　Key Points and Exercises / 030

　2.1　Measurement of unemployment / 030

　2.2　Types of unemployment / 035

　2.3　What factors determine the employment rate? / 038

　2.4　Economic cost of unemployment / 040

2.5 Measures of price level: CPI and PPI / 041

2.6 Correcting economic variables for the effects of inflation / 046

2.7 The effect of inflation / 049

Case Study / 051

Terms and Concepts / 055

Problems and Applications / 056

Answers to Problems and Applications / 061

3 **Economic Growth, the Financial System, and Business Cycles** / 066

Learning Objective / 066

Key Points and Exercises / 066

3.1 Long-run economic growth / 066

3.2 Saving, investment, and the financial system / 070

3.3 The business cycle / 074

Case Study / 077

Terms and Concepts / 080

Problems and Applications / 081

Answers to Problems and Applications / 084

4 **Long Run Economic Growth** / 086

Learning Objective / 086

Key Points and Exercises / 086

4.1 Economic growth over time and around the world / 086

4.2 What determines economic growth? / 088

4.3 Economic growth policies / 090

Case Study / 093

Terms and Concepts / 096

Problems and Applications / 097

Answers to Problems and Applications / 100

5 Determining the Level of Aggregate Expenditure in the Economy / 101

Learning Objective / 101

Key Points and Exercises / 101

5.1 An introduction to the aggregate expenditure model / 101

5.2 Aggregate expenditure / 102

5.3 The determinants of the four components of aggregate expenditure / 106

5.4 Graphing macroeconomic equilibrium / 113

5.5 The algebra of macroeconomic equilibrium / 117

5.6 The multiplier / 119

Case Study / 128

Terms and Concepts / 129

Problems and Applications / 130

Answers to Problems and Applications / 136

6 The IS-LM Model / 141

Learning Objective / 141

Key Points and Exercises / 141

6.1 What is the IS-LM model? / 141

6.2 The simple aggregate expenditure model / 143

6.3 The goods market and the IS curve / 144

6.4 The money market and the LM curve / 151

6.5 The short-run equilibrium / 161

6.6 Explaining the fluctuations with the IS-LM model / 164

6.7 Summary of the IS-LM model / 170

Case Study / 171

Terms and Concepts / 173

Problems and Applications / 174

Answers to Problems and Applications / 179

7 Aggregate Demand and Aggregate Supply Analysis / 184

Learning Objective / 184

Key Points and Exercises / 184

   7.1 The aggregate demand and aggregate supply model / 184

   7.2 Why is the aggregate demand curve downward sloping? / 186

   7.3 From the IS-LM model to the AD curve / 188

   7.4 Shifts of the aggregate demand curve vs. movements along it / 190

   7.5 What causes the aggregate demand curve to shift? / 191

   7.6 The aggregate supply curve / 194

   7.7 Macroeconomic equilibrium in the long run and the short run / 199

   7.8 Two extreme supply cases — Keynesian and classical / 206

   7.9 Supply-side economics / 208

Case Study / 209

Terms and Concepts / 212

Problems and Applications / 212

Answers to Problems and Applications / 218

8 Monetary System and Money Growth / 222

Learning Objective / 222

Key Points and Exercises / 222

   8.1 The meaning of money / 222

   8.2 How to measure money / 224

   8.3 Money supply / 224

   8.4 The role of banks / 225

   8.5 How does the central banks manage the money supply? / 231

   8.6 The quantity theory of money / 232

Case Study / 234

Terms and Concepts / 241

Problems and Applications / 242

Answers to Problems and Applications / 243

9 **Monetary Policy** / 245

Learning Objective / 245

Key Points and Exercises / 245

9.1 What is monetary policy? / 245

9.2 The money market and its equilibrium / 246

9.3 How monetary policy influences aggregate demand / 249

9.4 The Taylor rule / 252

Case Study / 253

Terms and Concepts / 258

Problems and Applications / 258

Answers to Problems and Applications / 261

10 **Fiscal Policy** / 263

Learning Objective / 263

Key Points and Exercises / 263

10.1 What is fiscal policy? / 263

10.2 The effects of fiscal policy on aggregate demand / 264

10.3 The multiplier effect / 265

10.4 The crowding out effect / 267

10.5 Budget deficits and budget surpluses / 269

Case Study / 272

Terms and Concepts / 273

Problems and Applications / 274

Answers to Problems and Applications / 277

1 GDP: Measuring Total Output and Total Income

Learning Objective

By the end of this chapter, students should understand:
- what macroeconomics is about.
- how gross domestic product (GDP) is defined and calculated.
- why total expenditure equals total income for an economy as a whole.
- the distinctions between real GDP and nominal GDP.
- other measures of total output and total income.
- the limitations of GDP as a measure of economic well-being.

Key Points and Exercises

1.1 What is macroeconomics?

1.1.1 Definition of macroeconomics

Macroeconomics is the study of the structure and performance of national economies and the policies that governments use to try to affect economic performance.

1.1.2 Macroeconomic issues

Macroeconomic issues include the following:
- What determines a nation's long-run economic growth?
- What causes the fluctuations of a nation's economic activity (business cycles)?
- What causes unemployment?
- What causes price to rise (inflation)?
- How does being part of economic system affect nation's economies (the interna-

tional economy)?

· Can government policies be used to improve a nation's economic performance?

In a word, Macroeconomics includes topics such as inflation, unemployment and economic growth.

1.1.3 Microeconomics and macroeconomics

Table 1-1 shows the differences between microeconomics and macroeconomics.

Table 1-1

Basis for comparison	Microeconomics	Macroeconomics
Object of study	The study of individual economic units and particular markets	The study of the whole economy
Variables	Individual economic variables	Aggregate economic variables
Issues	Covers various issues like demand, supply, product pricing, factor pricing, production, consumption, economic welfare, etc.	Covers various issues like national income, general price level, employment, government policies etc.
Business application	Labor economics, regulation economics, industrial organization	International economics, public finance, study of particular economic regions

1.2 Measurement of GDP

1.2.1 Definition of GDP

Economists use gross domestic product (GDP) to measure total production. Gross domestic product: the market value of all final goods and services produced in a country during a period of time, typically one year. In China, the National Bureau of Statistics compiles data used to compute GDP. This definition has five parts:

· Market value,

· Final goods and services,

· Produced,

· Within a country,

· In a given time period.

We'll examine each in turn.

1.2.2 Market value

GDP includes many different kinds of productions. We cannot add together the number of cars, melons, haircuts, since all other goods and services without agreeing on a common way to measure them. For example, which is the greater total production, 100 apples and 50 bananas or 50 apples and 100 bananas? It is not easy to answer, because we cannot just add together the quantities of apples and bananas.

Therefore, GDP use the market values of all different kinds of productions to measure the total productions. Market values are calculated by using market prices. If the price of a banana is 2 yuan, then the market values of 50 bananas equals one times 2 yuan, or 100 yuan in total. If the price of an apple is 3 yuan, then the market value of 100 apples is 300 yuan in total. By using market prices to value production, we can directly add up the value of the apples and bananas together. The market value of 100 apples and 50 bananas is 100 yuan plus 300 yuan, or 400 yuan. And the market value of 50 apples and 100 bananas is 350 yuan, which is less than the market value of 100 apples and 50 bananas.

1.2.3 Final goods vs. intermediate goods

A final good or service is a good or service purchased by a final user. An intermediate good or service is a good or service that is an input into another good or service. For example, a BYD car is a final good, but a tire on the car is an intermediate good. A Huawei computer is a final good, but an Intel chip inside it is an intermediate good.

Intermediate goods are not included in GDP, as the value of intermediate goods is already included as parts of the value of the final good. If we were to add the value of intermediate goods and services to the value of final goods and services, we would count the same thing many times — a problem called double counting. For example, in measuring GDP, we only include the value of BYD cars, but not the value of tires. Because the value of tires has been included in the value of BYD cars. If we were to add the value of ties and BYD cars together, we would count the value of tires twice.

Some goods can be intermediate goods in some situations, but in other situations, they also can be final goods. For example, the ice cream you buy in a hot summer is a final good, but the ice cream that a restaurant buys and uses to make dessert is an intermediate good.

However, when an intermediate good is produced, rather than being used, is added to a firm's inventory of goods for use or sale at a later date. In this case, the intermediate good can be a part of GDP as inventory investments. The definition of inventory investment will be discussed in more detail later in this chapter.

1.2.4 Used goods vs. new goods

GDP just includes new goods that are currently produced. It does not include used goods that are produced in the past. For example, GDP for 2018 includes all cellphones produced in 2018, whether these cellphones are sold in 2018 or 2019. And the cellphones produced in 2017 and sold in 2018 should be included in GDP for 2017, not included in GDP for 2018. Only current production is counted. Used goods that are sold do not count as part of GDP. For example, if you buy a new cellphone from JD. com, the purchase is included in GDP. If a month later you resell the cellphone on Taobao. com, that transaction is not included in GDP.

1.2.5 Stocks and flews

GDP measures the value of production that takes place within a specific interval of time. The interval usual is per quarter or per year. GDP measures the economy's flow of production during that interval. Therefore, GDP is a flew variable. A flew variable is a quantity measured per unit of time (for example, per quarter, per year), such as your income per year. In contrast, a stock variable is a quantity measured at a point in time, such as the amount of money in your bank account on January 1 of this year. In general, a flow variable is the rate of change in stock variable. The amount of water in the tub at any moment is a stock variable. The unit of a stock variable (liter or milliliter) doesn't have a time dimension. The rate of at which water enters the tube is a flow variable. Its unit (for example, liter per minute) have a time dimension. In this case the flow variable equals to change of the stock. For example, your income per year is a flew variable and your wealth on January 1, 2019 is a stock variable. Therefore, if china's GDP overtakes U. S. 's GDP in the future, which will mean China produces more goods and services in that year. It will not mean Chinese people are wealthier than American people. Because GDP is a flew variable, but wealth is a stock variable.

1.2.6 GDP vs. GNP

GDP (gross domestic product) measures the value of production within the geographic confines of a country. GNP (gross national product): The market value of all final goods and services produced by permanent residents of nation within a given period of time, even if the production takes place outside. For example, when a Chinese citizen works temporarily in the United States, his or her production is part of U. S. GDP, not part of U. S. GNP. But it is part of Chinese GNP.

Chinese firms have facilities in foreign countries and foreign firms have facilities in China. GNP includes foreign production by Chinese firms, but excludes the production by foreign firms in China. For China, GNP is almost the same as GDP. For example, in 2018, GDP in China was about 13.61 trillion U.S. dollar, and GNP was 13.56 trillion or only about 0.4 percent less than GDP.

▷ Exercise 1

Which of the following goods is directly counted in GDP of China in 2018?

ⅰ) The bread that Subway purchases for its sandwiches in 2018

ⅱ) A 12-inch Subway sandwich purchased by a student in 2018

ⅲ) Kitchen cabinets purchased from IKEA in 2018 to be installed in a house built in 1997

ⅳ) A used car that Tom bought from his friend in 2018

ⅴ) The income that a Chinese professor earned from American university in 2018

Answer:

ⅰ) No, the bread is an intermediate good that is not counted in GDP.

ⅱ) Yes, it is the final good produced in 2018.

ⅲ) Yes, if it's produced in 2018.

ⅳ) No, it's not produced in 2018.

ⅴ) No, the service offered by the professor is not happened in China. It is counted in the GDP of U.S.

1.3 The three approaches to measuring GDP

1.3.1 Total income = Total production = Total expenditure

GDP measures the total production of an economy. Also, GDP measures the total expenditure on an economy's output of goods and services, and the total income of everyone in the economy. For an economy as a whole, total income = total expenditure = total production. Because:

· Every transaction has a buyer and a seller.

· Every dollar of spending by some buyers is a dollar of income for some sellers.

· Everything that is produced and sold constitutes income for someone.

We can illustrate why these three variables are equivalent by an example. Figure

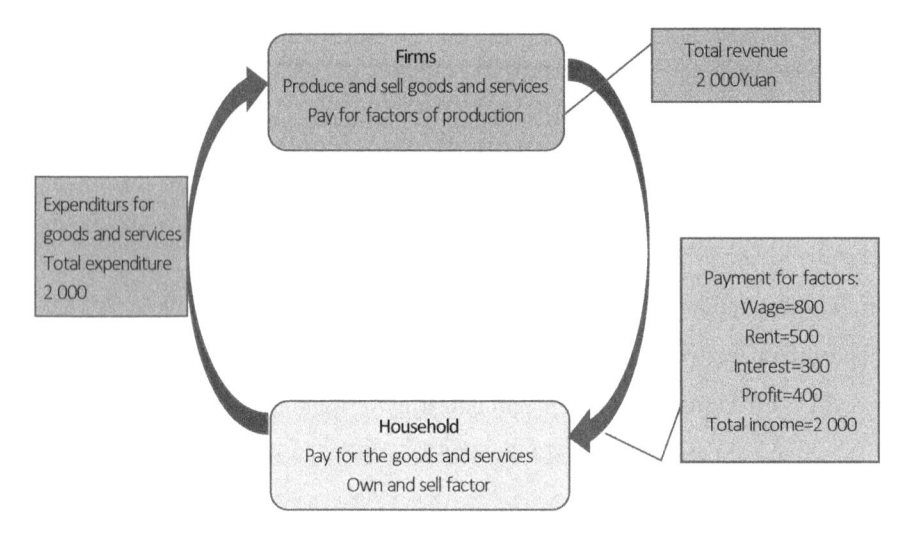

1-1 presents a visual model of economy called a circular-flow diagram.

Figure 1-1

(Diagram showing circular flow: Firms — Produce and sell goods and services, Pay for factors of production. Total revenue 2 000Yuan. Payment for factors: Wage=800, Rent=500, Interest=300, Profit=400, Total income=2 000. Household — Pay for the goods and services, Own and sell factor. Expenditurs for goods and services, Total expenditure 2 000.)

In a very simple model of the economy, there are two types of decision makers — households and firms. Firms produce and sell goods and services to households and buy factors of production from households. Households consume goods and services and sell factors of production to firms. For example, if firms produce 500kg of apples in one year. Apples' price is 4 yuan/kg. Then the market value of these apples is 2 000 yuan. So, the total production will increase by 2 000 yuan. When firms sell these apples to households, the total expenditure will increase by 2 000 yuan, at the same time, firms' revenues will increase by 2 000 yuan. Then firms might use the 2 000 yuan to pay wages of their workers, say 800 yuan, to pay rent of 500 yuan to their landlords, to pay interest of 300 yuan to some household. So, firms' profit equals 400 yuan (total revenue minus wage, rent and interest).

Therefore, the total income will be 2 000 yuan (Wage+Rent+Interest+Profit). In the example, Total expenditure=Total income=Total production=2 000 yuan. This simple model is somewhat unrealistic as it omits saving, taxes, government purchases, and investment purchases by firms. However, because a transaction always has a buyer and a seller, total expenditure in the economy must be equal to total income.

Therefore, there are three approaches to measure GDP:
- the product approach,
- the income approach,

· the expenditure approach.

1.3.2 The product approach to measuring GDP

For the product point of view, GDP is the market value of all final goods and services produced within a country during a fixed period of time. We have already talked about the definition before. An alternative method to measure GDP is to measure the value added: the market value a firm adds to a product. It is equal to the difference between the price for which the firm sells a good and the price it paid other firms for intermediate goods. For example, Xiao Ming is an artist painter. He purchases canvas, paints, brushes, and accessories for 75 yuan. He sells one of his original paintings to an art gallery for 1 500 yuan, which, in turn, sells it to an art lover for 4 500 yuan. From the production point of view, the painting increases GDP by 4 500 yuan (the market value of the only final good in this case is 4 500 yuan). If we add the value added by each firm involved in producing the paintings, we still can get the same answer. The value added by Xiao Ming is 1 425 yuan (1 500−75). And the value added by the art gallery is 3 000 yuan (4 500−1 500). The value added by some other firms is 75 yuan. So, we add the value added by all the firms involved in production of the paintings together, we can get 4 500 yuan (1 425+3 000+75). Notice that the retail price of the painting is exactly equal to the sum of the value added by each firm involved in the production of the painting. We can calculate GDP by adding up the market value of every final good and services produced during a particular period. Or, we can arrive at the same value for GDP by adding up the value added by every firm involved in producing those final goods and services.

1.3.3 The expenditure approach to measuring GDP

The expenditure approach measures GDP as total spending on final goods and services produced within a country during a specified period of time. Four major categories of expenditure are added to get GDP: consumption, investment, government purchases of goods and services, and net export of goods and services. In symbols, GDP can be expressed as the sum of these:

$$Y = C + I + G + NX$$

C = Consumption

I = Investment

G = Government purchases of goods and services

NX = Net exports of goods and services

1) Consumption

The expenditure is spending by households on final goods and services, with the exception of purchases of new housing. It includes expenditure on durable goods such as computers and microwave ovens. (but not house, which are classified under investment.) It also includes nondurable goods such as apples and lipsticks. And it also includes services like education, financial services and legal advice, which are shorter lived items.

2) Investment

The expenditure is spending on capital equipment, additions to inventories, and structures, including household purchases of new housing.

"Investment" in macroeconomics is different from the term we use in our daily conversation. When we hear the word "investment," we think of financial instruments such as stocks and bonds. However, in GDP accounting, investment means purchases of investment goods such as capital equipment, inventories, or structures, which will be used in the future to produce more goods and services. Spending on new housing by households, like investment, can earn income in the future when houses are rented or leased. Therefore, the accountants regard purchases of residential constructions as investment rather than consumption.

Increases in inventories (unsold goods) are assumed that firms have "purchased" the unsold goods for themselves. So, the accountants treat additions to inventories as investment. The accounting rule is useful because it guarantees production and expenditure are always equal in the national income accounts. For example, Huawei company may produce 2 000 cellphones, expecting to sell them all. If it does sell all, the expenditure by household will increase by 200 million yuan (suppose the price of cellphone is 1 000 yuan). Total expenditure equals total production. But if it sells only 150 million yuan, then the expenditure by household will increase by 150 million yuan. Since the unsold cellphones (valued as 50 million yuan) are considered as investments, which are assumed as the expenditure of the firm. Therefore, the total expenditure will still increase 200 million yuan which is equal to consumption by households (150 million yuan) plus investment by firms (50 million yuan).

In summary, investment includes three parts: spending on capital equipment, (such as machines, vehicles, computers, and furniture), additions to inventories, and structures purchased by firms and households. Please notice that the "Investment" here is gross investment. Gross investment is the total value of all newly produced capital goods produced in a given period. Net investment equals gross investment minus depreciation. Depreciation represents the amount of the capital stock that wears out in a given period. Therefore, net investment represents the extent to which the stock of capital changes in a given period. Net investment equal Gross investment minus Depreciation.

3) Government purchases of goods and services

The expenditure is spending on goods and services by governments at all levels, such as teachers' salaries, highways, defence spending.

Government purchases does not include transfer payments, as those do not result in immediate production of new goods and services. Transfer payments: payments by the government to households for which the government does not receive a new good or service in return, such as government payments for social security, unemployment insurance, welfare payments. They are excluded from the government purchases categories, because it does not result in the production of new good and services, and they are already included in consumption by the household.

4) Net exports of goods and services

The expenditure is spending on domestically produced goods by foreigners (exports) minus spending on foreign goods by domestic residents (imports).

Exports are added to total expenditure because they represent spending (by foreigners) on final goods and services produced in a country. Imports are subtracted from total expenditure because consumption, investment and government purchases include imported goods and services, which are not defined to be included in GDP. Therefore, subtracting imports ensures that total spending reflects spending only on output in the country.

▷ Exercise 2

Which component of GDP will be affected by the following transactions?

i) You buy a cell phone of Huawei from a supermarket.

ii) You buy a used cell phone of Huawei from your friend.

iii) Huawei company purchases new machines from an Indian manufactory.

ⅳ) Your mother buys a new house for you.

ⅴ) Your mother buys an old house from an American woman.

Answer:

ⅰ) Consumption.

ⅱ) None of the components of GDP will be affected because the cell phone is not new production.

ⅲ) The investment will increase, but the NX will decrease. So, the total expenditure is unchanged.

ⅳ) Investment.

ⅴ) None of the components of GDP will be affected because the house is not produced in this year.

1.3.4 The income approach to measuring GDP

The income approach calculates GDP by adding the incomes received by producers, including profits and taxes paid to government by the owners of firms and wages received by workers. Total income consists of five parts:

1) Compensation of employees

The income of workers includes wages, salaries, employee benefits, and employer contributions to social insurance and a variety of private pension, health, and welfare funds for workers.

2) Rents

The income is received by the households and businesses that supply property resources. They include the monthly payments tenants make to landlords and the lease payments corporations pay for the use of office space. Rents also include some miscellaneous types of income, such as royalty income paid to authors.

3) Interest

Interest is net interest received by individuals minus interest paid by individuals. It also includes such item as the interest households receive on saving deposits, certificates of deposit, and corporate bonds.

4) Profit

Profits include the profits of sole proprietor and the profits of corporation. They are the earning of corporations. There are three categories: corporate income taxes, dividends and undistributed corporate profits.

5) Taxes on production and imports

They are also called indirect business taxes, including sales taxes, excise taxed business property taxes, license fees and customs duties. For example, the government imposes 5% sales tax to an item whose original price is 1 yuan. Costumers will spend 1.05 yuan to buy it. The 1 yuan will go to the seller who will distribute it as income of factors. The remaining 5 cents will flow the revenue to the government. So, we may consider it to be income to government. So, we should add the indirect taxes to GDP using the income approach. In contrast, a direct tax is a tax on income. It is included in the income of factors. So, we only add the indirect taxes to GDP.

In addition to the five parts, to make national income equal to GDP, we need add a statistical discrepancy and depreciation to national income. Because depreciation is the cost of production and thus included in the GDP, but it does not add to anyone's income. in the expenditure approach, we add gross investment (Gross investment = Net investment+Depreciate) to GDP. However, in calculation of components of national income, depreciation is subtracted from total income. Thus, to make national income equal to GDP, we should add back in depreciation to national income. That's why both the measurement of aggregate income and the measurement of aggregate expenditure are called gross.

In summary , the GDP from the income points of view can be calculated as:

GDP = Compensation of employees+Rent+Interest+Profit+Indirect business
    taxes+Statistical discrepancy+Depreciation

▷ Exercise 3

Let's take your economics book for example. In producing a book, the first stage is a logger chop down tree to be used for paper production. The tree is sold to a paper manufacture. The paper manufacture sells the papers to the publisher, who prints and bounds the book. Then the publisher sells the book to the bookstore. From there it is sold to you. The various stages of producing the book are shown in Table 1-2.

Calculate the contributions to GDP of these transactions, showing that all three approaches give the same answer.

Table 1-2

	Logging operation	Paper production	Printing and publishing	Bookstore sales
Values of sales (yuan)	4	12	28	40
Payment to previous stage	0	4	12	28
Wages/salaries	2	3	8	5
Rent/interest	1	2	4	3
profit	1	3	4	4
Income generated at each stage	4	8	16	12

Answer:

i) The production approach: there are only one final goods and the market value of the final goods is 40 yuan. So, the contributions to GDP of these transaction is 40 yuan. We can also get the same answer by value added method. :

Value added by the logger: 4 yuan.

Value added by paper manufactory: 8 yuan(12-4).

Value added by the publisher: 16 yuan(28-12).

Value added by the bookstore: 12 yuan(40-28).

Together, the value added by the four producers is 4+8+16+12=40 yuan. Therefore, the contributions to GDP of these transaction is 40 yuan.

ii) The income approach: the logger receives 4 yuan from the paper producer. It pays 2 yuan of wages and salaries, and 1 yuan of rent and interest, so that it leaves 1 yuan of profit. Therefore, the total income generated by the first stage of production is 4 yuan. Then we can calculate the total income from these transaction by adding the incomes generated by the all stages of production. So, the total income is 40 yuan(4+8+16+12).

iii) The expenditure approach: for these transactions, there is only one expenditure for a final good which is you spend 40 yuan on the economics book. Because other goods like paper are not final goods.

Exercise 4

Table 1-3 table below contains data for country A for the year 2022.

Table 1-3

Household purchases of durable goods	$ 1 293
Household purchases of nondurable goods	$ 1 717
Household purchases of services	$ 301
Household purchases of new housing	$ 704
Purchases of capital equipment	$ 310
Inventory changes	$ 374
Purchases of new structures	$ 611
Depreciation	$ 117
Salaries of government workers	$ 1 422
Government expenditures on public works	$ 553
Transfer payments	$ 777
Foreign purchases of domestically produced goods	$ 88
Domestic purchases of foreign goods	$ 120

i) What was country A's consumption in 2022?

ii) What was country A's investment in 2022?

iii) What were country A's government purchases in 2022?

iv) What were country A's net exports in 2022?

Answer:

i) Country A's consumption = $ 1 293 + $ 1 717 + $ 301 = $ 3 311.

ii) Country A's investment = $ 704 + $ 310 + $ 374 + $ 611 = $ 1 999.

iii) Country A's government purchases = $ 1 422 + $ 553 = $ 1 975.

iv) Country A's net exports = $ 88 - $ 120 = $ -32.

1.4 Real GDP and nominal GDP

Since GDP is measured in "value" terms (prices × qualities), there are two possible reasons for total spending to rise from one year to the next. One possible reason is the economy may be producing a larger output of goods and services, the other is goods and services could be selling at higher prices. To separate the two reasons, economists calculate real GDP and nominal GDP:

· Nominal GDP — the value of final goods and services evaluated at current-year prices.

· Real GDP — the value of final goods and services evaluated at base-year prices.

A numerical example:

Let's say we are studying a simple and oversimplified country that only sells apples and bananas. Table 1-4 shows output and prices in 2010, 2022 and 2023.

Table 1-4

Year	Price of apples (yuan/kg)	Quantity of apples (kg)	Price of bananas (yuan/kg)	Quantity of bananas (kg)
2010	1	100	2	50
2022	2	150	3	100
2023	3	200	4	150

i) Nominal GDP: the production of goods and services valued at current prices.

Nominal GDP for 2010 = (1 yuan× 100) + (2 yuan× 50) = 200 yuan.

Nominal GDP for 2022 = (2 yuan× 150) + (3 yuan× 100) = 600 yuan.

Nominal GDP for 2023 = (3 yuan × 200) + (4 yuan × 150) = 1 200 yuan.

The GDP in 2022 is 600 yuan and the GDP in 2023 is 1200 yuan. The difference between GDP in 2022 and 2023 is 600 yuan. For the difference, some of it is due to the increase in quantities. But lot of it is also due to the increase in price. A simple way to remove the effects of price changes, and thus to focus on changes in quantities of output, is to measure the value of production in each year by using the price from some base year. it is called real GDP.

ii) Real GDP: the production of goods and services valued at base-year prices.

Let's assume that the base year is 2010.

For the base year real GDP equals nominal GDP (200 yuan), because they use the same price (current prices = base-year prices). Therefore, real GDP for 2010 is also 200 yuan. For real GDP for 2022, we use the prices from 2010 to value the production in 2022, as the following equation shows:

Real GDP for 2022 = (1 yuan× 150) + (2 yuan× 100) = 350 yuan.

Therefore, the value of real GDP in 2022 is 350 yuan, measured using the prices of year 2010. Using the same method, we can calculate real GDP for 2023.

Real GDP for 2023 = (1 yuan× 200) + (2 yuan× 150) = 500 yuan.

The difference between real GDP for 2022 and real GDP for 2023 is due to the increase in quantities not in price. In general, an economic variable that is measured by the prices of a base year is called a real variable. Real economic variables measure the physical quantity of economic activity, such as real interest rate.

iii) Economists and policy-makers also are interested in the price level. The difference between nominal GDP and real GDP is due to the increase in price not in quantities. So, Economists use GDP deflator to measure the price level.

$$\text{GDP deflator} = \frac{\text{Nominal GDP}}{\text{Real GDP}} \times 100$$

GDP deflator for 2010 = (200 / 200) × 100 = 100.

GDP deflator for 2022 = (600 / 350) × 100 = 171.

GDP deflator for 2023 = (1200 / 500) × 100 = 240.

The GDP deflator increased from 171 to 240 between 2022 and 2023. This is an increase:

$$\left(\frac{240-171}{171}\right) \times 100\% = 40.3\%.$$

So, we say the price level rose 40.3% over this period.

Summary: The definition of the GDP deflator allows us to separate nominal GDP into two parts: one-part measures quantities (real GDP) and the other measures prices (the GDP deflator). That is,

$$\text{Nominal GDP} = \text{Real GDP} \times \text{The GDP deflator}$$

Nominal GDP measures the output valued at current-year prices.

Real GDP measures output valued at the base-year prices.

The GDP deflator measures the price of output relative to its price in the base year.

1.5 Other measures of total production and total income

In addition to GDP, economists also care about the following four measures of production and income: gross national product, national income, personal income, and disposable personal income.

1.5.1 Gross national product (GNP)

GNP is the value of final goods and services produced by residents of an economy. China's GNP includes foreign production by Chinese firms but excludes production by foreign firms in China. Therefore:

$$GNP = GDP - \text{Income that foreigners earn in China} + \text{Income that Chinese citizens earn abroad}$$

1.5.2 National income (NI)

GNP minus depreciation is NI. Depreciation, which is also called capital consumption, is the value of capital that wears out during an interval of time. The market values of final goods include the depreciation, but depreciation is not really part of somebody's income. When we calculate NI, it is necessary to subtract capital consumption from the value of goods and services produced by factors supplied by a country.

$$NI = GNP - \text{Depreciation}$$

1.5.3 Personal income (PI)

PI is income received by households. To calculate personal income, we subtract the earnings that corporations retain rather than pay to shareholders in the form of dividends. We add in the payments received by households from the government in the form of transfer payments or interest on government bonds.

There is still a part of NI that is not included in Personal Income. They are indirect taxes. Indirect taxes consist of sales plus import duties. These fees are paid indirectly by consumers who pay taxes to product suppliers and then remitted to the government. Indirect taxes are part of net national product. However, they are not part of people's incomes. They may be considered as the income of government. Therefore, in calculating personal income, it is necessary to subtract indirect taxes from NI.

$$PI = NI - \text{Firms' retained earnings} - \text{Indirect taxes} + \text{Transfer payments}$$

1.5.4 Disposable personal income (DPI)

Disposable personal income is equal to personal income minus personal tax payments, such as personal income taxes. Disposable personal income is the best measure of the income households have available to spend.

$$DPI = PI - \text{Personal tax payments}$$

▷ Exercise 5

Base on Table 1-5, what is national income, personal income and deposit personal income of this economy?

Table 1-5

	Billions of dollars
GDP	$ 3 250
Depreciation	$ 300
Retained earnings	$ 1 000
Personal tax payments	$ 500
Transfer payments	$ 80

Answer:

NI = GDP - Depreciation

Substituting the table values:

NI = $ 3 250 - $ 300 = $ 2 950.

PI = NI - Retained earnings + Transfer payments

Substituting the table values:

PI = $ 2 950 - $ 1 000 + $ 80 = $ 2 030.

DPI = PI - Personal tax payments

Substituting the table values:

DPI = $ 2 030 - $ 500 = $ 1 530.

1.6 The limitations of real GDP

Economists use estimates of real GDP for two main purposes: To compare the standard of living over time and to compare the standard of living across counties. Government policy makers pay close attention to real GDP, often behaving as if the greater the GDP, the better. However, real GDP is not the same as economic well-being. Let's look at some limitations of real GDP.

1.6.1 GDP does not reflect the distribution of output

GDP emphasizes the quantity of goods produced. GDP does not tell us the way that output is distributed. The distribution of output may make a big difference for society's overall well-being. Therefore, GDP may not provide good information about the goods and services consumed by a typical person.

1.6.2 Household production are omitted from the measurement of GDP

Household production refers to goods and services people produce for themselves, such as childcare, cleaning, and cooking. Household production is not typically paid for with money, so such activities never show up in GDP. However, such contributions are real. If a person has been caring for children, cleaning the house and preparing the family meals, the value of such services is not included in GDP. But if they were performed by a non-household-member, they would be paid for and counted in GDP. Another example is volunteer services. These unpaid services are left out of GDP. From this point, GDP understates the value of production.

1.6.3 The underground economy are omitted from the measurement of GDP

The underground economy refers to buying and selling of goods and services that is concealed from the government to avoid taxes or regulations or because the goods and services are illegal. Since the buying and selling is concealed from government, GDP does not include the production in the underground economy. From this point, GDP understates the value of production.

1.6.4 GDP does not consider some social costs

The growth of GDP is inevitably accompanied with some negative affection on our economic well-being, such as dirty air, polluted water, congestion. Since these social costs are not deducted from total output, GDP overstates a nation's well-being. Ironically, when money is spent to clean up pollution, the expenses are added to the GDP. From this point, GDP overstates the social well-being.

In general, developing countries often have higher levels of pollution than high-income countries, because the lower GDP of the developing countries make them reluctant to spend resources on reducing pollution. With increase of Chinese GDP, China government will devote more resources to reduce pollution. The air quality in China will become better and better.

1.6.5 GDP does not reflect the quality of living

Some indicators of the good life are not shown in markets and so may be omitted from GDP. For example, GDP does not measure the value of leisure. the increasing in leisure time has a positive effect on overall well-being. But the measurement of GDP ignores leisure's value. Today, the typical person works fewer than 40 hours per week. If people worked more time per week, GDP would be much higher than it's now, but the well-being of a typical person would be lower, because less time would be available for leisure activities. Therefore, GDP understates well-being by ignoring leisure's value.

In addition, GDP also ignores the improvement in product quality. A ¥1 000 mobile phone purchased today is of very different quality than a mobile phone that cost ￥1 000 just a decade ago. Obviously quality improvement has a great effect on economic well-being, as does the quantity of goods produced. GDP fails to capture the full value of improvements in product quality.

Case Study

China's Economic Growth from 1978 to 2018

Since the reform and opening up, the life of Chinese people has undergone tremendous changes. In the 1970s and 1980s, people used to travel by bike and the green train. Now they take subway, high-speed train or plane, or use online car-hailing services instead. Bike, sewing machine, watch and tape recorder that were four must-have items for marriage have been replaced by house, car, bride price and deposits. All these signify the fast-changing life of Chinese people which is benefited from the rapid development of China's economy.

In 2018, China's Gross Domestic Product reached 90.03 trillion yuan, equivalent to 13.61 trillion US dollars. From the perspective of purchasing power parity, China's Gross Domestic Product increased by 1.4 trillion US dollars in 2018, contributing up to 30% to the global economic growth.

From the founding of People's republic of China in 1949 to reform and opening-up in 1978, China accounted for less than 5% of world GDP, over 20% of world population with per capita GDP at less than one fourth of world average. And export less than 1% of world's total export. Back then, China was poor, populous and largely isolated from the rest of the world. On December 18, 1978, China launched reform and opening-up. With great resolve and confidence, China created a socialist market economy with its own characteristics. The achievements of reform and opening-up are indisputable. Since reform and opening-up in 1978, China's economy has been growing at almost 10%. In 2000, China's nominal GDP surpassed that of Italy, France in 2005, the United Kingdom in 2006 and that of Germany in 2007. In 2010, China's GDP overtook that of Japan that made China the world's second largest economy after the United States. But adjusting for purchasing power parity (PPP), China become the world's second largest economy as early as 1999 surpassing Japan, and has toppled America to become the biggest economy since 2014. In 2016, China accounted for 18.8% of world population, 14.9% of world GDP and 13.2% of world total export. China's per capita GDP is also getting close to world average, as Table 1-6 shows.

Table 1-6   **Overview of China's Economic Performance**

Indicator variables	1952	1978	2016
Proportion of GDP against the global total	4.6%	4.9%	14.8%
Proportion of population against the global total	22.5%	22.3%	18.8%
Proportion of per capita GDP against the global average	23.8%	22.1%	88.3%
Proportion of exports against the global total	1.0%	0.8%	13.2%

Source: Maddison (2000) and WDI database.

Rapid growth of China and other emerging market economies has reshaped the world economy. In the post-crisis era, emerging market economies overtook advanced economies in terms of their share in world GDP. China and other BRIC countries contributed over 30% and 60% of world GDP growth respectively.

Recent years, the growth rate of Chinese economy become slower than before. Present Xi Jinping used the phrase 'new normal' in May 2014 to describe China's next period of economic growth. The features of "new normal" in economic development are: First, the economy has shifted gear from the previous high speed to a medium to high-speed growth. Second, the economic structure is constantly improved and upgraded. Third, the economy is increasingly driven by innovation instead of input and investment. In the "new normal", China's economic development will be guided by strategic mentality of patience, public interest, and sustainability. Hasty growth will give way to long-term horizons. "Although" remarkable and "instant" achievements become less easy, the "new normal" will lead to long term prosperity, stability and solid steps towards the Chinese dream.

Sources: https://en.wikipedia.org/wiki/Historical_GDP_of_China; "China's Economic Growth and Structural Transition since 1978" Zhang Ping and Nan Yu Institute of Economics, Chinese Academy of Social Sciences, Beijing, China, China Economist and "China's New Normal", China Economist

Terms and Concepts

· **Macroeconomics**：The study of the economy as a whole, including topics such as inflation, unemployment, and economic growth.

· **Gross domestic production (GDP)**：The market value of all final goods and services produced in a country during a period of time, typically one year.

· **Gross national production (GNP)**：The market value of all final goods and services produced by permanent residents of nation within a given period of time.

· **Nominal GDP**：The value of final goods and services evaluated at current-year prices.

· **Real GDP**：The value of final goods and services evaluated at base-year prices.

· **Transfer payment**：Payments by the government to households for which the government does not receive a new good or service in return.

· **GDP deflator**：A measure of the price level, calculated by dividing nominal GDP by real GDP and multiplying by 100.

· **Investment**：Spending by firms on new factories, office buildings, machinery, and additions to inventories, plus spending by households and firms on new houses.

· **Price level**：A measure of the average prices of goods and services in the economy.

Problems and Applications

Ⅰ. True or False

1. Macroeconomic statistics include GDP, the inflation rate, the unemployment rate, and the trade deficit.

2. In the circular flow diagram, the value of all the income in the economy is greater than the value of goods and services produced in the economy.

3. An economy's income is the same as its expenditure because every transaction has a buyer and a seller.

4. Government spending on transfer payments is included in government purchases

when calculating GDP because it results in the production of new goods and services.

5. U. S. GDP excludes the production of most illegal goods.

6. When an American doctor opens a practice in China, his production in China is part of China's GDP.

7. The GDP deflator is a measure of the average level of price of final goods and services in the economy

8. The purchase of new house by household is included in consumption expenditures.

9. China's GDP was almost 90.03 trillion yuan in 2018.

10. A sharp increase in the divorce rate increases the number of lawyers hired to determine divorce settlements. This will increase GDP and decrease well-being in the economy.

II. Choices

1. The purchase of rice produced this period is included in GDP if the rice is _____.

   A. used in a meal a restaurant sells during the same period they buy the rice

   B. purchased by a family who uses it for its supper

   C. purchased by a frozen food company to increase its inventory

   D. B and C are correct

2. Value added equals the market price of the firm's product minus _____.

   A. wages and salaries

   B. the price of intermediate goods

   C. the price of all factors of production

   D. depreciation on plant and equipment

3. Investment, as defined by economists, would include the purchase of a _____.

   A. corporate bond

   B. government bond

   C. share of stock in Bank of China

   D. computer by an accounting firm

4. Which of the following is not included in China's GDP? _____.

A. Additions of newly produced output to inventory

B. Production of U. S. citizens working in China

C. The estimated rental value of owner-occupied housing

D. Production of China citizens living in the United States

5. Which of the following is an example of depreciation? _____.

A. Falling stock prices

B. The retirement of several employees

C. Computers becoming obsolete

D. All of the above are examples of depreciation

6. An example of a transfer payment is _____.

A. teacher's paycheck

B. paycheck for a member of the National Guard

C. welfare payment

D. purchase of a new bridge in Chengdu

7. Which of the following would not be included in the expenditure category called investment expenditures? _____.

A. Spending on new houses

B. Purchase of shares of preferred stock

C. A purchase of a copy machine by Bank of China

D. The cars held in inventory on a local Ford dealer's lot

8. Which of the following statements is true? _____.

A. A decrease in the crime rate increases GDP as people will spend more on security

B. Household production is counted in GDP as it amounts to real production

C. GDP accounting rules do not adjust for production that pollutes the economy

D. GDP growth distributes income equally to people in the economy

9. Which of the following is counted in GDP? _____.

A. The value of goods and services produced in the underground economy

B. The cost of a speed boat purchased by drug smugglers

C. The value of do-it-yourself work

D. The value of leisure

10. Which of the following can cause an increase in national income? _____.

A. An increase in depreciation

B. An increase in personal taxes

C. A decrease in personal income

D. An increase in gross domestic product

III. Short Answer

1. Why do we subtract import spending from total expenditures?

2. Suppose that a very simple economy produces three goods: pizzas, haircuts, and backpacks. Suppose the quantities produced and their corresponding prices for 2007 and 2013 are shown in Table 1-7.

Table 1-7

Product	2007 Quantity	2007 Price	2013 Quantity	2013 Price
Pizzas	100	$ 10	120	$ 12
Haircuts	50	$ 15	45	$ 20
Backpacks	200	$ 40	210	$ 45

i) Use the information to Calculate real GDP in 2013 assuming the base year is 2007.

ii) Do the same calculation assuming the base year is 2013.

ii) Are the calculations different? Why?

iv) Calculate the GDP deflator in 2013 assuming the base year is 2007.

3. China's real GDP increased 6.9 percent in the first quarter of 2017 from a year earlier. Investment grew by 9.2 percent and retail sales by 10.9 percent. In current prices, GDP increased by 11.8 percent from a year earlier.

i) Explain how China's real GDP can grow at a 6.9 percent rate when consumption and investment grew faster than 6.9 percent.

ii) Explain why the growth rate of GDP in current prices does not provide information about how quickly the economy is really growing.

4. The United Nations' Human Development Index (HDI) is based on real GDP per person, life expectancy at birth, and indicators of the quality and quantity of education. Please give your opinions about the following questions.

i) Do you think the HDI might be better than real GDP as a measure of economic welfare? Please explain your reasons.

ii) Which items in the HDI are part of real GDP and which items are not in real GDP?

iii) Do you think the HDI should be expanded to include items such as pollution, resource depletion, and political freedom? Explain.

5. Identify the immediate effect of each of the following events on China's GDP and its components.

i) Your classmate receives a scholarship from Shanghai municipal government.

ii) Your teacher buys an Italian sports car.

ii) Your friend buys domestically produced tools for his construction company.

iv) Huawei company buys an equipment from a U.A. corporation for the production of cellphones.

v) Your parents bought an apartment that was newly constructed in 2007 for $ 275 000. They sold the home in 2009 for $ 205 000.

6. Briefly explain under what condition, if any, net investment can be negative. If so, explain what this implies about the capital stock.

7. Table 1-8 is a list of domestic output and national income figures for certain year. All figures are in billions.

Table 1-8

Personal consumption expenditure	245
Transfer payments	12
Rents	14
Statistical discrepancy	4
Consumption of fixed capital (depreciation)	23
interest	13
Proprietors' income	33
Net export	11
Dividends	16
Compensation of employees	223
Taxes on production and import	18
Undistributed corporate profits	21
Personal tax	26

	continued
Corporate income tax	19
Corporate profit	56
Government purchase	72
Net private domestic investment	33

ⅰ) Using the above data, determine GDP by both the expenditure and the income approaches. The results you obtain with the different methods should be the same.

ⅱ) Determine NI, PI and DPI.

Answers to Problems and Applications

Ⅰ. True or False

1	2	3	4	5	6	7	8	9	10
T	F	T	F	T	T	T	F	T	T

Ⅱ. Choice

1	2	3	4	5	6	7	8	9	10
D	B	D	D	C	C	B	C	B	D

Ⅲ. Short Answer

1. **Answer**: Import spending is defined as spending on goods and services that are produced in foreign countries. So, it is not included in GDP. However, when we total up consumption expenditures, investment spending, and government spending, this total includes some import spending. Therefore, we must then subtract the value of import spending from total expenditures.

2. **Answer**: Recall that real GDP is found by valuing GDP in a particular year using base year prices. When 2007 is the base year, real GDP for 2013 is found by multiplying 2007 prices by 2013 quantities and then adding the values up.

Therefore,

i) Real GDP for 2013(2007 base year) = 120× $ 10+45× $ 15+210× $ 40
$$= \$ \ 10\ 275.$$

ii) Real GDP for 2013 (2013 base year) = 120× $ 12+45× $ 20+210× $ 45
$$= \$ \ 11\ 790.$$

ii) When 2013 is used as the base year, the calculation of real GDP is larger as compared to the calculation of real GDP for 2013 assuming 2007 is the base year. The values differ because the prices are different in 2007 and 2013, so the value of real GDP does depend on the chosen base year.

iv) Nominal GDP for 2013 = real GDP for 2013(2013 base year) = $ 11 790.

GDP deflator in 2013 = nominal GDP for 2013×100/ real GDP for 2013(2007 base year)

$$= 11\ 790 \times 100 / 10\ 275$$
$$= 115.$$

3. Answer:

i) Even though consumption and investment both grew more rapidly than 6.9 percent, the other components of GDP, government expenditure and net exports grew more slowly, so the net effect from all four parts of GDP was 6.9 percent growth.

ii) GDP in current prices can grow because both production grows and prices grow. The growth in prices does represent growth in the economy. Growth in the economy is measured using the growth rate of real GDP because real GDP measures only production.

4. Answer:

i) The HDI might be a better measure of economic welfare because it includes some important factors that affect welfare and which are omitted from GDP. In particular, life expectancy is included in the HDI but not in GDP and on this count the HDI is superior. The HDI also includes direct measures of the quality and quantity of education. These are indirectly included in GDP because they affect GDP per person, but it might be the case that the direct inclusion in the HDI is better.

ii) The HDI is based on real GDP per person and so directly includes GDP. In addition, the quality and quantity of education affect people's productivity, which is closely related to GDP per person. So real GDP indirectly includes some of the education effects explicitly included in the HDI.

iii) Ideally factors such as pollution, political freedom, and so forth should be included in a broad measure of welfare. Two difficulties, however, occur. One difficulty comes when trying to measure these variables. For instance, how can political freedom be measured in a way that is accepted by all? A second difficulty is weighting these factors. For instance, how much political freedom should be weighted relative to GDP per person?

5. **Answer:**

i) Since this is a transfer payment, there is no change to GDP or to any of its components.

ii) Consumption and imports will rise and cancel each other out so that there is no change in China's GDP.

iii) This increases the investment component of GDP and so increases GDP.

iv) Investment and imports will rise, but they can cancel each other out. Therefore, there is no change in China's GDP.

v) The 2009 sale affected neither 2007 GDP nor 2009 GDP.

6. **Answer:** Net investment equals gross investment minus depreciation. If depreciation is greater than gross investment, net investment will be negative. In such a situation, there is insufficient gross investment to offset the effects of the depreciation of the capital stock. In this case, the capital stock would diminish in size during that period.

7. **Answer:**

i) From the expenditure view of GDP,
$$GDP = C+I+G+NX$$
Substituting the table values:
GDP = 245+33+23+72+11 = 384.

From the income view of GDP,

GDP = Compensation of employees+Rent+Interest+Profit+Indirect business taxes
+Statistical discrepancy+Depreciation

Substituting the table values:

GDP = 223+14+13+56+33+18+4+23 = 384.

The two approaches have the same results.

ii) NI = GDP−Depreciation = 384−23 = 361.

PI = NI−Indirect taxes−Corporation income taxes−Undistributed corporate profit+Transfer payment

= 361−18−21−19+12

= 315.

DPI = PI−Personal tax = 315−26 = 289.

2 Unemployment and Inflation

Learning Objective

By the end of this chapter, students should be able to understand:
- how to measure the unemployment rate for an economy.
- how to identify the three types of unemployment.
- what a full employment is.
- what factors determine the unemployment.
- economic cost of unemployment.
- how the consumer price index (CPI) is constructed.
- how to use a price index to correct the effects of inflation.
- the distinction between the real interest rate and the nominal interest rate.
- the effects of inflation on the economy.

Key Points and Exercises

2.1 Measurement of unemployment

2.1.1 Definition of unemployment

Unemployment and inflation are the macroeconomic problems that are most often discussed in the media and during political campaigns. The state of the economy can be measured roughly by the unemployment rate and the inflation rate. In this chapter, we will look closely at the statistics on unemployment and inflation.

The unemployment rate is the percentage of the labor force unemployed:

$$\text{Unemployment rate} = \frac{\text{Unemployed}}{\text{Labor force}} \times 100\%$$

2.1.2 Calculation of the unemployment rate

The unemployment rate is a key macroeconomic statistic. Government statisticians in nearly every nation in the world attempt to measure their respective unemployment rates. This is typically done with surveys. For example, to estimate the unemployment rate in the United States, the Bureau of Labor Statistics (BLS) surveys 60 000 households each month and asks questions about the age and job market status of household members. This survey is called the household survey. From the survey data, BLS divides the total working age population (over age 16) into three groups:

Employed[1], if the person worked during the week before the survey or if they were temporarily away from their jobs.

Unemployed, if the person did not work in the previous week but were available for work and had actively looked for work during the previous four weeks.

Not in the labor force, if the person did not work in the past week and did not looking for work during the past four weeks. Examples are full-time students, homemakers, retirees, those on active military service, in prison, or in mental hospitals, and discouraged workers. Discouraged workers are people who are available for work but have not looked for a job during the previous four weeks because they believe no jobs are available for them. The BLS classifies discouraged workers as not in the labor force.

Using the classification, we can calculate the other three important macroeconomic indicators:

The labor force is the sum of employed and unemployed workers in the economy.

Labor force = Number of people employed + Number of people unemployed

The labor force participation rate is the percentage of the labor force in the working-age population.

$$\text{Labor force participation rate} = \frac{\text{Labor force}}{\text{Working-age population}} \times 100\%$$

The employment-population ratio is the percentage of the working-age population

---

[1] National Bureau of Statistics of China explains that Employed Persons refers to persons above a specified age who had labor capacity and performed some social work for compensation or business gains. Specifically, it refers to persons, aged 16 and over, who performed some work for compensation or business gains for one hour or more during the reference period; or persons who do not work for the reasons of study or on holiday, but had work units or sites during the reference period; or persons temporary absence from a job for disorganization or suspension of work, recession, etc, But not exceeding three months during the reference period.

that is employed.

$$\text{Employment-population ratio} = \frac{\text{Number of people employed}}{\text{Working-age population}} \times 100\%$$

In summary, the employment status of the working age population can be shown in Figure 2-1.

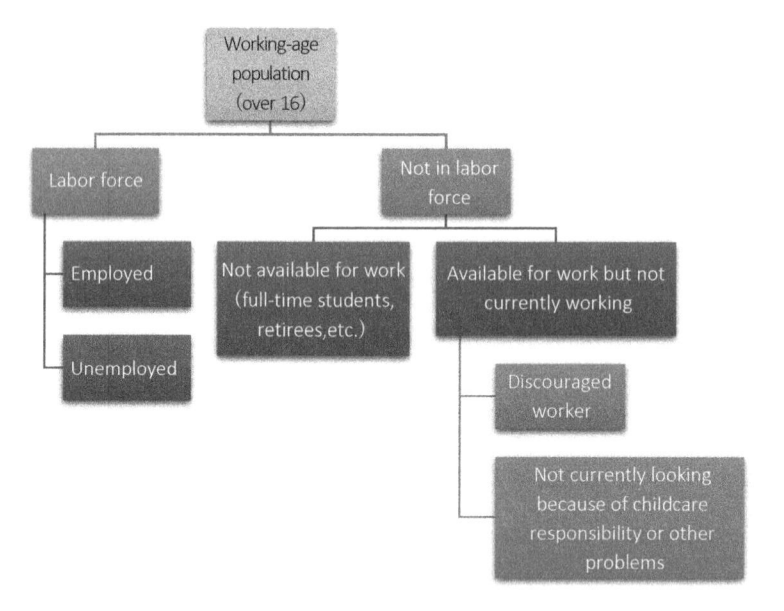

Figure 2-1

2.1.3 Problems with measuring the unemployment rate

The unemployment rate reported by the BLS is not a perfect measure of the actual state of joblessness in the economy. It may understate unemployment:

· Not counting discouraged workers as unemployed. During a recession, an increase in the number of discouraged workers occurs, as people who have had trouble finding a job stop actively looking. Because these workers are not counted as unemployed, the unemployment rate may understate the true degree of joblessness in the economy. Suppose discouraged workers were counted as unemployed, both the unemployment rate and the labor force participation rate would increase. The number of unemployed would rise, as would the labor force. The unemployment rate would rise because adding the same number to the numerator and the denominator of a fraction that is less than one increases the value of the fraction. The labor force participation rate would rise because the labor force increases with no change in the working-age population.

• Counting people as employed who are working part time. The BLS counts people as employed if they hold part-time jobs even if they would prefer to hold full-time jobs. Suppose these people were counted as unemployed, the unemployment will increase.

Not counting discouraged workers as unemployed and counting people as employed who are working part time, has a substantial effect on the measured unemployment. For example, in August 2013, using the broader definition of unemployment[①], the U. S. unemployment rate would have increased the measured unemployment rate from 7.3 percent to 13.7 percent.

There are other measurement problems that cause the measured unemployment rate to overstate the true extent of joblessness. Because the household survey does not verify the responses of people included in the survey, some people might offer false information such as:

• People might claim falsely to be actively looking for work to remain eligible for government programs. In this case, a person who is actually not in the labor force is counted as unemployed.

• People may claim not to be working to evade taxes or keep criminal activity unnoticed. In this case, people who are actually be employed are counted as unemployed.

In summary, these inaccurate responses to the survey bias the unemployment rate. Although the unemployment rate provides some useful information about the employment situation in the country, it is far from an exact measure of joblessness in the economy.

2.1.4 Another measure of employment: the establishment survey

In addition to the household survey, the BLS also uses the establishment survey, sometimes called the payroll survey, to measure total employment in the economy. This survey samples about 300 000 establishments, or places of employment, about their employees. In China, the data on basic conditions of employment, data by groups are collected and compiled by the Department of Population and Employment Statistics, the NBS, through *The National Monthly Sample Survey System on Labor Force*. And the data on the number of registered unemployed persons in urban areas are collected through *The Reporting Form System on Training and Employment Statistics*, which provided by the Ministry of Human Resources and Social Security. Therefore, now, China uses both

---

① The broader definition of unemployment would had counted as unemployed: all discouraged workers and all people who were in part-time jobs but wanted full-time jobs.

the household survey and the establishment survey.

The establishment survey is not also a perfect measure which has four drawbacks:

· First, self-employed people were not on a company payroll. Therefore, the survey does not provide information on the number of persons. In China, we can get the data on the number of employed persons in private enterprises and self-employed individuals from China statistical yearbook, which are provided by the State Administration for Market Regulation.

· Newly-opened firms were often omitted. Some people employed at newly opened firms are not included in the survey.

· Information on employment only, not unemployment.

· Numbers fluctuate depending on establishments included, often requiring large revisions.

However, a big advantage is that the data are determined by real payrolls, not self-reporting like the household survey. In recent years, some economists have come to rely more on establishment survey data than on household survey data in analyzing current labor market conditions.

▷ Exercise 1

Assume the following data for a country: total population, 245 800, population under 16 years of age or institutionalized, 9 900, labor force participation rate 65.5%, unemployment rate, 9.4%. What is the size of the labor force? What is the size of employment? What is the size of unemployment?

Answer:

Working-age population = Total population − Population under 16 years of age or institutionalized

So, Working-age population = 245 800 − 9 900 = 235 900.

$$\text{Labor force participation rate} = \frac{\text{Labor force}}{\text{Working-age population}} \times 100\%$$

Labor force = (Working-age population × Labor force participation rate)/100%

Labor force = (235 900 × 65.5%)/100% = 154 515.

$$\text{Unemployment rate} = \frac{\text{Unemployment}}{\text{Labor force}} \times 100\%$$

Unemployed = (Labor force × Unemployment rate)/100%

Unemployed = (154 515 × 9.4%)/100% = 14 524.

Labor force = Employed + Unemployed

Employed = Labor force − Unemployed

Employed = 154 515 − 14 524 = 139 991.

2.2 Types of unemployment

Unemployment rates rise when the economy is during recessions, and fall when the economy is doing well. But they never fall to zero. To understand why, we need to discuss the types of unemployment. The three types of unemployment are: frictional unemployment, structural unemployment and cyclical unemployment. We will examine each in turn.

2.2.1 Frictional unemployment

Frictional unemployment is short-term unemployment that arises from the process of matching workers with jobs.

• Frictional unemployment occurs mostly because of job search. Most workers spend time engaging in a job search, and most firms spend time searching for people to fill job openings. The flows into and out of the labor force and the processes of job creation and job destruction create the need for people to search for jobs and for business to search for workers. For example, a new worker entering the labor force or a worker who has lost a job probably will not find an acceptable job right away. The word "frictional" implies that the labor market does not operate perfectly and instantaneously (without friction) in matching workers and jobs.

• It also occurs because of seasonal unemployment: some jobs fluctuate in availability due to seasonal demand, like ski-instructor or farm-worker. This type of unemployment is due to factors such as weather, variations in tourism, and other calendar-related events.

• Frictional unemployment is unavoidable and, at least in part, desirable. The unemployment arises from the normal labor turnover. And some frictional unemployment actually increases economic efficiency by allowing a better match. Because both workers and firms need time to ensure a good match between the attributes of workers and the characteristics of jobs. By devoting time to job search, workers end up with jobs they find satisfying and in which they can be productive. Therefore, frictional unemployment is a permanent and healthy phenomenon in a dynamic growing economy.

2.2.2 Structural unemployment

Structural unemployment is unemployment that arises from a persistent mismatch between the skills or attributes of workers and the requirements of jobs.

· Structural unemployment occurs because of the changes in the "structure" of the total demand for labor, both occupationally and geographically. The demand for certain skills (for example, sewing clothes or working on farms) may decline or even vanish. The demand for other skills (for example, designing software or maintaining computer systems) will intensify. Unemployment results because the composition of the labor force does not respond immediately or completely to the new structure of job opportunities.

· Structural unemployment may last for longer periods than frictional unemployment because workers need retraining in order to obtain new jobs. For example, during the late 1990s and early 2000s, there are millions of Chinese workers who were laid off from state-owned businesses because of the reform of market-oriented economy. In return, the government gave laid-off workers and other unemployed people preferential treatment in seeking new jobs and setting up their own businesses, including tax reductions or exemptions.

2.2.3 Cyclical unemployment

Cyclical unemployment is unemployment caused by a business cycle recession.

· Cyclical unemployment results from insufficient demand for goods and services. When the economy moves into recession, many firms find their sales falling and cut back on production. As production falls, firms lay off workers. For example, Ford laid off works during the recession of 2007 – 2009. As the economy slowly recovered from the recession, Ford began rehiring those workers.

· Cyclical unemployment is a very serious problem when it occurs. We will say more about its high costs later, but first we need to define "full employment".

2.2.4 Full employment

Since frictional and structural unemployment is largely unavoidable in a dynamic economy, full employment is something less than 100 percent employment of the labor force. That is the reasons why the unemployment rate never fall to zero. Economists say that economy is "full employment" when it is experiencing only frictional and structural unemployment. That is, full employment occurs when there is no cyclical unemployment.

Notice that a fully employed economy does not mean zero unemployment.

The unemployment rate that is consistent with full employment is called the full-employment rate of unemployment, or the natural rate of unemployment (NRU). At NRU, the economy is said to be producing its potential output. Potential GDP is the real GDP that occurs when the economy is "full employed".

However, "natural" does not mean that economy will always operate at this rate and thus realize its potential output. When cyclical unemployment occurs, the economy has much more unemployment than which would occur at the natural rate of unemployment. Thus, the output would be less than potential output. Moreover, the economy can operate for a while at an unemployment rate below NRU, when the demand for labor may be so great that teenagers, retirees and some parents are trying to find a part-time or full-time job.

Also, the NRU can vary over time as job-search methods and public policies changes. Currently, most economists estimate the natural rate to be between 5 percent and 6 percent.

▷ Exercise 2

i) The advice to "keep searching, there are plenty of jobs around here for which you are qualified" would be most appropriate for which types of unemployment?

ii) A student who just graduated from college but has not found a job would most likely be which type of unemployment?

iii) If you have trouble finding a job because of a slowdown in the overall economy, what type of unemployment are you?

iv) The advice to "retrain" would be most appropriate for which of the following types of unemployment?

v) During the Great Depression, cyclical unemployment increased as the recession continued. Will this increase in cyclical unemployment have effect on natural unemployment rate?

Answer:

i) Frictional unemployment.

ii) Frictional unemployment.

iii) Cyclical unemployment.

ⅳ) Structural unemployment.

ⅴ) No. because the natural unemployment reflects unemployment owing to frictional and structural unemployment.

2.3 What factors determine the employment rate?

In this section, we will discuss some factors that determine the levels of frictional and structural unemployment. Governments can reduce the size of natural unemployment rate with some policies that aid workers in finding new jobs. For example, governments implement some policies that aid worker retaining to reduce structural unemployment. However, some government policies can add to the natural unemployment rate, such as unemployment insurance and minimum wage laws.

2.3.1 Unemployment insurance

In the United States and most industrial countries, the unemployed are eligible for unemployment insurance payments. These payments reduce the opportunity cost of a job search. So, the unemployed spend more time searching for jobs, which increases the natural rate of unemployment. Most economists believe that since in Canada and the countries of Western Europe, workers are eligible to receive more unemployment payments than in United States, the unemployment rates in those countries tend to be higher than in United states.

However, unemployment insurance helps the unemployed maintain their income and spending that can help reduce the severity of recessions. We will talk about this point in later chapters.

2.3.2 Minimum wage laws

Minimum wage laws are designed to help low-income workers. Raising the wage that firms have to pay, however, will likely result in them hiring fewer workers. And some workers will be unemployed who would have been employed if there are no minimum wage. Figure 2-2 shows the impact of a minimum wage.

The equilibrium wage is $ 6.5 per hour as the figure shows. If the government impose a minimum wage $ 8 that is greater than equilibrium wage, the demand of labors is 8 million of workers and the supply of labors is 12 million of workers. The result is 4 million of workers are unemployed. Actually, they are employed if government does not impose a minimum wage. Studies estimate that a 10 percent increase in the minimum wage

Price(dollars per hour)

[Figure 2-2: Labor supply and demand graph with S curve intersecting D curve at wage 6.50 and labor 10 million; dotted lines at wages 8.00 (labor 8 and 12) and 5.00]

Figure 2-2

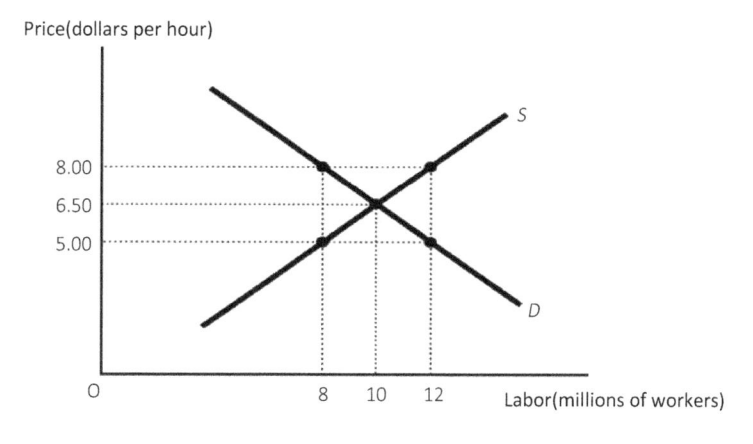

reduces teenage employment by about 2 percent.

To fully understand the minimum wage, keep in mind that minimum wage laws just have impact on the workers whose equilibrium wages are below the minimum wage, like teenagers. Highly skilled and experienced workers are not affected because their equilibrium wages are well above the minimum. For these workers, the minimum wage is not binding.

2.3.3 Labor unions

Labor unions are organizations of workers that bargain with employers for higher wages and better working conditions for their members. Higher wage than market wage results in unemployment as the minimum wage shows. But most economists believe that this does not result in an increase in the overall unemployment rate because only about 9 percent of workers outside the government sector are unionized. And most workers who can not find jobs in unionized industries can find jobs in other industries.

2.3.4 Efficiency wages

An efficiency wage is an above-market wage that a firm pays to increase workers' productivity, attract the most productive worker, get them work hard, and discourage them from quitting. Efficiency wages are another reason that economy experiences some unemployment even when cyclical unemployment is zero. The reason is the same as minimum wage.

▷ Exercise 3

Discuss the likely effect of each of the following on the unemployment rate:

i) The government passes a law to make labor unions illegal.

ii) The minimum wage is raised by 50 percent.

iii) The government funds an internet site where companies can post job openings at no charge.

iv) The length of time workers who are eligible to receive unemployment insurance payments doubles.

v) The minimum wage is abolished.

Answer:

i), iii) and v) are likely to decrease the unemployment rate. An increase in union membership pushes more wages above market wages will result in more workers are unemployed. So dissolving labor unions can reduce the unemployment rate. Abolishing the minimum wage lowers the wage from above the market wage for some workers. Making information on job openings more available shortens the search involved in frictional unemployment.

ii) and iv) are likely to increase the unemployment rate. Increasing minimum wage raises the wage from above the market wage for some workers, which results in higher unemployment rates. Lengthening the time workers are eligible to receive unemployment insurance lowers the opportunity cost of a job search.

2.4　Economic cost of unemployment

Unemployment that is excessive involves great economic and social costs. The basic economic cost of unemployment is forgone output. When unemployment rises, potential production will decline. At NRU, the economy can produce its potential output. When the unemployment rate is greater than NRU (the cyclical unemployment is greater than zero), the economy will produce less than potential output. Economists call the difference between actual and potential GDP as GDP gap. That is:

$$\text{GDP gap} = \text{Actual GDP} - \text{Potential GDP}$$

As actual GDP is greater than potential GDP, GDP gap is positive. Otherwise, GDP gap is negative. The statistical relationship between GDP gap and the unemployment rate can be described by Okun's law. According to Okun's law, for every 1 percentage point by which the actual unemployment rate exceeds the natural unemployment rate, a negative GDP gap of about 2 percent occurs.① We express Okun's law algebraically as:

$$\frac{Y-\overline{Y}}{\overline{Y}} = -2(U-\overline{U})$$

The left side of the equation above is the percentage growth rate of actual output (Y) to potential output ($\overline{Y}$). The right side of the equation is 2 times the cyclical unemployment rate [the actual unemployment (U) minuses the national rate of unemployment ($\overline{U}$)].

Okun's law is intended to tell us how much of a country's gross domestic product (GDP) may be lost when the unemployment rate is above its natural rate. The logic behind Okun's law is simple. Output depends on the amount of labor used in the production process, so there is a positive relationship between output and employment. Total employment equals the labor force minus the unemployed, so there is a negative relationship between output and unemployment.

Let's apply Okun's law by supposing the national rate of unemployment is 5% and that full-unemployment level of output is 5 000 billion yuan. If the actual unemployment rate is 7%, which is 2 percentage point above the national rate (cyclical unemployment equals 2%). According to Okun's law, the actual output will be 4% lower than full-employment output. Because the full-employment output is 5 000 billion yuan, the actual output will be 200 billion yuan below the full-employment output. (4% times 5 000 billion yuan).

As with any law in economics, science, or any discipline, it is important to determine if it holds true under varying conditions and over time. In regard to Okun's law, there appear to be conditions where it holds quite well and others where it doesn't. For instance, Okun's law has held up at various times but did not prove true during the 2008 financial crisis.

2.5 Measures of price level:CPI and PPI

Inflation is a general increase in the level of prices. When inflation occurs, each dollar of income will buy fewer goods and services than before. Inflation reduces the

---

① When the unemployment rate increases, for example, from 3% to 6%, we say that it increases by 3 percentage points (6%-3%), or that it increases by 3 percent (3%).

"purchasing power" of money. But inflation does not mean that all prices are rising. It means the price level (the average prices of goods and services in the economy) is increasing. So, a persistently rising price level is called inflation; a persistently falling price level is called deflation. In Macroeconomics, the price level measures the average prices of goods and services in the economy. In the previous chapter, we introduced the GDP deflator as a measure of the price level. The GDP deflator includes the price of every final good and service, so it is the broadest measure. But for some purposes it is too broad. Because it includes the prices of products such as large electric generators and machine tools that are not purchased by a typical household. Therefore, in this chapter, we will introduce two commonly measures of price level: Consumer Price Index (CPI) and Producer Price Index (PPI).

2.5.1 Consumer price index (CPI)

CPI is a measure of the average change over time in the prices a typical urban family of four pays for the goods and services they purchase.

The CPI tells you about the value of the money in your pocket. Each month the Bureau of Labor Statistics (BLS) surveys 14 000 households nationwide on their spending habits. The BLS uses the results of this survey to construct a market basket of 211 types of goods and services purchased by a typical urban family of four. The market basket includes eight broad categories: food and beverages, education and communication, recreation, medical care, transportation, housing, apparel and other goods and services. According to the households' spending habits, each price in the CPI is given a weight equal to the fraction of a typical family's budget spent on that goods and services. Then we can calculate the cost to a typical family of buying a representative basket of goods and services in each year. One year is chosen as the base year. In any year other than the base year, the value of the CPI is equal to the ratio of the dollar amount necessary to buy the market basket of goods in that year divided by the dollar amount necessary to buy the market basket of goods in the base year, multiplied by 100.

In general, constructing the CPI and calculating the inflation rate involve five stages:

· Selecting the CPI basket.

· Conducting the monthly price survey.

· Calculating the cost of the CPI basket in each month.

- Choosing one year as base year and calculating the CPI in each month.
- Calculating the inflation rate.

To see exactly how CPI is calculated, Let's consider a simple economy in which consumers buy only two goods: apples and bananas.

First, determine which goods should be in the market basket and the weight of each good in measuring the cost of living. To determine the CPI basket, the BLS conducts a periodic survey of consumer expenditure. In this example, we simply say a typical family of four buys a basket of 1 000 apples and 200 bananas for each year.

Second, find the prices of each of goods and services in the basket at each point in time. Table 2-1 shows the prices of apples and bananas for three years.

Table 2-1

Production	Quantity	2000 Price	2000 Expenditure	2022 Price	2022 Expenditure	2023 Price	2023 Expenditure
Apples	1 000	$ 1	$ 1 000	3	$ 3 000	3.5	$ 3 500
Bananas	200	$ 1	$ 200	2	$ 400	2	$ 400

Third, use the information in the table above to calculate the cost of the basket of goods and services at different times. The cost of the basket is $ 1 200 in 2000, $ 3 400 in 2022, and $ 3 900 in 2023. Notice only the prices change in the calculation and the quantity is fixed.

Forth, choose one year as a base year and compute the price index. Because the index is used to measure changes in the cost of living, the choice of base year is arbitrary. The price index is calculated as follows:

$$\text{CPI} = \frac{\text{The total expenditure in current year}}{\text{The total expenditure in base year}} \times 100$$

That is, the CPI in the current year is the cost to purchase the basket of goods this year, divided by the cost in the base year. By convention, we multiply this by 100, so that the CPI in the base year is 100. In this example, we choose 2000 as the base year. The total expenditure in 2000 is $ 1 200. The total expenditure in 2022 is $ 3 400. So, the consumer price index in 2022 equals 283 ($ 3 400 divided by $ 1 200 and multiplied by 100). This means the price level in 2022 is 283 percent of its price in the base year. And the CPI in 2023 equals 325, indicating that the price level in 2023 is 325 percent of the price level in 2000.

Fifth, compute the inflation rate. The inflation rate is the percentage change in the price index from the preceding period. It is calculated as follows:

$$\text{Inflation rate} = \frac{\text{CPI in current year} - \text{CPI in last year}}{\text{CPI in last year}} \times 100\%$$

In this example, the inflation rate in 2023 equals:

$$\frac{325-283}{283} \times 100\% = 14.8\%.$$

The inflation rate in 2023 is 14.8 percent.

From the example above, we know the CPI measures the cost to a typical family of buying a basket of goods and services, it is sometimes called the cost of living index. In addition, notice that the CPI measure the price level rather than the inflation rate. The inflation rate is the percentage increase in the price level (for example, the CPI) from the previous year, not the percentage increase from the base year.

2.5.2 Producer price index (PPI)

PPI is an average of the prices received by producers of goods and services at all stages of the production process.

It is conceptually similar to the CPI. The CPI tracks the prices of goods and services purchased by a typical household. And the PPI tracks the prices firms receive for goods and services at all stages of production. The PPI includes the prices of intermediate goods, such as flour, yarn, steel, and raw materials. If these prices rise, the cost to firms will rise. Because the costs of firms are eventually passed on the consumer prices, the PPI can give early warning of future movements in consumer prices.

2.5.3 Is the CPI accurate?

The CPI is sometimes called the cost-of-living index. Its goal is to measure changes in the cost of living. Although CPI is the most widely used measure of inflation, there are four biases that cause the CPI to overstate the true inflation rate: substitution bias, increase in quality bias, new product bias, and outlet bias. The BLS take steps to reduce the size of the bias.

1) Substitution bias

In calculating the CPI, we assume the basket is same for each year. But in fact, consumers are likely to buy fewer of those goods whose prices increase most and more of those goods whose prices increase least. For example, when apples' price increase more than bananas' price, consumers will buy more bananas and fewer apples in current year than in base year. Because of this, the prices of the market basket in current year are overstated by us.

2) Increase in quality bias

Most goods and services in the market basket improve in quality. The increase in prices partly due to the improvement in quality and partly due to pure inflation. Because the CPI ignores the improvement in quality, it overstates the pure inflation.

3) New product bias

Every 10 years, the BLS updates the market basket of goods used in computing the CPI. The market of goods does not include the new products introduced between updates. The price of many products, such as cellphone, decrease in the years immediately after they are introduced. These prices decreases are not included in the CPI.

4) Outlet bias

The BLS collects price statistics from traditional full-price retail stores, but many consumers often purchase goods from outlet or internet. So, the CPI does not reflect the real cost of living. It overstates the pure inflation.

The consumer price index suffers from these biases that cause it to overstate the true underlying rate of inflation. To make the calculation of cost of living more accurate, Economists compute the personal consumption expenditure price index (PCE), which is a so-called chain-type price index. Rather than assuming the basket is same for each year, PCE allows the mix of products to change each year. In 2000, the Fed announced that it would rely more on the PCE than on the CPI in tracking inflation.

▷ Exercise 4

Consider a simple economy that produces only three products: apples, hats, and golf balls. Use the information in Table 2-2 to calculate the inflation rate for 2023, as measured by the consumer price index.

Table 2-2

Products	Quantity	Base year prices(2001)	Prices(2022)	Prices(2023)
Apples	10	1.00	1.50	1.75
Hats	15	5.00	7.00	6.75
Golf balls	8	2.00	3.00	3.50

Answer:

Total expenditures for 2001 = (10 × $ 1.00) + (15 × $ 5.00) + (8 × $ 2.00)
= $ 101.00.

Total expenditures for 2022 = (10 × $ 1.50) + (15 × $ 7.00) + (8 × $ 3.00)
= $ 144.00.

Total expenditures for 2023 = (10 × $ 1.75) + (15 × $ 6.75) + (8 × $ 3.50)
= $ 146.75.

The CPI for 2022 = [($ 144.00/$ 101.00) × 100] = 142.57.

The CPI for 2023 = [($ 146.75/$ 101.00) × 100] = 145.30.

So,

The inflation rate for 2023 = (145.30−142.57)/142.57×100% = 1.9%.

2.6 Correcting economic variables for the effects of inflation

2.6.1 The value of money at different times

Price indexes give us a way to compare the values of money from different years. Suppose your mother's salary for her first job in 2000 was 2 000 yuan per month. And, in 2023, your sister's salary for her first job was 6 000 yuan per month. Was the salary of your sister's first job higher than that of your mother's first job? To answer this question, we need to know the level of prices in 2000 and the level of prices in 2023. According to the government statistics, the CPI for 2000 is 434 (the base year is 1978) and the CPI for 2023 is 708 (the base year is 1978). Because 708/434 = 1.63, the price level of 2023 is 1.63 times of the price level of 2000. That means if we could buy one apple in 2000 using 1 yuan, then in 2023, we needed 1.63 yuan to buy one apple. The value of 1.63 yuan in 2023 equals the value of 1 yuan in 2000. Then we can turn your mother's salary in 2000 yuan into the salary in 2023 yuan using the formula as follows:

$$\text{Amount in 2023 yuan} = \text{Amount in 2000 yuan} \times \frac{\text{CPI in 2023}}{\text{CPI in 2000}}$$

$$= 2\,000 \text{ yuan} \times \frac{708}{434}$$

$$= 3\,260 \text{ yuan}.$$

Your mother's salary in 2023 yuan is 3 260 yuan. Therefore, your sister's salary (6 000 yuan) per month is higher than your mother's salary per month.

In general, to correct for the effects of inflation, we can divide the nominal variable by a price index and multiply by 100 to obtain the real variable.

$$\text{The real variable} = \frac{\text{The nominal varialbe}}{\text{A price index}} \times 100$$

The real variable will be measured in money of the base year for the price index. For example, your sister nominal wage in 2023 was 6 000 yuan. Her real wage in 2023 was $\frac{6\ 000}{708} \times 100$ = 847 yuan. The base year for the CPI is 1978.

2.6.2 Real and nominal interest rate

When you deposit your money in a bank account, you will earn interest on your deposit. Conversely, when you borrow from a bank to pay for your apartment, you will pay interest on your loan. Interest represents a payment in the future for a transfer of money in the past. As a result, interest rate always involves comparing amounts of money at different points in time.

To fully understand interest rates, let's consider an example. Suppose you deposit 1 000 yuan in a bank account. The stated interest rate is 5% for one year. That means you will receive 1 050 yuan from the bank next year. But 1 050 yuan in next year is 5% more than 1 000 yuan now? If prices rise during the year, the values of 1 050 yuan next year will be less than the values of 1 050 yuan now. Why? Let's consider a question: how much more I can buy with this 1 050 yuan than I could buy with that 1 000 yuan before? Let's say that the inflation ended up being 2% between a year ago and today. If that's the case, what is 1 000 yuan a year ago in today's money? Because the inflation rate was 2%, so the 1 000 yuan a year ago would buy the same stuff as that 1 020 yuan would buy today. So, it would be 1 020 yuan. Therefore, the actual real return in today's money would be $\frac{1\ 050 - 1\ 020}{1\ 020} \times 100\% = 2.94\%$. That is the real interest rate which is 2.94%. We can do it in today's money and we also could do it either way. We could discount the 1 050 yuan back to a year ago money and figure out the real return there. You can try this method by yourself. Finally, you could get the same answer for the real return. Although the normal return is 5%, because of the inflation, the actual real return is only 2.94%.

The stated interest rate in bank is nominal interest rate. The interest rate corrected for inflation is called real interest rate. The real interest rate more accurately reflects the cost of borrowing and lending money. In this example, the real interest rate (2.94%) is approximately equal to the nominal interest rate (5%) minus the inflation rate (2%).

Therefore, in general, we say real interest rate equals the nominal interest rate minus the inflation rate.

$$\text{Real interest rate} = \text{Nominal interest rate} - \text{Inflation rate}$$

If nominal interest rate is 5% and the inflation rate is 2%, then the real interest rate for your saving is 3%. [1]

▶ Exercise 5

Use the information about nominal average yearly earnings of Shanghai and its CPI for each year as Table 2-3 shows, to calculate real average yearly earnings for each year. And What was the percentage change in real average yearly earnings between 2011 and 2015?

Table 2-3

Year	Earnings (yuan)	CPI (1978=100)
2011	51 968	676.7
2012	56 300	695.9
2013	60 435	711.9
2014	65 417	730.7
2015	71 268	748.4

Answer:

To calculate real average yearly earnings for each year, divide nominal average yearly earnings by the CPI and multiply by 100. For example, real average yearly earnings for 2011 are equal to:

(51 968/676.7) ×100 = 7 679.6.

Table 2-4 shows the results for all five years.

This percentage change is equal to: (9 527.8 − 7 679.6)/7 679.6 × 100% =

---

[1] We can also get the real interest rate using the following formula:

$$\text{Real interest rate} = \frac{1 + \text{Nominal interest rate}}{1 + \text{Inflation rate}} - 1$$

In the above example, Real interest rate = $\frac{1+5\%}{1+2\%}$ = 2.94%.

24%. We can conclude that real average yearly earnings in Shanghai increased by 24% between 2011 and 2015.

Table 2-4

Year	Nominal average yearly earnings (yuan)	CPI (1978=100)	Real average yearly earnings (yuan)
2011	51 968	676.7	7 679.6
2012	56 300	695.9	8 090.2
2013	60 435	711.9	8489.3
2014	65 417	730.7	8 952.6
2015	71 268	748.4	9 527.8

2.7 The effect of inflation

Sometimes inflation seems unimportant. After all, if all prices doubled overnight, it seems like nothing much would change: the prices of goods and services would have doubled, but so would your wage; so, you could afford exactly as much as before.

However, inflation effects the distribution of income and wealth. For example, nominal assets like cash decrease in value when there is a significant inflation. If you hold much of your wealth in cash, then inflation causes a significant decrease in real wealth for you. And people on fixed incomes such as a retired worker, are particularly likely to be hurt by inflation. The extent to which inflation redistributes income depends, in part, on whether the inflation is anticipated.

2.7.1 The effect of perfectly anticipated inflation

When inflation can be perfectly anticipated, people can prepare for it. For example, if everyone knows that inflation rate for the next 10 years will be 5% per year, workers will require their wage should be raised by 5% per year to keep their purchasing power unchanged. And firms will be willing to increase workers' wage, because they know the prices of their products will increase. Similarly, lenders will charge higher interest rates to compensate for inflation and borrowers will be willing to pay the higher interest rates. So far, there seem to be no costs in anticipated inflation.

However, an anticipated inflation still causes some economic costs:

1) Shoeleather costs

It is the cost in time and effort incurred by people and firms who are trying to minimize their holdings of cash.

As you know, inflation erodes the real value of the money in your wallet. One way to avoid the loss is to go to bank more often. For example, rather than withdrawing 2 000 yuan every month, you might withdraw 500 yuan every week. By making more frequent trips to the bank, you can keep more of your wealth in bank and less in your wallet, which reduces the cost of holding cash. But making more frequent trips to the bank causes your shoes to wear out more quickly. And you might also sacrifice your time and convenience to keep less money in hand. Therefore, any cost of reducing your money holdings is called the shoeleather cost.

2) Menu costs

It is the cost to firms of changing prices.

Frequently changing prices are inconvenient for firms (and consumers too!) to deal with. Most firms do no change the price of their products every day. They often keep their price unchanged for months or even years. But firms have to change their prices when an economy occurs inflation. The costs of adjustment are called menu costs. Menu costs include the cost of printing new price lists, the cost of persuading their dealers and customers to accept the new price lists, the cost of deciding on new price, and the cost of advertising the new prices. During hyperinflation, firms must change their prices daily to keep up with all other prices in the economy. They must bear the menu costs because of hyperinflation.

3) Inflation-induced tax distortions

Investors pay more taxes because of inflation.

Investors are taxed on nominal returns, rather than real returns. So, this can increase the tax due. For example, you bought a stock of 1 000 yuan in 2000, then you sold the stock in 2020 for 5 000 yuan. You have earned a capital gain of 4 000 yuan. Suppose the tax rate for capital gains is 10 percent. You had to pay 400 yuan for taxes. But suppose the overall price level doubled from 2000 to 2020. In this case, the 1 000 yuan you invested in 2000 is equivalent to 2 000 yuan in 2020. Your real gain is only 3 000 yuan and you should pay 300 yuan for taxes. Thus, inflation exaggerates the size of capital gains and inadvertently increase the tax burden on this type of income.

One solution to this problem is to index the tax system. The government could take account of the effects of inflation and tax only real interest income rather than nominal interest income.

2.7.2 The effect of unanticipated inflation

When people cannot predict the rate of inflation, they find it hard to make good borrowing and lending decisions. When people borrow money or banks lend money, they must forecast the rate of inflation, then they can calculate the real rate of interest on a loan. When the actual inflation rate turns out to be different from the expected rate, some people gain, and other people lose. For example, unanticipated inflation hurts fixed-income recipients, savers and creditors (lenders). Suppose a household may save 1 000 yuan in a commercial bank at 5% annual interest. But if inflation is 10%, the real value of that 1000 yuan will be cut to about 909 (1 000/1.1) yuan by the end of the year. Although the saver will receive 1050 yuan (1 000×1.05), its real value is only about 955 (1 050/1.1). So, the real interest rate is −4.5% [(955−1 000)/1 000] rather than 5%. The "borrower" gains because the "borrower" pays back less valuable money than those received from the lender. Therefore, unpredictable inflation makes borrowing and lending risky.

On the contrary, the effects of deflation — declines in price level are the reverse of those of inflation. People with fixed nominal incomes will find their real incomes enhanced. Creditors will benefit at the expense of debtors. And savers will discover that the purchasing power of their savings has grown because of the falling prices.

▷ Exercise 6

When the actual inflation rate turns out to be greater than the expected inflation rate, who gains — the borrower or the lender — and who loses? Explain why.

Answer:

The borrower gains because he pays back the loan in cheaper dollars — dollars that have lost more purchasing power than expected.

Case Study

China's Inflation and Its Characteristics from 1978 to 2020

The changes of inflation rates are closely related to people's life and therefore have been closely watched by the public. The outbreak of COVID-19 imposed unprecedented economic impacts on both China and the world, and greatly affected the production and life of people. In order to ensure economic operation, prevent liquidity crisis, and also stimulate the economy after the pandemic, various countries adopted loose monetary policies, proactive fiscal policies and even quantitative easing accordingly, so as to provide huge liquidity for the market. The Federal Reserve cut interest rates several times, lowered the target range of federal funds interest rate to 0~0.25%, and restarted quantitative easing, which expanded its balance sheet rapidly. Meanwhile, it implemented measures such as granting subsidies to the unemployed. The People's Bank of China adopted a combination of measures including interest rate cuts, RRR cuts, refinancing and rediscounting, aiming at providing moderate liquidity, guiding cutdown of entity financing costs and maintaining market confidence. According to the classic statement of Friedman, the Nobel laureate in economics, "Inflation is always and everywhere a monetary phenomenon", loose liquidity will inevitably lead to high inflation. So in actual observation, are the trends of money supply and inflation rate consistent with each other? Let us recall China's inflation and its characteristics since its reform and opening up.

Inflation is a common economic phenomenon in modern economic society, and China is no exception. Figure 2-3 shows the annual inflation rates of China from 1978 to 2020.

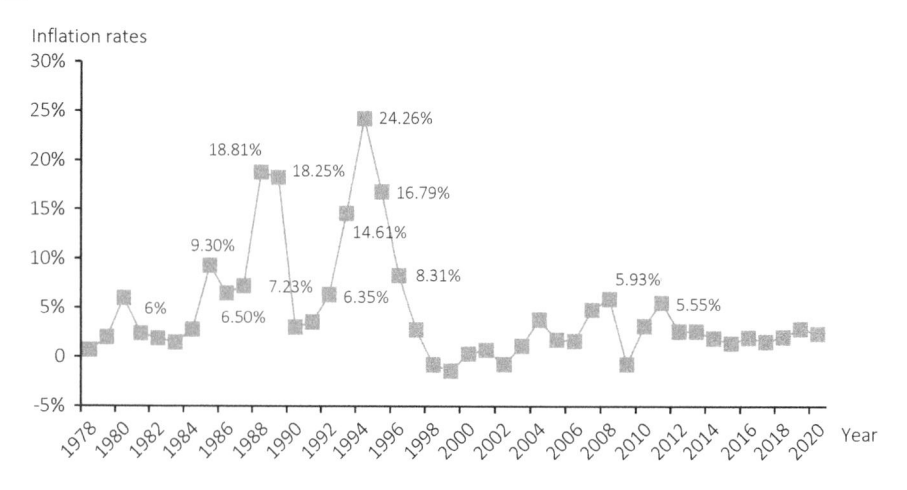

Figure 2-3

Source: China Statistical Yearbook.

So far, China has roughly experienced the following inflation peaks:

The first peak was in 1980, when the consumer price index reached 6.0%, forming the first peak of inflation since the reform and opening up. This high inflation started from and ended with the adjustment of macro-economic policies.

The second peak appeared in 1985, when the consumer price index reached 9.3%. It was mainly driven by costs. The government raised the purchase prices of major agricultural products such as grains, cotton, oil and oil plants, and the ex-factory prices of industrial products such as coal, iron ores, pig iron, steel ingots, steel billets, non-ferrous metals and cement. In order to curb inflation, the State Council implemented a series of measures to control the scale of investment in fixed assets, strengthen price control, supervision and inspection, and conducted a comprehensive credit inspection. After taking a series of measures, the CPI began to fall in early 1986 and returned to below 4% in August.

The third peak was from 1988 to 1989, when the CPIs rose to 18.81% and 18.25% respectively, reaching a new high. Since 1989, China began to implement a severe credit tightening policy. However, due to the widespread expectation on inflation in the market and the inertia characteristics of inflation itself, inflation was not immediately curbed, but lasted until July 1990.

The fourth peak was found in 1994, when the CPI reached a new high, reaching 24.26%. At the end of 1991, in order to invigorate large and medium-sized enterprises, the State Council announced 20 important measures, including further lowering interest rates to give off a strong signal of loosening monetary policy, leading to a nearly 50% credit supply growth rate nationwide in 1993, reaching a new high. From 1992 to 1994, there was a nationwide boom in real estate development, development zones and investment in China. After the comprehensive implementation of the austerity policy, and thanks to the fixed exchange rate system always pegged to the US dollar since 1995, it took China more than two years to get on the right track from the severe situation featuring both high economic growth and high inflation, and gradually shape a growth pattern of high growth and low inflation, realizing a "soft landing" of the economy.

Since the 21st century, the inflation rate in China has been growing steadily, basically below 5%. Affected by the international financial crisis in 2008, China's inflation rate reached 5.93%. In 2011, influenced by the 4 trillion yuan investment plan and a loose monetary policy, the inflation rate reached 5.55%.

Since the COVID-19, "monetary easing" and "low inflation" have coexisted. Affected by the COVID-19, the GDP in Q1 of 2020 decreased by 6.8% year-on-year. It was the first time that China had experienced negative growth since it announced its quarterly GDP. In response to the impacts of the pandemic, the People's Bank of China launched a series of powerful support measures, including three RRR cuts, an additional quota of 1.8 trillion yuan for refinancing and rediscounting, guidance on the continuous declines of market interest rates, introducing a support plan for small-scale corporate credit loans, and implementing the policy of delaying the repayment of principal and interest by stages for loans to small and medium-sized enterprises. Because of the loose monetary policy, the growth rates of broad money supply (M2) balance and social financing balance were significantly higher than those of 2019. However, the monetary policy during the COVID-19 did not cause inflation. Taking the industrial added value as an example, the cumulative year-on-year decline in May 2020 narrowed to 2.8%, close to the same level last year. However, the recovery of the demand side was far below expectation. In May 2020, the cumulative year-on-year declines in total retail sales of consumer goods and investment in fixed assets were also narrowing, yet still down 13.5% and 6.3% respectively. In the case that the recovery of domestic demand was weaker than domestic supply, the positive impacts of monetary policy easing on the price level were relatively weakened, and thus inflation continued to fall.

Inflation theory is one of the major issues in the studies on macro-economics. Inflation rate is the most important reference factor for formulating relevant policies to achieve monetary policy objectives. Its changes are closely related to people's life and thus has been closely watched by the public. This case reviews the changes of China's inflation rates over the years since the reform and opening up, briefly analyzes the causes of several high inflations, and focuses on discussing and analyzing the reasons why China managed to keep a low inflation rate during COVID-19 when other countries around the world suffered from high inflation. It can be seen that in the short term, loose monetary policies do not necessarily lead to a high inflation rate. There are many reasons behind inflation, such as the velocity of money, economic growth rate, the flow direction of new money, the implementation and effects of monetary policy, and so forth. A loose monetary policy is not exactly the same as the increase in money supply.

Whether the money supply increases or not depends on the size of the money multiplier. Even if the money supply increases, whether it will cause inflation is related to whether the output increases. Therefore, whether there will be inflation in the future should not be simply based on whether a loose monetary policy has been adopted, but also on other factors that affect inflation.

Source: https://www.jiemian.com/article/4644184.html.; https://www.sohu.com/a/102238449_227249.

Terms and Concepts

· **Consumer price index (CPI)**: Measure of the average change over time in the prices a typical urban family of four pays for the goods and services they purchase.

· **Frictional unemployment**: Short-term unemployment that arises from the process of matching workers with jobs.

· **Structural unemployment**: Unemployment that arises from a persistent mismatch between the skills or attributes of workers and the requirements of jobs.

· **Cyclical unemployment**: Unemployment caused by a business cycle recession.

· **Full employment**: a situation in which the unemployment rate equals the natural unemployment rate.

· **Natural rate of unemployment**: The normal rate of unemployment, consisting of frictional unemployment and structural unemployment.

· **Producer price index (PPI)**: An average of the prices received by producers of goods and services at all stages of the production process.

· **Real interest rate**: The nominal interest rate minus the inflation rate.

· **Nominal interest rate**: The stated interest rate on a loan.

· **Inflation rate**: The percentage increase in the price level from one year to the next.

· **Discourage workers**: People who are available for work but have not looked for a job during the previous four weeks because they believe no jobs are available for them.

· **Menu cost**: The costs to firms of changing prices.

Problems and Applications

I. True or False

1. Counting part-time workers who are looking for full-time work as employed overstates the degree of joblessness in the economy.

2. Eliminating frictional unemployment would be good for the economy.

3. The natural rate of unemployment consists of frictional unemployment plus cyclical unemployment.

4. The unemployment rate is higher with a minimum wage law than it would be without a minimum wage law.

5. Price level can be measured using either the GDP deflator or the consumer price index.

6. Because an increase in gasoline prices causes consumers to ride their bikes more and drive their cars less, the CPI tends to underestimate the cost of living.

7. The content of the basket of goods and services used to compute the CPI changes every month.

8. The producer price index tracks the prices firms receive for goods and services at all stages of production.

9. If inflation is higher than expected, this helps borrowers (by reducing the real interest rate they pay) and hurts lenders (by reducing the real interest rate they receive).

10. The CPI is always 1 in the base year.

11. When a new good is introduced, consumers have more variety from which to choose, and this in turn increases the cost of maintaining the same level of economic well-being.

II. Choices

1. Suppose that homemakers are included as employed in the labor force statistics, rather than being counted as out of the labor force. This would _____.

  A. increase the measured unemployment rate

  B. increase the measured labor force participation rate

C. decrease the number of persons in the labor force

D. decrease the number of persons in the working-age population

2. Someone who is available for work but has not actively looked for work in the previous four weeks would be classified as _____.

A. employed

B. unemployed

C. not in the labor force

D. not in the working-age population

3. An advantage of the establishment survey over the household survey of the labor market is that the establishment survey _____.

A. is based on actual payrolls, rather than on unverified answers

B. includes the number of self-employed persons

C. includes persons employed at newly opened firms

D. provides an estimate of the number of persons unemployed

4. Full employment is not considered to be zero unemployment, because _____.

A. some cyclical unemployment always exists

B. some people do not want a job

C. there are not enough jobs for everyone who wants one

D. people do not find jobs instantaneously

5. Xiaoming is a full-time student who is not looking for work. What kind of unemployment is Xiaoming experiencing? _____.

A. Cyclical

B. Structural

C. Frictional

D. Xiaoming is not experiencing unemployment of any kind, because he is not currently part of the labor force

6. Why might firms pay wages that are above the equilibrium wage in a market? _____.

A. To increase the productivity of their workers

B. To reduce the unemployment rate

C. To encourage workers to form labor unions

D. To reduce profit

7. The substitution bias in the consumer price index refers to the idea that consumers _____ the quantity of products they buy in response to price, and the CPI does not reflect this and _____ the cost of the market basket.

A. change; overestimates

B. change; underestimates

C. do not change; overestimates

D. do not change; underestimates

8. In a particular economy, the price index was 270 in 2005 and 300 in 2006. Which of the following statements is correct? _____.

A. The economy experienced a rising price level between 2005 and 2006

B. The economy experienced a higher inflation rate between 2005 and 2006 than it had experienced between 2004 and 2005

C. The inflation rate between 2005 and 2006 was 30 percent

D. All of the above are correct

9. Suppose prices of personal computers fall significantly and consumers respond by buying more personal computers. The consumer price index _____.

A. reflects this price decrease accurately

B. understates this price decrease due to the substitution bias

C. overstates this price decrease due to the income bias

D. overstates this price decrease due to the substitution bias

10. Which of the following statements is true? _____.

A. Even if we know the values of the consumer price index for the years 2009 and 2010, we cannot calculate the inflation rate for 2010 if we do not know which year is the base year

B. If we know the base year is 1990, and if we know the value of the consumer price index for the year 2010, then we have all the information we need to calculate the inflation rate for 2010

C. If we know the base year is 2000, and if we know the value of the consumer price index for the year 1995, then we have all the information we need to calculate the inflation rate for 1995

D. If we know the base year is 2000, and if we know the value of the consumer price index for the year 1995, then we have all the information we need to calculate the percentage change in the cost of living between 1995 and 2000

11. You agree to lend $ 1 000 for one year at a nominal interest rate of 10%. You anticipate that inflation will be 4% over that year. If inflation is instead 3% over that year, which of the following is true? _____.

A. The real interest rate you earn on your money is lower than you expected

B. The purchasing power of the money that will be repaid to you will be lower than you expected

C. The person who borrowed the $ 1 000 will be worse off as a result of the unanticipated decrease in inflation

D. The real interest rate you earn on your money will be negative

12. If inflation is positive and is perfectly anticipated _____.

A. those that borrow money lose

B. those that lend money lose

C. those that hold paper money lose

D. no one in the economy loses

13. Which of the following do not suffer the costs of inflation? _____.

A. Persons on fixed incomes

B. Persons whose incomes rise more rapidly than inflation

C. Firms that have to devote more time and labor to raising prices

D. An investor that has to pay higher taxes because of the inflation

14. Okun's law states that a 1 percentage point increase in the unemployment rate, _____ output by _____ of full-employment level of output.

A. reduces; 2%

B. rises; 2%

C. reduces; 1%

D. rises; 1%

Ⅲ. Short Answer

1. If the number of unemployed workers is 19 million, the number in the working-age population is 500 million, and the unemployment rate is 4%, how many workers are in the labor force? what is the labor force participation rate? How many people are employed?

2. How would the unemployment rate and the labor force participation rate change if discouraged workers were counted as unemployed rather than counted as out of the labor force? Show using the formula for both measurements.

3. To understand why someone cannot get a job, it helps to know the three types of unemployment. List the three types of unemployment and explain what causes each type. What advice for finding a job would be appropriate for someone in each type of unemployment?

4. In a simple economy, people consume only 2 goods, food and clothing. The prices information as Table 2-5 shows.

Table 2-5

Products	Quantity	Prices in 2010	Prices in 2022	Prices in 2023
Food	100 unit	¥80	¥100	¥130
Clothing	50 unit	¥200	¥250	¥300

i) What are the percentage increases in the price of food and in the price of clothing from 2022 to 2023?

ii) Using 2010 as the base year, compute the CPI for each year, and the inflation rate in 2023.

iii) Using 2022 as the base year, what is the percentage increase in CPI?

iv) Do ii) and iii) have the same results? Explain.

5. List the four major problems in using the CPI as a measure of the cost of living. And explain which of the problems might be illustrated by each of the following situations.

i) The tendency for households to spend their money at discount stores as prices rise.

ii) In 2008, more and more households accessed the Internet through a broadband connection that would not have existed ten years ago.

iii) Consumers increased air-condition purchases in response to a decline in their prices.

iv) Smart cellphone become faster and have more memory recently.

6. Using the information in Table 2-6 to determine:

Table 2-6

Year	Shanghai Minimum wage per month	CPI	New York Minimum wage per hour	CPI
2000	¥ 445	547	$ 7	215
2018	¥ 2 420	798	$ 12	260

i) The percentage changes in shanghai and in New York minimum wages from 2000 to 2018 in both nominal terms and in real terms.

ii) Does it matter for your answer that you have not been told the base year for the New York CPI and the Shanghai CPI?

iii) Was the percentage increase in price level greater in shanghai or in Nork York during these years?

7. You lend $ 5 000 to a friend for one year at a nominal interest rate of 10%. The CPI over that year rises from 180 to 190. What is the real rate of interest you will earn? How much will you receive at the end of the year? What is the purchasing power of that money in current dollar?

8. You are given the following data (Table 2-7) on the unemployment rate and output.

Table 2-7

Year	1	2	3	4
Unemployment rate	8%	6%	7%	5%
Output	950	1 030	1 033.5	1 127.5

Assume that the national rate of unemployment is 6%, according to Okun's law, find the full employment level of output in each year.

Answers to Problems and Applications

I. True or False

1	2	3	4	5	6	7	8	9	10	11
F	F	F	T	T	F	F	T	T	F	F

II. Choice

1	2	3	4	5	6	7	8	9	10
B	C	A	D	D	A	A	A	B	D
11	12	13	14						
C	C	B	A						

III. Short Answer

1. **Answer:** Unemployment rate $=\dfrac{\text{Number of unemployed}}{\text{Labor force}} \times 100\%$

$$\text{Labor force} = \dfrac{\text{Number of unemployed}}{\text{Unemployment rate}}$$

$$\text{Labor force} = \dfrac{19}{4\%} = 475 \text{ million.}$$

$$\text{Labor force participation rate} = \dfrac{\text{Labor force}}{\text{Working-age population}} \times 100\%$$

$$\text{Labor force participation rate} = \dfrac{475}{500} \times 100\% = 95\%.$$

$$\text{Labor force} = \text{Unemployed} + \text{Employed}$$

$$\text{Employed} = \text{Labor force} - \text{Unemployed}$$

Employed = 475 − 19 = 456 million.

2. **Answer:** The unemployment rate is calculated as:

$$\text{Unemployment rate} = \dfrac{\text{Number of unemployed}}{\text{Labor force}} \times 100\%$$

Including discouraged workers would increase the number of people counted as being in the labor force and would increase the number of people counted as unemployed. In terms of our calculation, the numerator would rise, and the denominator would rise. However, the numerator would rise by a greater percentage than the denominator as the denominator is the sum of employment plus unemployment. If the top number rises more quickly than the bottom number, then the whole number rises. This would increase the unemployment rate.

The labor force participation rate is calculated as:

$$\text{Labor force participation rate} = \frac{\text{Labor force}}{\text{Working-age population}} \times 100\%$$

Including discouraged workers would increase the number of people in the labor force, but not change the number of people in the working-age population. This would increase the labor force participation rate because the numerator increases. Increasing the numerator of a fraction increases the fraction.

3. **Answer**: Frictional unemployment is the unemployment that arises from the process of matching workers with jobs. These workers are qualified; they just need to search for a job. The advice for finding a job would be to keep searching, because there are jobs available for which they are qualified.

Structural unemployment is unemployment arising from a persistent mismatch between the skills and characteristics of workers and the requirements of the jobs. The advice for finding a job would be to retrain so that they can match up with the requirements of current jobs.

Cyclical unemployment is unemployment caused by a business cycle recession. The advice for finding a job would be to hang in there and continue searching, but realize that there are less jobs available than the number of applicants. The cyclically unemployed person could perhaps get a temporary job until the economy picks up, or perhaps consider continuing his or her education while the business cycle slowdown lasts.

4. **Answer**:

ⅰ) The price of food increased by 30 percent [(130−100)/100×100%]. The price of clothing increased by 20 percent [(300−250)/250×100%].

ⅱ) In 2000, the market basket cost ￥18 000 (100×80 + 50×200);

In 2022, it cost ￥22 500 (100×100 + 50×250);

In 2023, it cost ￥28 000 (100×130 + 50×300).

Using 2000 as base year, the CPI in 2017 is 125 (22 500×100/18 000);

The CPI for 2023 is 155 (28 000×100/18 000);

The percentage increase in the CPI is 24 percent [(155−125)/125×100%].

ⅲ) Using 2022 as base year, the CPI for 2022 is 100. The CPI for 2023 is 124 (28 000×100/22 500). The inflation rate is 24%[(124−100)/100].

ⅳ) ⅱ) and ⅲ) have the same results. the choice of base year has effect on the value of consumer price index for each year. But it has no effect on the percentage change of the overall price level. Because we use the index to measure the changes in the cost of living. The choice of base year is arbitrary.

5. **Answer**: a) Substitution bias. The CPI ignores the fact that consumers substitute toward goods that have become relatively less expensive. b) Introduction of new goods. Because the CPI uses a fixed basket of goods, it does not take into account the increased well-being of consumers created when new goods are introduced. c) increase in quality bias. Not all quality changes can be measured. d) Outlet bias. The CPI did not reflect the prices some consumers actually paid.

ⅰ) Outlet bias.

ⅱ) Introduction of new goods.

ⅲ) Substitution bias.

ⅳ) Increase in quality bias.

6. **Answer**:

ⅰ) In Shanghai, the percentage changes in nominal minimum wage is 444 percent from 2000 to 2018. The real minimum wage per month in 2000 was ￥81 (445×100/547), and in 2018 it was ￥303 (2 420×100/798). Therefore, from 2000 to 2018, the percentage changes in real minimum wage is 274 percent.

In New York, the percentage changes in nominal minimum wage is 71.4 percent from 2000 to 2018.

In New York, the real minimum wage per hour in 2000 was $ 3.25 and in 2018 it was $ 4.61.

Therefore, between 2000 and 2018, there was a 41.8 percent increase in the real minimum wage per hour in New York.

ⅱ) It does not matter whether we have information about the base year as long as we have the CPI data. Whatever the base year is, we would get the same percentage increase in prices.

ⅲ) The percentage increase in the price level was less in the Shanghai {[(798−547)/547 × 100] = 45.9%} than in New York {[(260−215)/215 × 100] = 20.9%}.

7. **Answer**: The inflation rate $= \dfrac{190-180}{180} \times 100 = 5.6\%$;

Real interest rate = Nominal interest rate−Inflation rate

Therefore, Real interest rate = 10% − 5.6% = 4.4%.

At the end of the year, I will receive $ 5 500. Because the prices have increased in the year, the purchasing power of the $ 5500 will be $ 5 220 ($ 5 000×1.044) in current dollar.

8. **Answer**: The Okun's law can be expressed by the following equation:

$$\frac{Y-\overline{Y}}{\overline{Y}} = -2(U-\overline{U})$$

The natural rate of unemployment is 6%, so for year 2, the unemployment rate is equal to the natural rate of unemployment, then the actual output should be equal to the full-employment output. Therefore, for year 2, the full-employment output is 1 030.

For year 1, the unemployment is 8%, which is 2 percentage point above the natural rate, so the actual output should be 4% lower than full-employment output. As the actual output in year 1 is 950, the full employment should be 989.6 [950/ (1−4%)].

Then, we can get the full-employment outputs of year 3 and year 4:

The full-employment of year 3 = 1 033.5/ (1−2%) = 1 054.6,

And the full employment of year 4 = 1 127.5/ (1+2%) = 1 105.4.

3 Economic Growth, the Financial System, and Business Cycles

Learning Objective

By the end of this chapter, students should understand:
- the importance of long-run economic growth.
- how to calculate growth rates.
- how to calculate growth rates over longer periods.
- the role of the financial system in facilitating long-run economic growth.
- the definition of business cycle.
- the characteristics of business cycle.
- what happens during the business cycle.
- to explain actual situation with business cycle.

Key Points and Exercises

3.1 Long-run economic growth

3.1.1 Definition of long-run economic growth

People living in rich countries tend to take economic growth and rising standard of living for granted. But unfortunately, some economics around the world are not growing at all or growing very slowly. An important macroeconomic topic is why some countries grow much faster than others.

Long-run economic growth is the process by which rising productivity increases the average standard of living. How to calculate the average standard of living, the most commonly used measure is real GDP per capita.

As Figure 3-1 shows, measured in 1978 RMB, real GDP per capita in China grew from about 382 yuan in 1978 to about 10 537.6 yuan in 2018. The Real GDP per capita in China has risen more than twenty-six-fold during the last forty years. An average Chinese in 2018 could buy more than twenty-six times as many goods and services as an average Chinese in 1978.

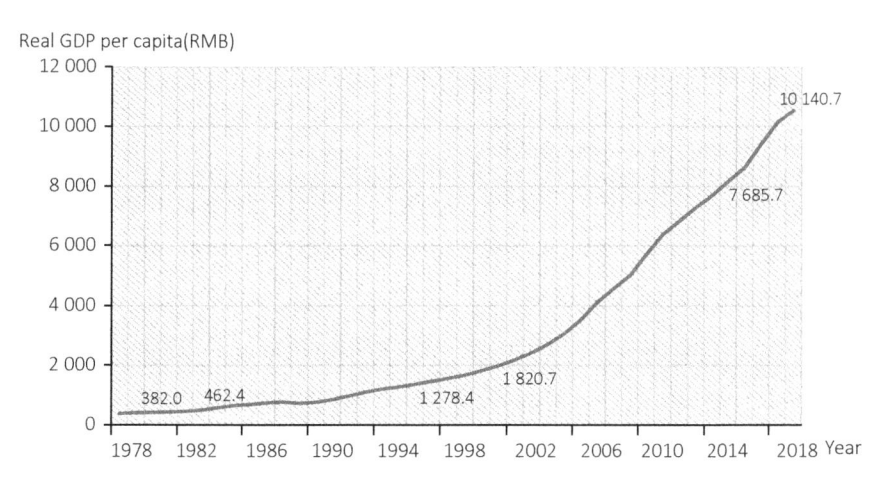

Figure 3-1

3.1.2 Calculating growth rates

1) The growth rates

The growth rate of real GDP or real GDP per capita during particular year is equal to the percentage change from the previous year. For example, if real GDP is shown in Table 3-1, we can get the growth rates as follows.

Table 3-1

Year	Real GDP
2011	$ 15 052 billion
2012	$ 15 471 billion

$$\text{Growth Rate} = \left（\frac{\$\ 15\ 471\ \text{billion} - \$\ 15\ 052\ \text{billion}}{\$\ 15\ 052\ \text{billion}}\right） \times 100\% = 2.8\%$$

2) Annual rate of growth

Over periods of a few years, we can average the growth rates to find the approximate annual rate of growth, as Table 3-2 shows.

Table 3-2

Year	Growth in real GDP
2010	2.5%
2011	1.8%
2012	2.8%

$$\text{Annual rate of growth} = \frac{2.5\% + 1.8\% + 2.8\%}{3} = 2.4\%$$

3) Growth rates over longer periods

In the longer term, we don't want to calculate the annual growth rates and then take an average in order to get the average annual growth rate; instead we would find the solution for the growth rate g, where:

$$\text{Previous real GDP} \times (1+g)^t = \text{Current real GDP}$$

in which t is the number of time periods between the previous and current periods.

4) Rule of 70

Rule of 70 is an easy way to calculate how many years it would take real GDP per capita to double. The formula for the rule is:

$$\text{Number of years to double} = \frac{70}{\text{Growth rate}}$$

Thus, we can easily judge how rapidly an economic variable is growing. So, if the growth rate is 4%, it will take about 17.5 years for the economic variable to double. If it is 2%, 35 years to double.

It also tells us that small differences in growth rates can have significant effects on how rapidly the living standard increases in a country. The rule of 70 applies not just to growth in real GDP per capita but to growth in any variable. If your income is 60 000 yuan a year, and your income grows at an average annual rate of 10 percent, your income will double to 120 000 yuan in 7 years.

▷ Exercise 1

If you invest $ 20 000 in a bond that earns 5% interest per year, how many years will it take to double your money?

A. 1 year and 3 months

B. 2 years and 6 months

C. 14 years

D. 14 years and 9 months

Answer:

C

3.1.3 What determines the rate of long-run growth?

It depends on what determines the increases in real GDP per capita. That is labor productivity, the quantity of goods and services that can be produced by one worker or by one hour of work. So, the question is transferred to what determines the increases in labor productivity growth.

Two key factors determine the increases in labor productivity are the increase in capital per hour worked and the level of technology. Capital refers to manufactured goods that are used to produce other goods and services. Country's capital stock means total amount of physical capital available in a country. The more capital a worker has available to use (including human capital), the more productive he or she will be, thus worker productivity increases. Human capital refers to the accumulated knowledge and skills workers acquire from education and training or life experiences. Increases in human capital stimulate economic growth.

Technology is the processes a firm uses to turn inputs into outputs of goods and services. Technological change is an increase in the quantity of output firms can produce using a given quantity of inputs. Economic growth depends more on technological change than on increases in capital per hour worked. Just accumulating more inputs, such as natural resources, labor, physical capital per worker will not ensure an economy experiences growth unless technological change also occurs. Most technological changes are reflected in new machines, equipments, and software.

In implementing technological changes, entrepreneurs are important because they make the key decisions about whether to introduce new technology to produce better or lower-cost products. Entrepreneurs also decide whether to allocate the firm's resources to research and development to generate new technologies.

3.1.4 Potential GDP

Potential GDP refers to the level of real GDP attained when all firms are producing at capacity. Capacity here refers to "normal" hours and a "normal" sized workforce. Potential GDP will increase gradually as the labor force expands, new factories and office buildings are built, new machinery and equipment are installed, and new technology are created.

▶ Exercise 2

According to many economists, productivity is considered to be the cornerstone of economic growth, would you agree with such a statement? Why?

Answer:

I agree with such a statement. Productivity is the cornerstone of economic growth because it is very much related to progress and to increases in standards of living. Rising productivity increases the average standard of living leading to long-run economic growth.

3.2 Saving, investment, and the financial system

3.2.1 Financial system

Economic growth depends on the ability of firms to expand their operations. Firms can finance some of their own expansion through retained earnings, reinvesting profits back into the firm. But firms want to obtain more funds for expansion via the financial system than are available in this way. The financial system is the system of financial markets (such as stock and bond markets) and financial intermediaries (such as banks) through which firms acquire funds from households.

1) Financial markets

Financial markets are markets where financial securities, such as stocks and bonds, are bought and sold. Financial markets allow firms to borrow directly from those that wish to lend. A financial security is a document, maybe electronic, that states the terms under which funds pass from the buyer of the security to the seller. Stocks are financial securities that represent partial ownership of a firm. Stock allows firms to raise funds by taking on additional partners or owners of the firms. Bonds are financial securities that represent promises to repay a fixed amount of funds. Bonds specifies the date of maturity. The buyer of the bond is the lender.

2) Financial Intermediaries

Financial intermediaries are firms, such as banks, mutual funds, pension funds, and insurance companies, which savers can indirectly loan funds to borrowers. Financial intermediaries are middlepersons between borrowers and lenders.

The financial system provides three key services for savers and borrowers, which are risk sharing, liquidity and information.

· Risk sharing. Risk is the chance that the value of a financial security will change relative to what you expect. By allowing investors to spread their money over many different assets, investors can reduce their risk while maintaining a high expected return on their investment.

· Liquidity. This is the ease with which a financial security can be exchanged for money. The financial system allows savers to quickly convert their investments into cash.

· Information. The prices of financial securities represent the beliefs of other investors and financial intermediaries about the future revenue stream from holding those securities. This aggregation of information makes funds flow to the right firms.

3.2.2 The macroeconomics of savings and investment

In the economy, the total value of saving must equal the total value of investment. There are two categories of saving in the economy: private saving by households and public saving by the government. We can use some relationships from national income accounting to derive the result that the total saving must equal the total investment. We know the relationships between GDP (Y) and its components, consumption (C), investment (I), government purchases (G), and net exports (NX):

$$Y = C + I + G + NX$$

For the sake of simplicity, we develop the relationship between saving and investment for a closed economy. Net exports are zero, so:

$$Y = C + I + G$$

We can rearrange this to obtain an expression for investment in terms of the other variables:

$$I = Y - C - G$$

That is, investment in a closed economy is equal to income minus consumption and government purchases.

Savings is composed of private savings (S_{Private}) and public savings (S_{Public}).

S_{Private} is equal to all household income that is not spent; household incomes derive from the payments for factors of production to firms (Y) and from government in the form of transfer payments (TR); households spend money on consumption (C) and taxes (T). So

$$S_{\text{Private}} = Y + TR - C - T$$

The government "saves" whatever it brings in but does not spend (this may be negative, known as dissaving), so public saving (S_{Public}) equals the amount of tax revenue the government retains after paying for government purchases and making transfer payments to households:

$$S_{\text{Public}} = T - G - TR$$

So, total saving is:

$$\begin{aligned} S &= S_{\text{Private}} + S_{\text{Public}} \\ &= Y + TR - C - T + T - G - TR \\ &= Y - C - G \end{aligned}$$

Thus, we can conclude that total savings must equal total investment:

$$S = I$$

When S_{Public} is zero, the government spends as much as it brings in; this is known as a balanced budget. When the government spends more than it collects in taxes, there is a budget deficit, which means that public saving is negative or dissaving. When the government spends less than it collects in taxes, there is a budget surplus. A budget surplus increases public saving and the total level of saving in the economy. A higher level of saving results in a higher level of investment spending.

3.2.3 The market for loanable funds

The market for loanable funds refers to the interaction of borrowers and lenders that determines the market interest rate and the quantity of loanable funds exchanged.

Firms borrow loanable funds from households. They borrow more when households demand a lower return on their money — a lower real interest rate.

Households supply loanable funds to firms. They provide more when firms offer them a greater reward for delaying consumption — a higher real interest rate.

Governments, through their saving or dissaving, affect the quantity of funds that "pass through" to firms. So, the supply of loanable funds is determined by the willingness of households to save and by the extent of government saving or dissaving. The higher the interest rate, the greater the reward for saving and the larger the amount of funds households will save. Because both borrowers and lenders are interested in the real interest rate they will receive or pay, equilibrium in the market for loanable funds determines the real interest rate.

We draw the demand curve for loanable funds by holding constant all factors, other than the interest rate, that affect the willingness of borrowers to demand funds (Figure 3-2). We draw the supply curve by holding constant all factors, other than the interest rate, that affect the willingness of lenders to supply funds (Figure 3-2). An increase in the demand for loanable funds increases the equilibrium interest rate. As a result, the equilibrium quantity of loanable funds increases. All else equal, as the interest rate rises, the quantity of loanable funds supplied will increase. All else equal, as the interest rate rises, the quantity of loanable funds demanded will fall.

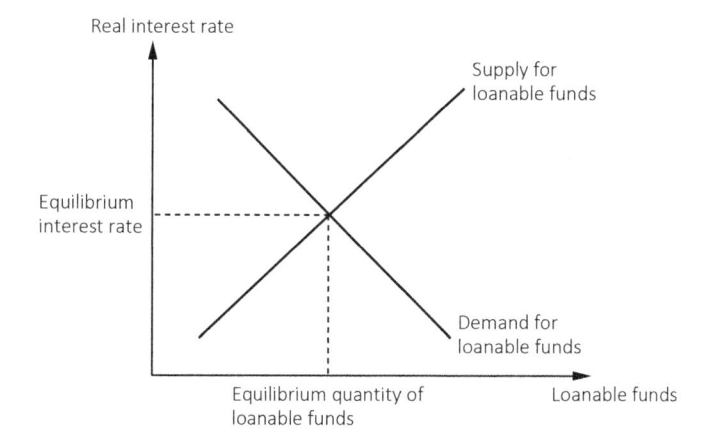

Figure 3-2

- Suppose that technological change occurs, so that investments become more profitable for firms. This will increase the demand for loanable funds. The real interest rate will rise, as will the quantity of funds loaned.

- Suppose the government runs a budget deficit. To fund the deficit, it sells bonds to households, decreasing the supply of funds available to firms. This raises the equilibrium real interest rate, and decreases the funds loaned to firms. This is referred to as crowding out: the decline in private expenditures as a result of increases in government purchases.

- In practice, the effect of government budget deficits and surpluses on the equilibrium interest rate is relatively small. According to one study, increasing borrowing by 1% of GDP would increase the real interest rate 0.003 points. Why would the effect be so small? Because interest rates are influenced by global markets, even a few hundred billion dollars is a relatively minor amount.

▶ Exercise 3

Use the saving and investment identity from the national income accounts to answer the following questions. Suppose the following values are from the national income accounts of a country with a closed economy (all values are in billions).

Y = $ 6 050

T = $ 1 050

C = $ 4 000

G = $ 1 200

i) What is the value of saving and investment in this country?

ii) What is the value of private saving?

iii) What is the value of public saving?

iv) Is the government's budget policy contributing to growth in this country or harming it? Why?

Answer:

i) ($ 6 050 − $ 1 050 − $ 4 000) + ($ 1 050 − $ 1 200) = $ 850 billion.

ii) $ 6 050 − $ 1 050 − $ 4 000 = $ 1 000 billion.

iii) $ 1 050 − $ 1 200 = − $ 150 billion.

iv) It is harming growth because public saving is negative, and less is available for investment.

3.3 The business cycle

On average, real GDP of China grows about 6 percent per year. Although the average China has experienced a tremendous increase in the standard of living over the past century, this does not mean the economy's output of goods and services grows smoothly. Growth is higher in some years than in others; sometimes the economy loses ground, and growth turns negative.

3.3.1 Definition

Business cycles consist of alternating periods of expanding and contracting economic activity. For a typical idealized business cycle, real GDP rises, falls then rises again⋯

The phases of rising are expansion and the periods of falling are recessions. The points at which the economy changes from one phase to another is referred to as peaks or troughs respectively. When the economy experiences expansion phase of a business cycle, production, employment, and income are increasing. The expansion phase ends with a business cycle peak. Followed by the recession phase of the cycle, production, employment, and income are declining. The recession comes to an end with a business cycle trough, after which another period of expansion begins.

3.3.2 How do we know when the economy is in a recession?

From the term, it seems that economic fluctuations are regular and predictable, but they are not. Recessions are actually irregular, sometimes they occur close together, while at other times they are much farther apart.

How to determine whether a downturn in the economy is sufficiently severe to be a recession? There is no simple answer and no timely official announcement. According to an old rule of thumb, a recession is a period of at least two consecutive quarters of declining real GDP. But this rule does not always hold. For example, the 2001 American recession had two inconsecutive quarters of negative growth. Most economists accept the decisions of the Business Cycle Dating Committee of the National Bureau of Economic Research (NBER). The committee is fairly slow in announcing the dates because it takes time to gather economic statistics and make analysis.

3.3.3 What happens during the business cycle?

Each business cycle is different, but most business cycles share certain characteristics. Toward the end of an expansion, interest rates are usually rising, and the workers' wages are usually rising faster than prices. Thus, profits of firms are falling. Near the end of an expansion, households and firms will have increased their debts greatly.

· When a recession hits, households respond to the expectations about their current and future incomes decreasing by consuming less. But this reduction in spending on durable goods, such as furniture, appliances and automobiles is even more substantial. Consumers mostly have to buy nondurables like food and clothing continuously. Since durable goods (by definition) are expected to last three or more years, consumers can continue to use for a little longer period when their purchasing power decreases. So, consumers are likely to postpone spending on durables. Therefore, firms selling durable goods seem to be hit hard by a recession. Of course, households reduce spending on housing, either.

· When a recession hits, firms experience declining sales and profits, they often cut back on production, purchases of capital goods and begin to lay off workers.

· During recessions, demand for products is low relative to supply, resulting in prices increasing more slowly or even decreasing — low inflation or deflation.

· Recessions cause the unemployment rate to rise. Sometimes the unemployment rates even continue to rise after recessions, such as USA unemployment rates after 1990 – 1991, 2001, and 2007 – 2009 recessions ended. There are two reasons. First, though employment begins to increase as the recession ends, it may increase more slowly than the increase in the labor force from population growth. Second, some firms continue to operate well below their capacity even after a recession has ended and production has begun to increase. Firms may not hire back all the workers they had laid off and may continue for a while to lay off more workers.

· As the recession continues, economic conditions gradually improve. Declines in spending eventually end, households and firms reduce their debts and firms begin to increase their spending on capital goods as they anticipate additional production during the next expansion. Household spending on consumer durables and business spending on capital goods will bring the recession to an end.

· During economic expansions, the inflation rate usually increases and unemployment rate falls.

▷ Exercise 4

What are the four phases of the business cycle? Why does the business cycle affect output and employment in capital goods industries and consumer durable goods industries more severely than in industries producing consumer nondurable?

Answer:

The typical business cycle goes through four phases: peak, recession, trough, and expansion. During a recession, industries producing capital goods and consumer durables are affected mostly in the business cycle. Because, firms and can postpone the purchase of capital goods. And consumers can defer the purchases of durable goods such as automobiles and major appliances. In contrast, for nondurable goods, consumers find it difficult to cut back on needed goods and services.

Case Study

China's Economic Growth over the Past 40 Years of Reform and Opening up Compared to Foreign Countries

Key Points:

I. Rapid economic growth of China over the four decades of reform and opening up

Since the reform and opening up, China's economic growth has maintained a growth rate of nearly 10%. From 1978 to 2002, its average GDP growth rate was 9.7% in the first 25 years. During this period, China went through several exploration stages of reform and opening up, including the stage featuring "bringing order out of chaos" and rural land contract system implementation from 1978 to 1984, the stage when the development was driven by township enterprises from 1985 to 1988, and the stage of economic adjustment from 1989 to 1991. In 1992, Deng Xiaoping's remarks during his inspection tour to the south ushered in another historical period when China was fully open to the outside world. In 1993, the Third Plenary Session of the 14th CPC Central Committee laid the foundation for the theory of socialist market economy, which was tested by the impacts of the Asian financial crisis in 1997 and the bursting of the Internet bubble in 2001. On December 11th, 2001, we witnessed China's successful entry into the WTO.

The growth in the first 25 years since 1978 laid the foundation for China's reform and opening up to become mature from the exploration stage. China has firmly and confidently embarked on the road of socialist market economy with China characteristics, and made great achievements in reform and opening up that are deeply rooted in the hearts of Chinese people. In 2003, China began to shift rapidly from a new starting point of industrialization and opening to the outside world to all-round industrialization and urbanization. In 2011, the urbanization rate of China exceeded 50%. Since then, China has changed from an agricultural country with a dominant agricultural population to a modern economy based on urban population. In 2012, its service sector surpassed the industrial sector and became the new engine for economic development, which starts the shifting process towards a service-oriented economic structure in China. Since then,

China's economic growth rate has gradually turned from high to medium high, maintaining at 9% from 2003 to 2018. For 40 years, China has taken the lead in terms of economic growth in the world at all stages.

II. China's economic growth compared to other countries

Table 3-3 shows GDP growth rates and per capita GDP growth rates of different countries. Through comparison with other countries, it is found that China's economic growth rate is more than twice that of the developed countries, and over 30% higher than that of emerging East Asian countries such as South Korea, Singapore, Malaysia, Indonesia, Thailand and the Philippines.

Table 3-3

Country	GDP growth rate		Per capita GDP growth rate	
	1978-2002	2003-2016	1978-2002	2003-2016
China	9.7%	9.59%	8.37%	9.01%
U.S.	3.17%	1.85%	2.08%	1.01%
U.K.	2.58%	1.63%	2.36%	0.90%
Germany	2.14%	1.25%	1.92%	1.24%
France	2.33%	1.09%	1.83%	0.52%
Japan	2.96%	0.86%	2.50%	0.89%
South Korea	7.89%	3.59%	6.82%	3.05%
Singapore	7.25%	5.60%	4.76%	3.42%
Malaysia	6.48%	5.10%	3.80%	3.21%
Thailand	6.19%	3.89%	4.64%	3.36%
Indonesia	5.12%	5.49%	3.20%	4.12%
Philippines	2.78%	5.56%	0.25%	3.77%

Source: WID database of World Bank.

The above table compares the growth scale between China with other major economies in the world. It will take some time for China to surpass the US in terms of the GDP. However, China boasts a much higher economic growth rate and has always been among top three largest economies in the world, with a great potential to surpass the United States. After the global financial crisis in 2008, China's GDP surpassed Japan and became the second largest economy in the world, when there was a huge gap between India and China. As a subsequent contender, India has outpaced China in growth rate after 2015. However, it is still a middle-low income country, while China is on the way to be a high-income country.

III. China's economy has shifted from one featuring high fluctuation and high growth to a mature one characterized by low fluctuation and medium-high growth

In the first 25 years of China's economic reform and opening up, the rapid growth was basically accompanied by high fluctuations. Moreover, inflation was the major target for regulation before 1997 as the inflation rate was 9.3% in 1985, 18.8% in 1988, 18% in 1989, 14.7% in 1993, 24% in 1994, and 17.1% in 1995, respectively. The economy maintained stable in 1997, and then faced deflation from 1999 to 2001, with the prices of commodities fluctuating sharply. Of the last 15 years, only two years experienced an inflation rate exceeding 5%, without deflation. Measured by the variance of fluctuation (the square of the differences between the numerical value and the average value each year), the price fluctuation in the first 20 years is ten times greater than that in the following 20 years. According to the fluctuation of growth, the economic growth fluctuated greatly in the first 20 years. In 1984, the economic growth rate exceeded 15%, while in 1989 and 1990, it fell back to about 4%. This great change was accompanied by inflation. The fluctuation variance of growth indicates that the fluctuation of growth in the first 20 years is 2.55 times larger than that in the following 20 years, during which period the economic growth showed an obvious converging trend. After 2012, the economic growth rate that kept declining from 7.8% was significantly lower than the original average trajectory of 8%. The report of the 19th CPC National Congress put forward for the first time that China's economy has stepped from the "high-rate growth stage" to the "high-quality development stage". This shows a greater tolerance of the government towards the slowdown in growth rate, i.e., from the high growth range of 8%~10% to the medium-high growth range of 6%~8%.

The increased China's economic stability is directly reflected in three aspects. First, the establishment of the market system has led to more rational choices and greater self-risk constraints for micro-entities. Second, the establishment of a mature macro-management system has enriched the macro-management experience, contributing to better control of the complex economic situation. Third, the reform begins to be deepened, and the impacts of institutional reform on economy have declined. For instance, the price control removal in 1988 and the reform of state-owned enterprises after 1998 both aggravated the shock against the economic system. In contrast, the existing reforms, adhering to the concept of "gradual" pace, have become more and more mature under the rule of law, thus producing relatively weak impacts. The increasingly mature economy of China has reduced the fluctuations. Nevertheless, greater openness will unavoidably bring more impacts from the outside, which is a risk factor China needs to pay special attention to and guard against for future development.

Terms and Concepts

· **Business cycle**: Alternating periods of economic expansion and economic recession.

· **Crowding out**: A decline in private expenditures as a result of an increase in government purchases.

· **Financial intermediaries**: Financial intermediaries are firms, such as banks, mutual funds, pension funds, and insurance companies, which savers can indirectly loan funds to borrowers.

· **Financial markets**: Financial markets are markets where financial securities, such as stocks and bonds, are bought and sold.

· **Financial system**: The financial system is the system of financial markets (such as stock and bond markets) and financial intermediaries (such as banks) through which firms acquire funds from households.

· **Labor productivity**: The quantity of goods and services that can be produced by one worker or by one hour of work.

· **Long-run economic growth**: Long-Run Economic Growth is the process by which rising productivity increases the average standard of living.

· **Potential GDP**: The level of real GDP attained when all firms are producing at capacity.

Problems and Applications

I. True or False

1. Potential GDP is the maximum output a firm is capable of producing.

2. The key to sustained economic growth is increasing labor productivity.

3. If there is public dissaving, investment spending in the economy will decline, holding everything else constant.

4. Financial markets and financial intermediaries comprise the financial system.

5. In an open economy, the relationship between GDP (Y) and expenditures is $Y=C+I+G$.

6. An increase in the real interest rate will decrease consumption and investment.

7. At the end of an expansion, wages of workers are usually rising faster than prices.

8. The lengths of the recession and expansion phases and which sectors of the economy are most affected will rarely be the same in any two business cycles.

9. A period of economic expansion ends with a business cycle trough.

10. Inflation usually increases during a recession and decreases during an expansion.

II. Choices

1. Technological advances generally result in _____.

A. decreased incomes

B. increased life expectancy

C. increased infant mortality rates

D. increased average number of hours worked per day

2. A good measure of the standard of living is _____.

A. real GDP per capita

B. nominal GDP per capita

C. total real GDP

D. total nominal GDP

3. A country will likely experience an increase in poverty if _____.

A. its population decreases over time

B. its real GDP growth rate decreases

C. its inflation rate decreases or slows over time

D. its real GDP per person growth rate increases over time

4. The growth rate of real GDP equals _____.

A. [(Employment in the current year − Employment in previous year) ÷ Employment in previous year] × 100

B. [(Real GDP in current year − Real GDP in previous year) ÷ Real GDP in previous year] × 100

C. [(Real GDP in previous year − Real GDP in current year) ÷ Real GDP in previous year] × 100

D. [(Real GDP in current year − Real GDP in previous year) ÷ Real GDP in current year] × 100

5. If real GDP was $13.1 trillion in 2013 and $13.2 in 2014, what is the growth rate? _____.

A. 8.0 percent

B. −0.8 percent

C. 0.8 percent

D. $0.1 trillion

6. A measure of growth in the standard of living is the growth in _____.

A. real GDP

B. population

C. real GDP minus the growth in population

D. population minus the growth in real GDP

7. The Rule of _____ can be used to calculate the number of years that it takes for the level of a variable to _____.

A. 20; double

B. 70; triple

C. 70; double

D. 20; triple

8. All of the following are preconditions for economic growth EXCEPT _____.

i) property rights　　ii) democracy　　iii) free markets

A. i) only

B. ii) only

C. iii) only

D. i), ii), and iii)

9. An increase in the government budget deficit will shift the _____ curve for loanable funds to the _____ and the equilibrium real interest rate will _____.

A. supply; right; fall

B. supply; left; rise

C. demand; right; rise

D. demand; left; fall

10. Which of the following will increase the real interest rate? _____.

A. An increase in the supply of loanable funds

B. An increase in household saving

C. An increase in the demand for loanable funds

D. An increase in the budget surplus

Ⅲ. Short Answer

1. There is a presidential debate. When the candidate is asked about his position on economic growth, the presidential candidate says, "It is necessary to get our country growing again. We can use tax incentives to stimulate saving and investment, and it is necessary to get government budget deficit down so that the government can stop absorbing the nation's saving."

　　i) If government spending remains unchanged, what inconsistency is implied by the presidential candidate's statement?

　　ii) If the candidate wishes to reduce taxes and decrease the budget deficit, what has he implied about his plans for government spending?

　　iii) If policymakers want to increase growth, and if policymakers have to select between tax incentives to stimulate saving and tax incentives to stimulate investment, what may they should to know about supply and demand in the loanable-funds market before making decision? And why?

2. When you explain the concept of an "inflation tax" to your friend, you tell him,

"When a government prints more money to cover its expenditures instead of borrowing or taxing, this causes inflation. An inflation tax is simply the erosion of the money value because of this inflation. Therefore, the burden of the tax imposes on the public who hold money." Your friend replies, "So, what's bad about it? The rich have almost all the money, so an inflation tax seems fair to us. Maybe the government can cover all of its expenditures by printing money."

ⅰ) Rich people may hold more money than poor people, is that right?

ⅱ) Do the rich hold a larger percent of their income as money than the poor?

ⅲ) Does an inflation tax impose a greater or lesser burden on the poor than an income tax? Why?

ⅳ) Are there any other reasons why an inflation tax is not a good policy?

3. If net taxes rise by $150 billion, would you expect household saving to fall by $150 billion, by more than $150 billion, or by less than $150 billion?

Answers to Problems and Applications

Ⅰ. True or False

1	2	3	4	5	6	7	8	9	10
F	T	T	T	F	T	T	T	F	F

Ⅱ. Choices

1	2	3	4	5	6	7	8	9	10
B	A	B	B	C	C	C	B	B	C

Ⅲ. Short Answer

1. Answer:

ⅰ) Tax incentives to stimulate saving and investment allow a reduction in taxes. This would increase government deficit, which would reduce national saving and investment in turn.

ⅱ) The candidate plans to reduce government's expenditure.

ⅲ) Policymakers would want to know the elasticity (similar to the steepness) of the supply and demand curves. If loanable funds demand is inelastic, changes in loanable funds supply have little effect on saving and investment, so tax incentives to increase saving at each interest rate do little for growth. If loanable funds supply is inelastic, changes in loanable funds demand have little effect on saving and investment, so tax incentives to increase investment at each interest rate do little for growth.

2. **Answer**:

ⅰ) Yes, the rich probably hold more dollars than the poor do.

ⅱ) No, by a wide margin, poor people hold a higher percent of their income as money. In fact, poor people may have no other kinds of financial asset except money at all.

ⅲ) An inflation tax imposes a far greater burden on the poor than on the rich. The rich are able to keep most of their assets in inflation-adjusted, interest bearing assets, such as house, funds and stocks... But the poor can just keep currency, which bear all the inflation tax. We observed this in Brazil and Argentina during periods of high inflation

ⅳ) Inflation imposes many other costs on the economy besides the inflation tax: menu costs, tax distortions, shoe leather costs, confusion, etc.

3. **Answer**: Private saving is equal to $Y-C-T$, so if taxes increase, private saving will fall. When taxes increase, however, disposable income also falls, so households will consume less. With the increase in taxes and the decrease in consumption, saving will fall, but by less than $150 billion. Some of the decrease in taxes will be reflected by reduced consumption, not simply reduced saving.

4 Long-Run Economic Growth

Learning Objective

By the end of this chapter, students should understand:
- how to explain global economic growth trends.
- the causes and effects of long-run economic growth.
- why productivity is the key determinant of people's living standard.
- how government policies speed economic growth.

Key Points and Exercises

4.1 Economic growth over time and around the world

4.1.1 Sustained economic growth did not begin until the Industrial Revolution

Brad DeLong, a famous Economist, estimates in his working paper "Estimating World GDP, One Million B. C. – Present" that, our ancestors had a GDP per capita of approximately $ 145 in 1 000 000 B. C. and GDP per capita in 1300 A. D. was also about $ 145. This means there was almost no economic growth occurred in that period (Figure 4-1). He estimates world economic growth was an average of only 0.2% per year between 1300 and 1800 (Figure 4-1). Continually rising living standards are a recent phenomenon, which started with the Industrial Revolution in the late 1700s. Instead of human or animal power, the application of mechanical power to the production of goods and services greatly increased the quantity of goods each worker could produce. The use of mechanical power allowed England and other countries — like the United

States, France, and Germany — to begin to experience long-run economic growth. As the graph below shows, from 1800 to 1900, the average annual growth rate for the world economy was 1.3% and during the next century, it raised to 2.3% (Figure 4-1). As we learned in the last chapter that small differences in economic growth rates can lead to big differences in peoples' standards of living because of compounding. Over 50 years, a 1.3% growth rate leads to about a 91% increase in real GDP per capita. But a 2.3% growth rate leads to about a 212% increase.

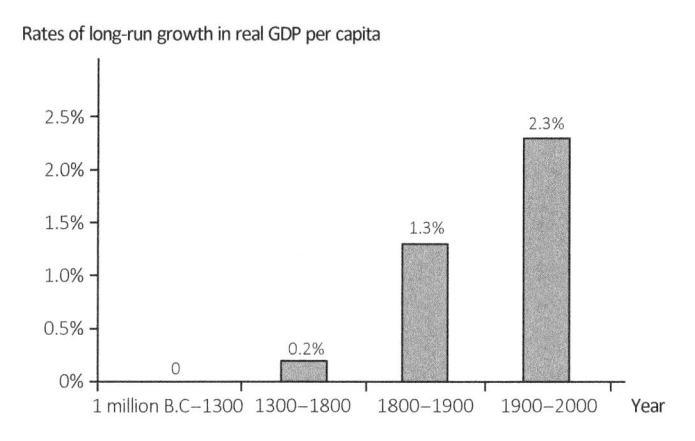

Rates of long-run growth in real GDP per capita

Figure 4-1

4.1.2 The uneven distribution of growth

Countries vary widely in terms of real GDP per capita and the growth rate of real GDP per capita. The high GDP per capita countries include Western Europe, the United States, Australia, Canada, Japan, and New Zealand. However, as growth rates of real GDP per capita vary from country to country, the ranking of countries by real GDP per capita varies over time. For example, over the past 100 years, Japan's ranking has risen relative to other countries, as the average growth rate in Japan has been above average, while the United Kingdom's ranking has declined because of below-average growth rates.

In 2012, GDP per capita in the United States was more than five times higher than GDP per capita in China. The growth rate of real GDP per capita in China has averaged 8.9 percent per year since 1980, but United States has averaged only 1.7 percent during the same time. If both of their growth rates were to keep unchanged and continue, China's standard of living are expected to exceed the U.S standard of living in the year

2037.

4.2　What determines economic growth?

We know from last chapter that the key to economic growth is labor productivity, which is the quantity of goods and services that can be produced by one worker or by one hour of work. Two key factors determine the increases in labor productivity are the increase in capital per hour worked and the level of technology. Technological change is a change in the quantity of output a firm can produce using a given quantity of inputs. Its main sources are as followed.

· Better machinery and equipment.

· Increases in human capital, the knowledge and skills that people have accumulated from education, training and life experiences.

· Better means of managing and organizing production, such as JIT production system.

The better the machinery and equipment, the more the human capital works have, people's living standard in a country will be higher.

The economic growth model can be expressed by per-worker production function (Figure 4-2), which shows the relationship between real GDP per hour worked and capital per hour worked, assuming the level of technology constant. Increases in the quantity of capital per hour worked will increase the output per hour worked, and there is a movement up along the per-worker production function. Given technology constant, equal increases in the amount of capital per hour worked lead to diminishing increases in output per hour worked. In other words, the extra output produced from an additional unit of capital falls as the capital rises.

Figure 4-2 shows the per-worker production function. From the figure, we can find that an increase in capital per hour worked from 50 to 100 increases the real GDP per hour worked from 50 to 55. The change in the real GDP is 5. But same increase of 50 in capital per hour worked from 100 to 150 increases the real GDP per hour worked from 55 to 59, which is 4, and it is a smaller amount. Each additional 50 increase in capital per hour worked results in a gradually smaller increase in real GDP per hour worked. This shows the diminishing returns of real GDP per hour worked from an equal increase in capital per hour worked.

Real GDP per hour worked, Y/L

62
59
55
50

50 100 150 200   Capital per hour worked, K/L

Per-worker production function

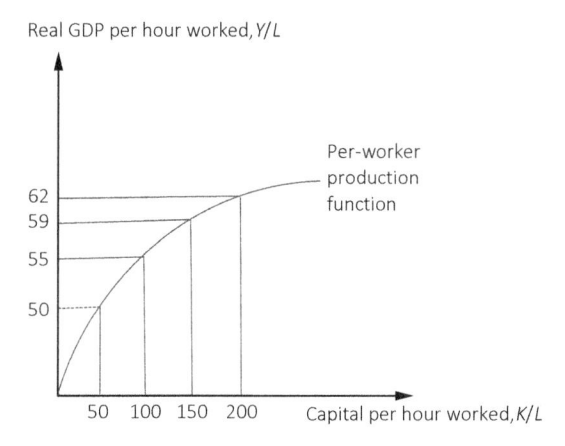

Figure 4-2

How to avoid diminishing returns to capital? Technological change helps here. Technological change improves production function. For the same quantity of inputs, technological change allows an economy to produce more output today than it could in the past. In the long run, a country can have an increasing living standard only if it has continuing technological change. That is, technological change can explain sustained growth and persistently rising living standards.

New growth theory is a model of long-term economic growth, emphasizing that technological change is affected by economic incentives and therefore is decided by the running of the market system. Paul Romer created the new growth theory. How individuals and firms respond to economic incentives is affecting the speed of technological change, he believes. When firms engage in R&D, they increase an economy's knowledge capital stock and therefore contribute to technological change. Romer believes that the accumulation of knowledge capital is subject to diminishing returns at the firm level, but at the overall economy level, returns on knowledge capital could be increase. Knowledge is largely a public good, so one firm's use of that knowledge does not prevent another firm from using it. Because of the nonrival of knowledge capital, Romer argues that firms may be unlikely to employ themselves in research and development because other firms can get most of the marginal returns and they can produce the next generation of innovations built on that one. Government policy can increase the accumulation of knowledge capital in three ways, thus encourage firms to devote resources to technological changes.

· Protecting intellectual property with patents and copyrights.

Patents are the exclusive right to produce a product for a period of 20 years from the date the patent is applied for. This period is projected to balance the opportunities for enterprises to benefit from inventions against the need of societies to benefit from inventions. Copyrights are granting the exclusive rights to use the creation during and 70 years after the creator's lifetime. It acts similarly for creative works such as records and books.

· Subsidizing research and development.

Governments subsidize scientists and researchers at researching organizations such as universities, or governments may carry out research work directly.

Similarly, they can provide tax-incentives to firms performing R&D.

· Subsidizing education.

For example, government subsidizes public colleges and universities. 9 years of compulsory education is another example.

The new growth theory has revived interest in Joseph Schumpeter's ideas. In his book Capitalism, Socialism, and Democracy, Joseph Schumpeter suggested that economic progress comes through a process of creative destruction. He emphasized driving force behind progress is the entrepreneur with an idea for a new product, a new way to produce an old product, or some other innovation. And new products drive older products — and the firms that produce them — out of the market which is, Creative Destruction. So according to Schumpeter, the key to continually rising living standards is new products development.

A recent example of creative destruction involves the retailing giant Walmart. While retailing may seem like a relatively static activity, it is a sector that has made considerable progress in the past few decades. For example, through personnel-management techniques, better inventory control (especially famous cross-docking) and marketing, Walmart has found ways to bring consumers' goods at lower cost than traditional retailers. These changes benefit consumers, who can buy goods at lower prices, and the stockholders of Walmart, who share in the profitability. But these adversely affect small mom-and-pop stores, which find it hard to compete with nearby Walmart.

4.3　Economic growth policies

4.3.1　Protecting property rights and enhancing the rule of law

Property rights refer to a right to specific property, intangible and tangible. Only if property rights are protected, a market system can run well. People must be confident that their property, production and capital are safe from being stolen and arbitrarily seized, and their agreements and contracts will be enforced, otherwise they won't make investment to do R&D, enlarge production, even they lose incentive to work and save. A well-functioning legal system is necessary.

4.3.2 Policies that encourage technological change, research and development

More research and development provide possibility for technological changes. Policies can help technology progress by funding research and development, such as grants, tax breaks, and patents. Policies also can guide funds to financing basic research.

Foreign Direct Investment is the easiest way for developing countries to access technology. Foreign Direct Investment is capital investment that is owned and operated by a foreign entity. Foreign Portfolio Investment is capital investment that is financed with foreign money but is operated by domestic residents. The World Bank and the International Monetary Fund help guide foreign investment to necessary countries.

4.3.3 Policies that encourage saving and investment

Increased saving can increase the growth of capital and investment. Encouraging saving and investment is a way that government can stimulate economic growth and raise living standard finally. By investment tax credits or tax breaks, governments can encourage firms to invest in more physical capital.

4.3.4 Improving health and education

Research shows that people will get more productive if their health are improved, thus labor productivity can be increased significantly. Encourage education and investment on education is another way to accumulate human capital. Education has a positive externality. It can not only increase the recipients' productivity, but raise the entire social productivity. Subsidies to education, from early childhood programs such as Head Start to on-the job training for adults in the labor force have played an important role to improve economic growth. The rising incomes and improved living standard from economic growth can reduce brain drain, too.

Exercise 1

Table 4-1

Country	Current real GDP/person	Current growth rate
A	$ 15 400	1.97%
B	$ 13 600	2.04%
C	$ 6 300	3.14%
D	$ 1 090	0.62%

i) Which country is the richest one? Why?

ii) Which country is advancing most quickly? Why?

iii) Which country would likely have the greatest benefits from an increase in capital investment? How do you know? Would this country have the same benefits from an increase in capital investment forever? What's your opinion?

iv) Do you think investment in R&D and human capital exhibit the same degree of diminishing returns as investment in physical capital?

v) Do you think which country has the potential to grow most quickly? Why?

vi) If real GDP per person in Country A next year is $ 15,920, what is its annual growth rate?

Answer:

i) Country A, because it has the largest real GDP per person.

ii) Country C, because it has the largest growth rate.

iii) Country D, because it is the poorest and has the least capital.

As we know, given technology constant, equal increases in the amount of capital per hour worked lead to diminishing increases in output per hour worked. That means capital exhibits diminishing returns, it is most productive when it is relatively scarce.

iv) No. Because of diminishing returns to capital, the additional growth from increasing capital declines as a country has more capital.

Human capital has a positive externality. Research and development is largely a public good.

v) Country D, because it is currently the poorest country and could easily benefit from capital investment. But It perhaps has trade restrictions, unstable government, few courts, and a lack of established property rights, health and education problems etc.

vi) ($ 15 920- $ 15 400)/$ 15 400 = 0.034 = 3.4%.

Case Study

Is the Middle-Income Trap a False Proposition for China?

In 2011, China's per capita income reached 5 577 US dollars, making it one of the middle and high income countries. In 2016, the Chinese Government stated that China's economic development has entered a new normal, and people will see an "L-shaped trend" in the future. So, will China encounter the "middle-income trap" and fall into it? Li Yining believes that as long as the response is proper and the reform measures are put in place in a timely manner, China can skip the "middle-income trap". Michael Spence, winner of the Nobel Prize in Economics in 2001, said at the "Jinjialing Fortune Forum 2014" that China is committed to promoting economic restructuring and pushing the market mechanism to play its role, so it will not fall into the "middle-income trap". However, some economists argue that China has fallen into the "middle-income trap". So, what is the "middle-income trap"? Is there really a "middle-income trap" in the world economy? How can China successfully enter the ranks of high-income countries from middle-income countries?

I. What is the "middle-income trap"?

The so-called "middle-income trap" refers to a state of economic stagnation where a country's per capita income reaches a medium level, and its failure to realize the smooth transformation between two economic development modes results in insufficient economic growth momentum. In today's world, as most countries are developing countries, there is the so-called "middle-income trap" problem. Countries like Brazil, Argentina, Mexico, Chile and Malaysia all entered the ranks of middle-income countries in 1970s, but until 2007, they were still struggling in the development stage with a per capita GDP of 3 000~5 000 US dollars, with no impetus and hope for growth.

The concept of "middle-income trap" was put forward by the World Bank in the *An East Asian Renaissance: Ideas for Economic Growth* published in 2007. According to the criteria of the World Bank, countries with a GNI per capita below 975 US dollars are low-income countries, those between 976 and 3 855 US dollars are lower-middle-income countries, those between 3 856 and 11 905 US dollars are upper-middle-income countries, and those above 11 905 US dollars are high-income countries. According to the criteria of income classifications in 2018, low-income countries have a per capita GNI below 995 US dollars, lower-middle-income countries between 996 and 3 895 US dollars, upper-middle-income countries between 3 896 and 12 055 US dollars, and high-income countries above 12 055 US dollars. Among the 218 economies included by the World Bank in 2018, there were 81 high-income countries, 56 upper-middle-income countries, 47 lower-middle-income countries and 34 low-income countries. If a middle-income country fails to enter the ranks of high-income countries after a period of time, it will fall into the "middle-income trap".

Table 4-2

Classifications	Criteria in 2007	Criteria in 2018
Low-income countries	Below 975 US dollars	Below 995 US dollars
Lower-middle-income countries	976~3 855 US dollars	996~3 895 US dollars
Upper-middle-income countries	3 856~11 905 US dollars	3 896~12 055 US dollars
High-income countries	Above 11 905 US dollars	Above 12 055 US dollars

II. Is the middle-income trap a false proposition for China?

The rise of China is a great epic in the contemporary world. In 1950, one year after the People's Republic of China was founded, China was one of the poorest countries in the world, as it lagged far behind neighboring countries and regions and even African countries. At that time, among the 25 African countries with data, 21 have a per capita GDP much higher than that of China. For example, at that time, the per capita GDP of Angola was 10 times that of China. The first 30 years of reform and opening-up laid a solid political, social and economic foundation for the development of the next 40 years. However, even in 1978, China's GNI per capita was still less than half of the average level of low-income countries.

According to the data of the World Bank, China finally got rid of the poverty trap that has plagued Chinese people for thousands of years in 1999, and entered the lower-middle income stage from the low income stage. It is a historic event that more than one billion people are lifted out of poverty, but there are always some in the world who hope to see and predict that China will fall into the "middle-income trap". Will China fall into the "middle-income trap"? On the one hand, we should admit that the transition from a middle-income country to a high-income country is a special stage for the economic development of any country, which is more complicated than the transition from a low-income country to a middle-income country. China will face challenges in all aspects at this stage. In this sense, the concept of "middle-income trap" has a warning significance for the development of China at this stage. On the other hand, we can also find a lot of favorable conditions for China to skip the "middle-income trap", and we have every reason to believe that China can smoothly make it and complete the leap from the middle income stage to the high income stage.

More than 20 years have passed since China entered the lower-middle income stage in 1999. Standing on this node to forecast the prospects of China, we are fully confident that our fundamental direction for the future is to enter the high income stage, skipping the "middle-income trap", and successfully enter the ranks of high-income countries in the next 10 years. Chinese people's confidence is by no means based on an illusory fantasy, but supported by solid data. According to the classification criteria of the World Bank, China only stayed in the lower-middle income stage for 12 years (1999 – 2011) and then entered the next stage: the upper-middle income stage. Another study quoted earlier also shows that compared with any other economy with historical data, China has the shortest transition period from the lower-middle income stage to the upper-middle income stage. In the history of world economic development over the past 100 years, the transition period from the lower-middle income stage to the upper-middle income stage is generally longer than that from the upper-middle income stage to the high income stage. The median of the previous transition period is 55 years, while that of the latter one only takes 15 years. In recent years, although the economic development of China has slowed down, it still maintains the trend of medium-high growth. This gives us every reason to believe that it will take less than 15 years for China to complete the transition from the upper-middle income stage to the high income stage. In other words, from 2012 when China entered the upper-middle income stage, China will complete the leap and enter the ranks of high-income countries by 2025 or so.

As a matter of fact, a number of provinces in China have provided examples for this successful leap. As we all know, 27 of the 31 provinces, autonomous regions and municipalities in China have a population over 15 million, with the top three provinces (Guangdong, Shandong and Henan) having around 100 million. It means that the population of these provinces, autonomous regions and municipalities is equivalent to that of a medium-sized or large country. To judge whether China as a whole can leapfrog the middle-income stage, we can first look into the performance of different provinces, autonomous regions and municipalities. By 2015, five provinces, autonomous regions and municipalities (Jiangsu, Zhejiang, Shanghai, Beijing and Tianjin) in China had reached the high income level, among which the population of Jiangsu and Zhejiang surpassed that of South Korea, and the population of Shanghai was larger that of Taiwan Province, China. Meanwhile, the per capita GDP of Guangdong, Shandong, Liaoning, Fujian, Inner Mongolia and other provinces, autonomous regions and municipalities also exceeded 10 000 US dollars, close to the threshold of the high income stage. These two types of provinces, autonomous regions and municipalities have a total population of 507.8 million, accounting for 36.9% of China's total population (1 374.6 million), equivalent to the total population of the European Union (509.6 million) and 1.58 times that of the U.S. (321.4 million). Now that the regions with over one third of China's population have successfully skipped the "middle-income trap" and entered or approached the high-income stage, other provinces, autonomous regions and municipalities will undoubtedly make it.

Terms and Concepts

· **Economic growth model**: The economic growth model can be expressed by per-worker production function, which shows the relationship between real GDP per hour worked and capital per hour.

· **Human capital**: The knowledge and skills that people have accumulated from education, training and life experiences.

· **Technological change**: A change in the quantity of output a firm can produce using a given quantity of inputs.

· **Labor productivity**: The quantity of goods and services that can be produced by one worker or by one hour of work.

· **New growth theory**: A model of long-term economic growth, emphasizing that technological change is affected by economic incentives and therefore is decided by the running of the market system.

· **Per-worker production function**: Shows the relationship between real GDP per hour worked and capital per hour worked, assuming the level of technology constant.

· **Creative Destruction**: New products drive older products — and the firms that produce them — out of the market.

Problems and Applications

I. True or False

1. Small differences in economic growth rates result in small differences in living standards.

2. Technological change is the key to sustaining economic growth.

3. One drawback of the patent system is that firms must disclose to the public information about the product or process.

4. Technological change allows the economy to produce more output with the same amount of capital and labor.

5. The lower-income industrial countries are catching up to the higher-income industrial countries in terms of economic growth.

6. One reason why many low-income countries experience low rates of growth is because of low rates of saving and investment in those countries.

7. The purchase of stocks and bonds issued in another country is known as foreign direct investment.

8. Political stability is not a prerequisite to economic growth.

9. Foreign portfolio investment occurs when an individual or firm buys stock or bonds issued in another country.

10. Recent rapid economic growth in India and China has reduced the amount of "brain drain" in those countries.

II. Choices

1. Suppose that in 2014, real GDP grew in Country A by 4% and the population in-

creased by 6%. Therefore, in 2014, Country A experienced _____.

A. economic growth, but not an increase in living standards

B. economic growth and an increase in living standards

C. no economic growth, but an increase in living standards

D. no economic growth and no increase in living standards

2. Protecting property rights in an economy will _____.

A. make the market system to work less efficiently

B. reduce the level of foreign portfolio investment

C. encourage corruption and expand the underground economy

D. increase the level of investment

3. According to Figure 4-3, diminishing marginal returns is illustrated in the per-worker production function by a movement from _____.

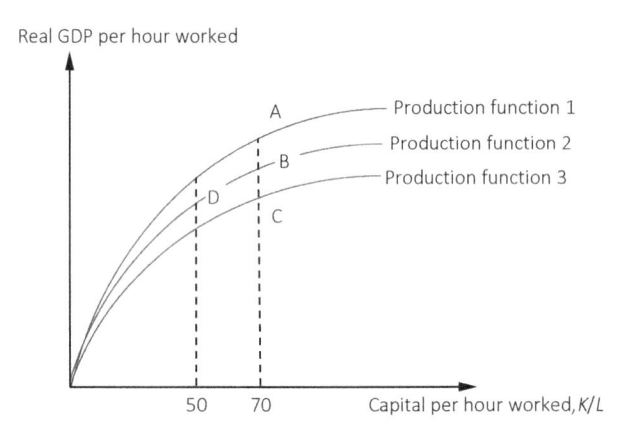

Figure 4-3

A. D to B

B. C to B

C. B to A

D. A to B

4. According to Figure 4-3, technological change is illustrated in the per-worker production function by a movement from _____.

A. D to C

B. C to B

C. C to D

D. A to B

5. According to Figure 4-3, using the per-worker production function, the greatest changes in an economy's living standard would be reached by a movement from _____.

A. D to C to B
B. C to B to A
C. B to C to D
d. A to B to C.

6. According to Figure 4-3, suppose the per-worker production function represents the production function for the Chinese economy. If China decided to double the support of R&D, this would cause a movement from _____.

A. D to C
B. C to B
C. C to D
D. A to B

7. According to Figure 4-3, within a country, the impact of wars and the subsequent destruction of capital is embodied in the per-worker production function by a movement from _____.

A. D to C
B. C to B
C. C to D
D. B to D

8. According to Figure 4-3, many countries in Africa strongly discouraged foreign direct investment in the 1950s and 1960s. So, these countries were preventing a moment from _____.

A. D to C
B. C to B
C. C to D
D. A to B

III. Short Answer

You are having a discussion with other Generation. The conversation turns to a supposed lack of growth and opportunity in the United States when compared to some Asian countries such as Japan, South Korea, China, and Singapore. Your roommate says, "These Asian countries must have cheated somehow. That's the only way they could have possibly grown so quickly."

ⅰ) Have you learned anything in this chapter that would make you question your roommate's assertion?

ⅱ) The phenomenal growth rate of Japan since World War Ⅱ has often been referred to as the "Japanese miracle". Is it a miracle or is it explainable?

ⅲ) Are the high growth rates found in these Asian countries without cost?

Answers to Problems and Applications

Ⅰ. True or False

1	2	3	4	5	6	7	8	9	10
F	T	T	T	T	T	F	F	T	T

Ⅱ. Choice

1	2	3	4	5	6	7	8
A	D	A	B	B	B	D	B

Ⅲ. Short Answer

Answer:

ⅰ) Yes. There are many sources of growth and a country can influence all of them except natural resources.

ⅱ) Japan's growth is explainable. Indeed, all of the high-growth Asian countries have extremely high investment as a percentage of GDP.

ⅲ) No. The opportunity cost of investment is that someone must forgo current consumption in order to save and invest.

5 Determining the Level of Aggregate Expenditure in the Economy

Learning Objective

By the end of this chapter, students should understand:

· how macroeconomic equilibrium is determined in the aggregate expenditure model.

· the determinants of the four components of aggregate expenditure.

· marginal propensity to consume and marginal propensity to save.

· how to use a 45°-line diagram to illustrate macroeconomic equilibrium.

· the definition of the multiplier effect.

· how to use the multiplier formula to calculate changes in equilibrium GDP.

Key Points and Exercises

5.1 An introduction to the aggregate expenditure model

The aggregate expenditure model is a macroeconomic model that focuses on the short-run relationship between total spending and real GDP, assuming that the price level is constant. This model is also known as the Keynesian Cross model, first suggested by the famous British economist John Maynard Keynes. It has had an enormous impact on the way economists analyze the reasons why economic performance can change in the short run and also on the ways policy makers can manage the economy.

The key idea of the model is that in any particular year, the level of GDP is determined mainly by the level of aggregate spending. If planned spending is low and the economy reaches equilibrium GDP below potential GDP, economic contraction occurs. On the contrary, when planned spending is high, resulting in equilibrium in excess of potential GDP, economic expansion occurs. In this chapter, we outline a relatively simple version of the Keynesian Cross Model. However, you will find that this theory provides a very powerful explanation for how contractions and expansions might evolve over the short run. In addition, an implication of this model is that government policies that affect the level of spending can be used to reduce or eliminate output gaps.

It is important to remember that the basic Keynesian model is built on a key assumption: the price level is fixed. It applies only to relatively short period during which firms tend to keep their prices fixed and meet the demand that is forthcoming at those prices. This model does not address the determination of inflation. In later chapter, we will extend the basic Keynesian Cross model to incorporate inflation and other important features of the economy.

5.2 Aggregate expenditure

5.2.1 Definition of aggregate expenditure

Aggregate expenditure (AE) is total spending in the economy. Keynes identified four components of aggregate expenditure: consumption, planned investment, government purchases, and net exports.

1) Consumption (C)

The expenditure is spending by households on final goods and services. Examples of consumer expenditure are spending on food, clothes and entertainment, and on consumer durable goods like cars and furniture. But, spending on new houses by households are not included in consumption.

2) Planned investment (I)

This is a planned spending by firms on new capital goods, such as office buildings, factories and equipment. And Spending on new houses and apartment buildings by households and planned inventory investment are also included in investment. As we discussed earlier, we use "investment" here to mean spending on new capital goods, such as factories, housing and equipment, which is not the same as financial investment. This distinction is important to keep in mind.

3) Government purchases (G)

This is spending of all levels of governments on final goods and services. For example, government purchases new schools, new hospitals, military hardware and services of government employees, such as soldiers, police and government office workers. However, transfer payments such as social security payments, unemployment benefits, and interest on the government debt are not included in government purchases. Because transfer payments and interest contribute to aggregate expenditure only at the point when they are spent by their recipients. For example, when a recipient of a welfare payment uses the funds to buy food, clothing or other consumption goods, they are included in consumption, not in government purchases.

4) Net exports (NX)

Net exports is the value of exports minus the value of imports. Since exports are sales of domestically produced goods and services to foreigner, aggregate expenditure should include exports. And since imports are purchases by domestic residents of goods and services produced abroad, it should be subtracted from aggregate expenditures.

To add these four types of spending — by households, firms, the government and the rest of the world together, or aggregate expenditure:

Aggregate expenditure = Consumption+Planned Investment
+Government purchases+Net exports

or

$$AE = C+I+G+NX$$

5.2.2 Planned expenditure vs. actual expenditure

I am not sure whether you notice that in aggregate expenditure model, we call it planned aggregate expenditure and add planned investment in total expending rather than actual investment. In this way, the definition of aggregate expenditures is slightly different from GDP. The difference is that planned investment spending does not include the build-up of inventories: goods that have been produced but not yet sold. For the purposes of measuring GDP, government statisticians treat the unsold output as being purchased by its producer, which can ensure actual production and actual expenditure are equal. So, in Chapter 1, we say the total expenditure always equals the total production. However, when a firm's actual sales are less than expected, the increase in its' inventory is unplanned inventory. In this case, the firm's actual investment, including the unplanned inventories, is greater than its planned investment. That means the actual aggregate expenditure is greater than planned aggregate expenditure. Because the actual aggregate expenditure always equals the actual aggregate production, the actual production (Y) is greater than planned expenditure (AE), or $Y > AE$.

For the economy as a whole, we can say that actual investment spending will be greater than planned investment spending when there is an unplanned increase in inventories. Conversely, actual investment spending will be less than planned investment spending when there is an unplanned decrease in inventories. Actual investment will equal planned investment only when there is no unplanned change in inventories. The relationship among actual investment, planned investment, and unplanned investment can be written as the format:

Actual investment (I) = Planned investment (I^P) + Unplanned investment (I^U)

when firms sell less of its output than expected, $I^U > 0$, actual investment is greater than planned investment, or $I > I^P$. On the contrary, when firms sell more of its output than expected (selling the inventories from last year), $I^U < 0$, actual investment is less than planned investment, or $I < I^P$. Actual investment equals planned investment only when $I^U = 0$.

For example: Suppose Huawei Company produces 2 000-million-yuan worth of cell phones, expecting to sell them all. What is the planned investment? If Huawei does sell all cell phones, what is the change in inventories? What is the actual investment? But if Huawei company sells only 1 500-million-yuan worth of cell phones, what is the unplanned inventories? What is the actual investment?

· The planned investment is 0. Because Huawei expects to sell the 2 000-million-yuan worth of cell phones out, there is no change in inventories. Therefore, the planned investment is 0. Please notice that the production of the cell phones is not investment. "Investment" here includes spending by firms on factories, office building, equipment and spending by households on new house. Productions are not the part of "investment."

· If all cell phones are sold, the change in inventories is 0. The actual investment is 0. In this case, actual investment equals planned investment.

· If it sells only 1 500-million-yuan worth of cell phones, then the unplanned inventories increase by 500 million yuan. The planned inventories are still 0, because Huawei Company expects to sell all the phones. However, since there are 500 million yuan of increase in inventories, actual investments are 500 million yuan. Because actual investment includes the change in inventories.

Therefore, the actual investment (500 million yuan) equals the planned inventories (0 yuan) plus the unplanned inventories (500 million yuan). When unplanned inventories are zero, actual investment equals the planned inventories.

5.2.3 Macroeconomic equilibrium and adjustment to it

For the economy as a whole, macroeconomic equilibrium occurs where planned aggregate expenditure equals total production. Or $AE = GDP$ or the unplanned investment is zero. Let's explain why macroeconomic equilibrium occurs when $AE = GDP$ or why the economy disequilibrium occurs when $AE \neq GDP$.

If planned aggregation expenditure is less than total production ($AE < GDP$), then firms will not be selling as many goods and services as they had expected. Inventories of goods will start to build up. This sends a signal that the retail firms cut back on orders of goods from their distributors. Distributors cut back purchases from manufacturers. Manufacturers of the goods will cut back on production of the goods, reduce purchases from their suppliers, and lay off workers. The reduction in production will continue until inventories equal their desired levels, or until spending equals production. If this happens across many different industries, GDP and total employment will decline. The decline in GDP will continue until $AE = GDP$.

On the contrary, if aggregate expenditure is greater than GDP ($AE > GDP$). Then firms will be selling more than their expectations. And Inventories will decline. The retail firms will increase their orders of goods from their distributors. Eventually, GDP and total employment will increase until $AE = GDP$.

Only when planned aggregate expenditure equals GDP will firms sell what they expected to sell. In this case, their inventories will be unchanged, and they will not have an incentive to increase or decrease production. The economy will be in macroeconomic equilibrium.

The relationship between planned aggregate expenditure and GDP can be summarized as Table 5-1.

Table 5-1

If	Then	And
AE = GDP	Inventories are unchanged	The economy is in macroeconomic equilibrium
AE > GDP	Inventories fall	GDP and employment increase
AE < GDP	Inventories rise	GDP and employment decrease

When aggregate expenditure is greater than GDP, inventories will decline, and GDP will increase; when aggregate expenditure is less than GDP, inventories will increase, and GDP will decrease. Increases and decreases in aggregate expenditure cause changes in GDP over different years. Economists devote considerable energy and time to forecasting what will happen to aggregate expenditure in the future. When economists forecast that aggregate expenditure is likely to decline and the economy is headed for a recession, the government may implement macroeconomic policies in an attempt to head off the fall in expenditure and keep the economy from falling into recession.

5.3 The determinants of the four components of aggregate expenditure

Base on the analysis above, we can conclude that the level of GDP is determined mainly by the level of aggregate expenditure. So, let's now focus on the determinants of aggregate expenditure, which is the sum of consumption, planned investment, government purchase and net export.

5.3.1 Consumption

Several factors influence consumption expenditure and saving plans. The five most important variables that determine the level of consumption are: current disposable income, household wealth, expected future income, the price level, and the interest rate.

1) Current disposable income

Consumer expenditure is largely determined by how much money consumers receive in a given year. All else being equal, households and individuals with higher disposable incomes will consume more than those with lower disposable incomes. The current disposable income equals aggregate income minus taxes plus transfer payment. So, the current disposable income depends on real GDP.

2) Household wealth

Households with greater wealth will spend more on consumption, even with similar incomes.

3) Expected future

Most people prefer to keep their consumption fairly stable from year to year, a process known as consumption-smoothing. So, if consumers become more optimistic about the future, they will increase their current consumption. Otherwise, they will decrease their current consumption.

4) Interest rate

Higher real interest rates encourage saving rather than spending. So, higher real interest rates result in lower spending, especially on durable goods.

5) The price level

As prices rise, household wealth falls. If you have $ 100 000 in the bank, that will buy fewer products at higher prices. Consequently, higher prices result in lower consumption spending. In this chapter, we assume the price level is unchanged. We will discuss the relationship between the price level and aggregate consumption in next chapter. Then, you will understand the effect of an increase in the price of one product on the quantity demanded of that product is different from the effect of changes in the price level on total spending by households on goods and services.

The five variables are the important factors that influence the level of consumption expenditure. However, both commonsense and available statistical data suggest that the most important determinant of consumption expenditure is current disposable income of households. Keynes himself stressed the importance of disposable income is determining household consumption decisions.

Therefore, we define the consumption function is the relationship between consumption spending and current disposable income, given other factors unchanged, as the following shows:

$$C = C(Y_d)$$

And let's define the current disposable income of households, Y_d, equals the total production (total income) of the economy, Y, minus net taxes (taxes minus transfer payment), T. That is:

$$Y_d = Y - T$$

A general equation that captures the link between consumption expenditure and the current disposable income is:

$$C = \alpha + \beta(Y-T)$$

The right side of the consumption function, contains two terms, α and $\beta(Y-T)$. The first term is known as exogenous consumption or autonomous consumption. The term exogenous has a very precise meaning in economics. In general, the value of an exogenous variable is determined from outside of the model under consideration. This means that the model does not provide an explanation for why exogenous variable takes any particular value. However, this does not mean that changes in an exogenous variable cannot affect other parts of the model. In fact, as we will see, changes in exogenous variables are central to the basic Keynesian model. In general, exogenous variables are constant variables. In the consumption function, the exogenous consumption α is intended to capture factors other than disposable income that affect consumption. For example, suppose consumers become more optimistic about the future, so, they would consume more given the level of their current disposable incomes. An increase in consumption at any given level of disposable income would be interpreted as an increase in exogenous consumption, α. In addition, α is also known as autonomous consumption, which would take place in an economy when households have no income.

The second term on the right side of the consumption function, $\beta(Y-T)$, reflects the effect of disposable income on consumption. This component of consumption is known as induced consumption, since it is consumption that is induced by disposable income. The parameter β, a fixed number, is called the marginal propensity to consume. The marginal propensity to consume (MPC) is the slope of the consumption function: The amount by which consumption spending changes when disposable income changes. We can write the expression for the MPC as:

$$MPC = \frac{\text{Change in consumption}}{\text{Change in disposable income}} = \frac{\Delta C}{\Delta Y_d}$$

From the above formula, the MPC can be considered as the amount by which consumption rises when current disposable income rises by one yuan. If people receive an extra yuan of income, they will consume part of the extra yuan and save the rest. In other words, their consumption will increase, but less than the full of the extra income. So, it is realistic to assume that marginal propensity to consume is greater than 0 but less than 1. Mathematically, we can summarize these assumption as:

$$0 < MPC < 1$$

Because the increase in the disposable income leads to an increase in consumption, the MPC is greater than zero. And because the increase in consumption is less than the full increase in income, the MPC is less than 1.

Next, let's talk about a saving function. As saving function is corollary of consumption function, we can derive the corresponding saving function from consumption function. By definition, disposable income not spent is saved given the net taxed unchanged. Therefore, we can write:

$$\text{Saving} = \text{Disposable income} - \text{Consumption}$$
$$S = Y_d - C$$

Because of

$$Y_d = Y - T$$

and

$$C = \alpha + \beta(Y - T)$$

We can get:

$$S = Y - T - C$$
$$S = Y - T - \alpha - \beta(Y - T)$$
$$S = -\alpha + (1 - \beta)(Y - T)$$

Where, $-\alpha$ represents dissaving, which is needed to finance autonomous consumption, at the zero level of disposable income. $1 - \beta$ is the marginal propensity to save (MPS). The MPS is the amount by which saving changes when disposable income changes.

$$MPS = \frac{\text{Change in saving}}{\text{Change in disposable income}} = \frac{\Delta S}{\Delta Y_d}$$

From the expression of MPS and MPC, we will find the marginal propensity to consume plus the marginal propensity to save equal 1. In fact, *MPC+MPS* always equal 1. We can prove this using the following method.

For the economy as a whole:

$$\text{National income} = \text{Consumption} + \text{Saving} + \text{Taxes}$$

When national income increases, there must be a combination of increases in consumption, saving, and taxes:

Change in national income = Change in consumption + Change in saving + Change in taxes

Using symbols, where Y represents national income (and GDP), C represents consumption, S represents saving and T represents net taxes, we can write:

$$Y = C + S + T$$

and

$$\Delta Y = \Delta C + \Delta S + \Delta T$$

We can assume that taxes are always a constant amount, so the following is also true:

$$\Delta Y = \Delta C + \Delta S$$

If we divide the previous equation by ΔY, we get:

$$\frac{\Delta Y}{\Delta Y} = \frac{\Delta C}{\Delta Y} + \frac{\Delta S}{\Delta Y}$$

$$1 = MPC + MPS$$

This equation tells us that when taxes are constant, the marginal propensity to consume plus the marginal propensity to save must always equal 1.

▷ Exercise 1

Fill in the blank in Table 5-2. Show that $MPC + MPS = 1$. Assume taxes equal to zero.

Table 5-2

National Income	Consumption	Saving	MPC	MPS
$ 8 600	$ 8 000			
9 000	8 300			
9 400	8 600			
9 800	8 900			

Answer:

$Y = C + S + T$. With taxes equal to zero, this equation becomes $Y = C + S$, and can be used to fill in the saving column.

To fill in the MPC and MPS columns, use the expressions:

$$MPC = \Delta C / \Delta Y$$

$$MPS = \Delta S / \Delta Y$$

For example, to calculate the value of the MPC in the second row:

$$MPC = \Delta C / \Delta Y$$

$= (\$8\,300 - \$8\,000)/(\$9\,000 - \$8\,600)$

$= \$300/\$400$

$= 0.75.$

To calculate the value of the MPS in the second row:

$MPS = \Delta S/\Delta Y$

$= (\$700 - \$600)/(\$9\,000 - \$8\,600)$

$= \$100/\$400$

$= 0.25.$

Therefore, we can get Table 5-3.

Table 5-3

National income (Y)	Consumption (C)	Saving (S)	Marginal propensity to consume (MPC)	Marginal propensity to save (MPS)
8 600	8 000	600	—	—
9 000	8 300	700	0.75	0.25
9 400	8 600	800	0.75	0.25
9 800	8 900	900	0.75	0.25

5.3.2 Investment

Let's now turn to the second major component of total expenditure: investment spending by firms. The decision about how much to invest depends on the four most important variables:

1) Expectations of future profitability

Investment goods, such as factories, office buildings, machinery, and equipment, are long-lived. Firms build more of investment goods when they are optimistic about future profitability. Recessions reduce confidence in future profitability, hence during recessions, firms reduce planned investment. Purchases of new housing are included in planned investment. In recessions, households have less incentive to invest in new housing.

2) The interest rate

Since business investment is sometimes financed by borrowing, the real interest rate is an important consideration for investing. A higher real interest rate results in less investment spending, and a lower real interest rate results in more investment spending.

3) Taxes

Firms focus on the after-tax profitability of investment spending. A reduction in taxes increases the profits that remain after they have paid taxes, which increase investment spending, like investment tax incentives.

4) Cash flow

Cash flow is the difference between the cash revenues received by a firm and the cash spending by the firm. Firms often pay for investments out of their own cash flow. The largest contributor to cash flow is profit. During recessions, profits fall for most firms, decreasing their ability to finance investment.

5.3.3 Government purchase

Government purchase includes purchases of consumption as well as investment goods such as infrastructure development, for example roads and railways. However, this category does not include transfer payments, such as social security payments or pension payments. Because the government does not receive a good or service in return. Therefore, government purchase here only refers to purchases for which the government receives some good or service. The main source of revenue of finance government purchases is taxation receipts. The choice of government purchases depends on the policies of the government. These purchases do not depend directly on the level of income in the economy. We therefore assume that government purchases are autonomous or independent of the level of income.

5.3.4 Net export

Net exports equal exports minus imports. The three most important variables that determine the level of net exports are:

· The price level in China relative to the price levels in other countries. If the price level in China rises faster than foreign price levels, then Chinese goods and services become more expensive relative to foreign goods and services. So, export of China falls and import of China rises, which leads the net export of China to fall. The opposite is true.

· The growth rate of GDP in China relative to the growth rates of GDP in other countries. If China GDP grows faster than foreign GDP, then China demand for foreign goods rises faster than foreign demand for Chinese export. Therefore, the net export will decrease.

• The exchange rate between Chinese yuan and other currencies. If the value of Chinese yuan become higher relative to other currencies, then Chinese goods and services become more expensive than foreign goods and services. So, imports rise and exports fall. The net export will decrease.

5.4 Graphing macroeconomic equilibrium

5.4.1 The Keynesian Cross

We can use a 45°-line diagram to illustrate macroeconomic equilibrium. In a graph, the 45°-line represents all the points that are equal distances from both axes. For example, suppose in the whole economy there is a single product: apples. For the economy to be in equilibrium, the number of apples produced must equal the number of apples purchased. As Figure 5-1 shows:

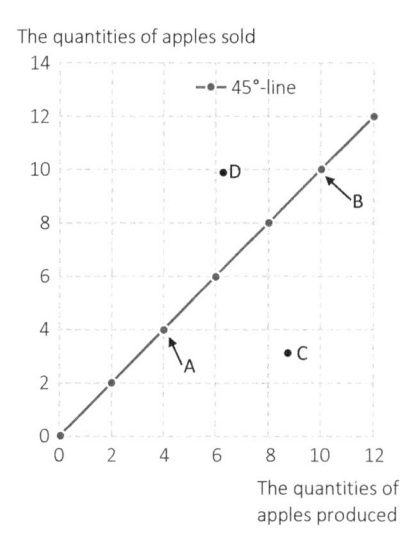

Figure 5-1

The 45°-line shows all the points that are equal distances from both axes. Points such as A and B, at which the quantity produced equals the quantity sold, are on the 45°-line. Points such as D, at which the quantity sold is greater than the quantity produced, lie above the line. Points such as C, at which the quantity sold is less than the quantity produced, lie below the line.

We can apply this model to a real economy, with real national income (GDP) on the x-axis, and real aggregate expenditure on the y-axis. This model is also known as the

Keynesian Cross, because it is based on the analysis of economist John Maynard Keynes. Because macroeconomic equilibrium occurs where planned aggregate expenditure equals GDP, we know that all points of macroeconomic equilibrium must lie along the 45°-line. At points above the line, planned aggregate expenditure is greater than GDP. At points below the line, planned aggregate expenditure is less than GDP. As Figure 5-2 shows: the aggregate expenditure equals real GDP at point K. The aggregate expenditure is less than real GDP at point L and greater than real GDP at point J.

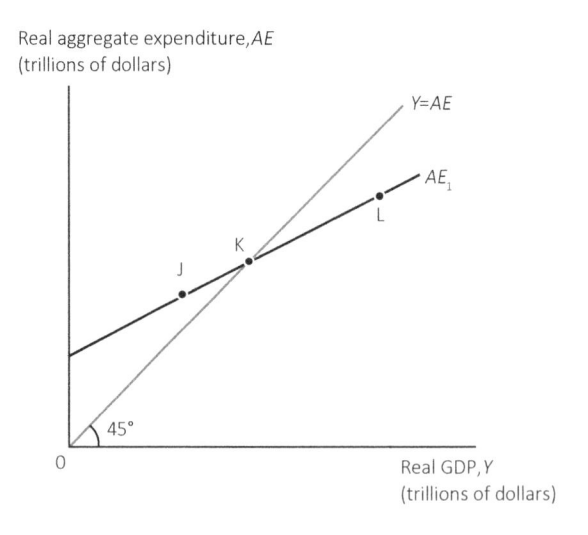

Figure 5-2

Any point on the 45°-line could be an equilibrium. However, how do we know which one will be the equilibrium in a given year? First of all, we should determine the line of AE. Then the intersection of the line of AE and the 45°-line should be an equilibrium. To determine this, recall that the aggregate expenditure, $Y = C + I + G + NX$. In this chapter, we assume that investment, government purchase and net exports are exogenous. They are predetermined and not affected by the GDP. And the consumption depends on the current disposable income. For each level of income, we will get a level of consumption. Therefore, we can place consumption function on the diagram, as Figure 5-3 shows.

The slope of consumption function is the MPC. If there was no other expenditure in the economy, then the macroeconomic equilibrium would be where the consumption function crossed the 45°-line; There, income (GDP) equals expenditure. But there are other expenditures: investment, government purchase and net export. They are not affect-

5 Determining the Level of Aggregate Expenditure in the Economy | 115

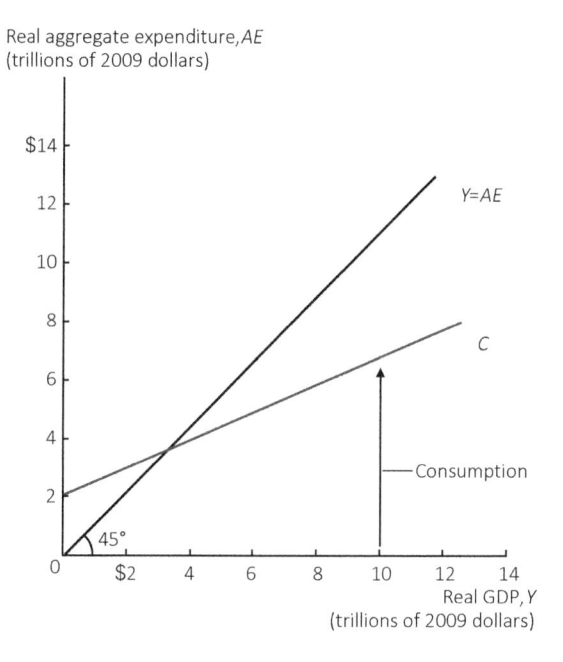

Figure 5–3

ed by the income, so they are the horizontal lines in the diagram. To add other expenditures to consumption function, there are vertical shifts in real expenditure, as Figure 5–4 shows.

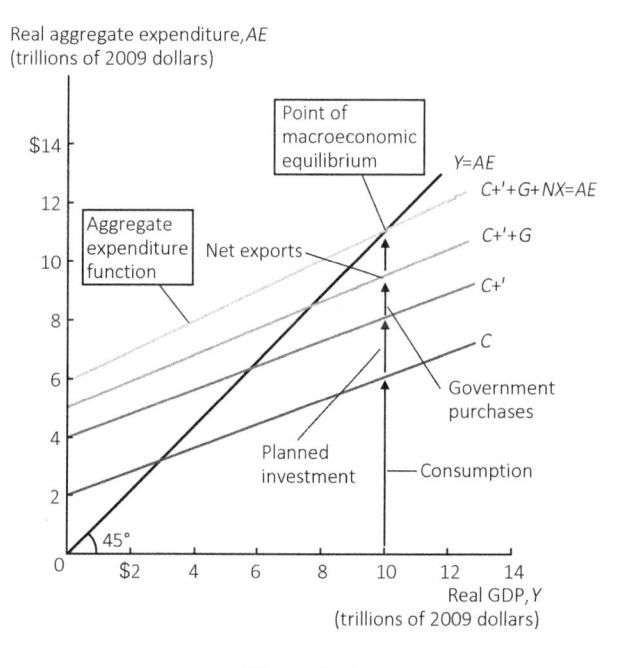

Figure 5–4

The vertical distance between the consumption line and the $C+I$ line will match exactly the height of the investment schedule above the horizontal axis. With the shifts of the consumption function, finally, we determine the line of aggregate expenditure. As Figure 5-4 shows, the intersection of the line of AE and the 45°-line is the point of macroeconomic equilibrium.

▶ Exercise 2

Figure 5-5 illustrates planned aggregate expenditure on the economy of X country. The grey line is aggregate expenditure line and the black line is the 45°-line. Use the figure to work problem i), ii), iii) and iv).

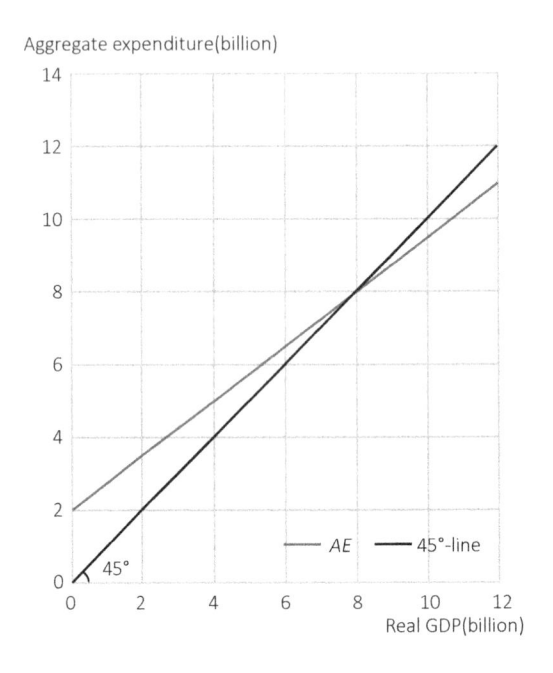

Figure 5-5

i) What is aggregate planned expenditure when real GDP is 10 billion?

ii) If real GDP is 4 billion, what is happening to inventories?

iii) If real GDP is 8 billion, what is happening to inventories?

iv) What is the equilibrium GDP?

Answer:

i) Figure 5-5 shows that planned aggregate expenditure is 9.5 billion when real GDP is 10 billion. in this case, planned aggregate expenditure is less than real GDP. The inventories will increase.

ii) Firms' inventories are decreasing. When real GDP is 4 billion, planned aggregate expenditure exceeds real GDP, so firms sell all that they produce and more. As a result, inventories decrease. And GDP will increase.

iii) Firms' inventories are unchanged. When real GDP is 8 billion, planned aggregate expenditure equals real GDP. So, there is no change to inventories.

iv) The equilibrium GDP is 8 billion.

5.4.2 Equilibrium vs. full employment GDP

Ideally, we would like macroeconomic equilibrium to occur at the level of potential GDP. If equilibrium occurs at this level, unemployment will be low — at the natural rate of unemployment, or the full employment level. But for various reasons, this might not occur. We know that we need a particular level of aggregate expenditure that induces businesses to produce a full-employment, non-inflationary level of output. However, for example, maybe firms are pessimistic and reduce investment spending. Then the equilibrium will occur below potential GDP — a recession. As the figure at exercise 2 shows that the full employment, non-inflationary level of output is 10 billion. But the AE intersects the 45°-line to 8 billion, in the left of full-employment output. This causes the economy's aggregate production to fall 2 billion shorts of its capacity production. The amount by which aggregate expenditure fall short of the full-employment level of GDP is called recessionary gap. On the contrary, if firms are optimistic and rise investment spending, which lead the AE line to shift upward. Then the equilibrium GDP will occur in the right of full-employment output. And the amount by which aggregate expenditures exceeds that required to achieve the full-employment level of GDP is called inflationary gap. The effect of this inflationary gap, because of this excess demand, is to pull up the prices on the economy's fixed physical volume of production. Businesses as a whole cannot respond to the excess demand by expanding their real outputs, so demand-pull inflation occurs.

5.5 The algebra of macroeconomic equilibrium

We can use equations to represent the aggregate expenditure model described in this chapter. Suppose the consumption function as the following:

$$C = \alpha + \beta Y_d$$

α is autonomous consumption. β is the MPC and Y_d is the disposable income, which equals $Y-T+TR$. T stands for taxes and TR stands for transfer payment. We assume other expenditures are exogenous and constant. So,

$$I = \bar{I}$$
$$G = \bar{G}$$
$$NX = \overline{NX}$$
$$T = \bar{T}$$
$$TR = \overline{TR}$$

So, the aggregate expenditure will be written as the following equation:

$$AE = \alpha + \beta(Y - \bar{T} + \overline{TR}) + \bar{I} + \bar{G} + \overline{NX}$$

The equilibrium condition is $Y = AE$, so:

$$Y = AE = \alpha + \beta(Y - \bar{T} + \overline{TR}) + \bar{I} + \bar{G} + \overline{NX}$$

or

$$Y - \beta Y = \alpha - \beta \bar{T} + \beta \overline{TR} + \bar{I} + \bar{G} + \overline{NX}$$

Solve the equation for Y, then we get:

$$Y^* = \frac{\alpha - \beta \bar{T} + \beta \overline{TR} + \bar{I} + \bar{G} + \overline{NX}}{1 - \beta}$$

So, Y^* is the equilibrium income.

▶ Exercise 3

In a particular economy, the consumption function is:

$$C = 2\,000 + 0.9 Y_d$$

So that the intercept term in the consumption function, exogenous consumption α, equals 2 000 and the marginal propensity to consume, β equals 0.9. Also, suppose that we are given that planned investment spending $I = 2\,500$, government purchases $G = 3\,000$, exports $NX = 400$ and net taxes $T = 1\,000$. what is the equilibrium level of GDP?

Answer:

The definition of planned expenditure:

$$AE = C + I + G + NX$$

To find a numerical equation for planned aggregate expenditure, we need to find numerical expressions for each of its four components. The first component of spending, consumption, is defined by the consumption function,

$$C = 2\,000 + 0.9Y_d$$

Since the taxes, $T = 1\,000$. We can substitute for T to write the consumption function as

$$C = 2\,000 + 0.9(Y - 1\,000)$$

Now plug this expression for C into the definition of planned aggregate expenditure above to get:

$$AE = 2\,000 + 0.9(Y - 1\,000) + I + G + NX$$

Where we have just replaced C by its value as determined by the consumption function. Similarly, we can substitute the given numerical values of planned investment I, government purchases G, and net exports NX into the definition of planned aggregate expenditure to get:

$$AE = 2\,000 + 0.9(Y - 1\,000) + 2\,500 + 3\,000 + 400$$

To simplify this equation, the result is:

$$AE = 0.9Y + 7\,000$$

The final expression shows the relationship between planned aggregate expenditure and output in this numerical example.

The equilibrium condition is:

$$Y = AE$$

Plug the expression of AE into the equilibrium condition to get:

$$Y = 0.9Y + 7\,000$$

Solve the equation to get the equilibrium GDP, $Y = 70\,000$.

5.6 The multiplier

5.6.1 The basic idea of the multiplier

Let us analyze the above exercise again. If the potential output Y^* equals 70 000, which equals the equilibrium output, the output gap is 0. Given that this equilibrium is the economy's potential output, this will be associated with full employment of the labor force (cyclical unemployment will be zero). Suppose that consumers become more pessimistic about the future, so that they begin to spend less at every level of current disposable income. Then, what is the effect of this reduction in exogenous consumption on the economy?

To answer this question, let us try to find the new equilibrium GDP. To be specific, suppose the exogenous consumption falls by 100 units, then $a = 1\ 900$. The consumption function will be:

$$C = 1\ 900 + 0.9(Y - 1\ 000)$$

So, the equation of aggregate expenditure will be:

$$AE = 1\ 900 + 0.9(Y - 1\ 000) + 2\ 500 + 3\ 000 + 400$$

Plug this expression of AE to the equilibrium condition and solve the equation to get $Y = 69\ 000$. As a result, a 100-unit decline in exogenous expenditure has led to 1 000 units decline in short run equilibrium output. This surprising result is called the multiplier effect. Specifically, the multiplier is the ratio of a change in equilibrium GDP to the original change in autonomous expenditures that caused that change in real GDP, that is:

$$\text{Multiplier} = \frac{\text{Change in real GDP}}{\text{Change in autonomous expenditure}}$$

In this case, the multiplier of autonomous consumption is 10 (1 000/100). As we have seen, the equilibrium GDP changes by more than the change in autonomous expenditure. This makes the multiplier greater than 1. How come? Why does equilibrium expenditure increase by more than the increase in autonomous expenditure? Let's answer these questions by taking the multiplier of planned investment as an example.

5.6.2 The multiplier: planned investment

Although changes in consumption, government purchases, or exports are also subject to the multiplier effect, the "initial change in spending" usually associated with investment spending. Because the investment seems to be the most volatile component of aggregate expenditures. Therefore, let's take the multiplier of planned investment as example to illustrate multiplier effects.

Graphically, an increase in planned investment spending will shift up the aggregate expenditure function and lead to a multiplied increase in equilibrium real GDP. If planned investment increases by ΔI, then the AE curve will shift upward by ΔI. As Figure 5-6 shows: the equilibrium of economy moves from A to B. The graph shows the increase in planned investment leads to an even greater increase in income. That is ΔY is greater than ΔI. The investment multiplier is greater than one, since investment multiplier equals the ratio $\frac{\Delta Y}{\Delta I}$.

Why is there a multiplier effect in this model? The reason is that, according to the

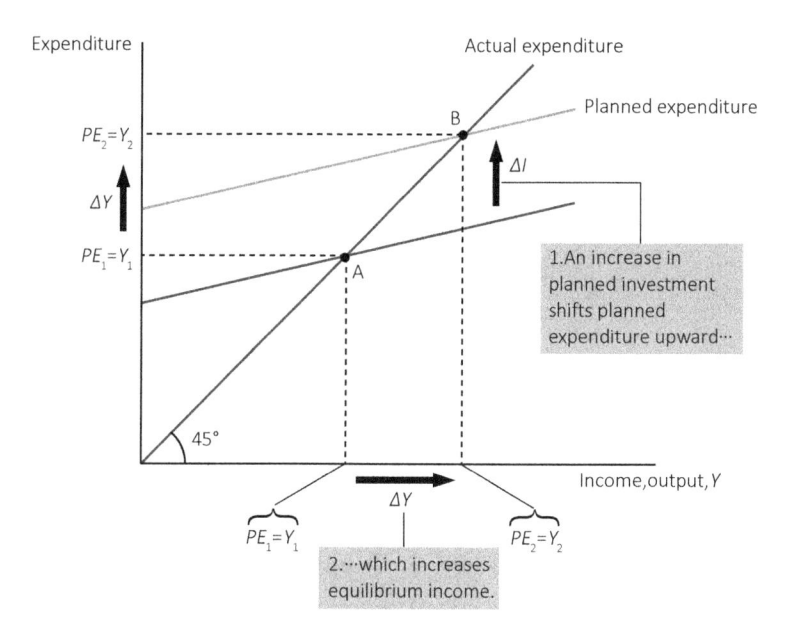

Figure 5-6

consumption function, higher income causes higher consumption. When the initial increase in planned investment raises income, it also raises consumption, which further raises income, which further raises consumption, and so on. Therefore, in this model, an expenditure causes a greater increase in income.

How big is the multiplier of planned investment? To answer this question, let's look at Table 5-4.

Table 5-4

	Additional investment	Additional induced consumption	Total additional expenditure
Round 1	$ 100 billion	$ 0	$ 100 billion
Round 2	$ 0	$ 75 billion	$ 175 billion
Round 3	$ 0	$ 56 billion	$ 231 billion
Round 4	$ 0	$ 42 billion	$ 273 billion
Round 5	$ 0	$ 32 billion	$ 305 billion
⋮	⋮	⋮	⋮
Round 10	$ 0	$ 8 billion	$ 377 billion
⋮	⋮	⋮	⋮

	Additional investment	Additional induced consumption	Total additional expenditure
Round 15	$ 0	$ 2 billion	$ 395 billion
⋮	⋮	⋮	⋮
Round 19	$ 0	$ 1 billion	$ 398 billion
⋮	⋮	⋮	⋮
Round n	$ 0	$ 0	$ 400 billion

As Table 5-4 shows, the initial increase in the planned investment is $ 100 billion. Initially, real GDP rises by the amount of the increase in autonomous expenditure, $ 100 billion. Suppose *MPC* is 0.75. In the second round, the $ 100 billion increase in real GDP will raise the consumption by $ 75 billion ($MPC \times$ $ 100 billion). The increase in consumption raises the real GDP by $ 75 in the second round. In each "round", the additional income prompts households to consume some fraction (the marginal propensity to consume). The process continues, as the following shows:

The initial increase in planned investment spending = $ 100 billion

Plus the first induced increase in consumption = $MPC \times$ $ 100 billion

Plus the second induced increase in consumption = $MPC \times (MPC \times$ $ 100 billion)

$= MPC^2 \times$ $ 100 billion

Plus the third induced increase in consumption = $MPC \times (MPC^2 \times$ $ 100 billion)

$= MPC^3 \times$ $ 100 billion

Plus the fourth induced increase in consumption = $MPC \times (MPC^3 \times$ $ 100 billion)

$= MPC^4 \times$ $ 100 billion

This becomes the infinite sum:

Total change in GDP = $ 100 billion

+ $MPC \times$ $ 100 billion

+ $MPC^2 \times$ $ 100 billion

+ $MPC^3 \times$ $ 100 billion

+ $MPC^4 \times$ $ 100 billion

+ ⋯

Which we can rewrite the equation above as:

Total change in GDP = $ 100 billion $\times (1 + MPC + MPC^2 + MPC^3 + MPC^4 + \cdots)$

Since *MPC* is less than 1, the expression in parentheses equals[①]:

$$\frac{1}{1-MPC}$$

Therefore, the total change in GDP (ΔY):

$$\Delta Y = \Delta I \times \frac{1}{1-MPC}$$

Divide both side of the equation by ΔI, We can get the multiplier of planned investment:

$$\text{Multiplier} = \frac{\Delta Y}{\Delta I} = \frac{1}{1-MPC}$$

In our case, *MPC* = 0.75, so, the multiplier is 1/(1-0.75) = 4. A $100 billion increase in investment eventually results in a $400 billion increase in equilibrium real GDP.

The general formula for the multiplier is:

$$\text{Multiplier} = \frac{\text{Change in equilibrium real GDP}}{\text{Change in autonomous expenditure}} = \frac{1}{1-MPC}$$

As the equation shows, the magnitude of the multiplier depends on the MPC. The greater the MPC is, the larger the multiplier is. For example, if *MPC* is 0.75 and the multiplier, therefore, is 4. A $100 billion rise (decline) in investment increases (decrease) the equilibrium GDP by $400 billion. However, if *MPC* is 0.8 and the multiplier is then 5, the same changes in investment cause the equilibrium GDP to change by $500 billion. This makes sense intuitively — a large MPC means the chain of induced consumption changes quickly and cumulates to a large change in income. Conversely, a small MPC causes induced consumption to change slowly, so, the cumulative change in income is small.

The MPC also is the slope of AE. The AE curve is steeper, then the multiplier is larger. We can get the relationship between the multiplier and the slope of AE using the

---

[①] Mathematical note: we prove this algebraic result as follows. For $|a|<1$, let

$$z = 1 + a + a^2 + \cdots$$

Multiply both sides of this equation by α:

$$az = a + a^2 + a^3 + \cdots$$

Subtract the second equation from the first one:

$$z - \alpha z = 1$$

Solve for z, we get:

$$z = 1/(1-x)$$

following figure.

As Figure 5-7 shows, the change in equilibrium GDP (ΔY) equals the change in induced expenditure (ΔN) plus the change in autonomous expenditure (ΔI). That is,

$$\Delta Y = \Delta N + \Delta I$$

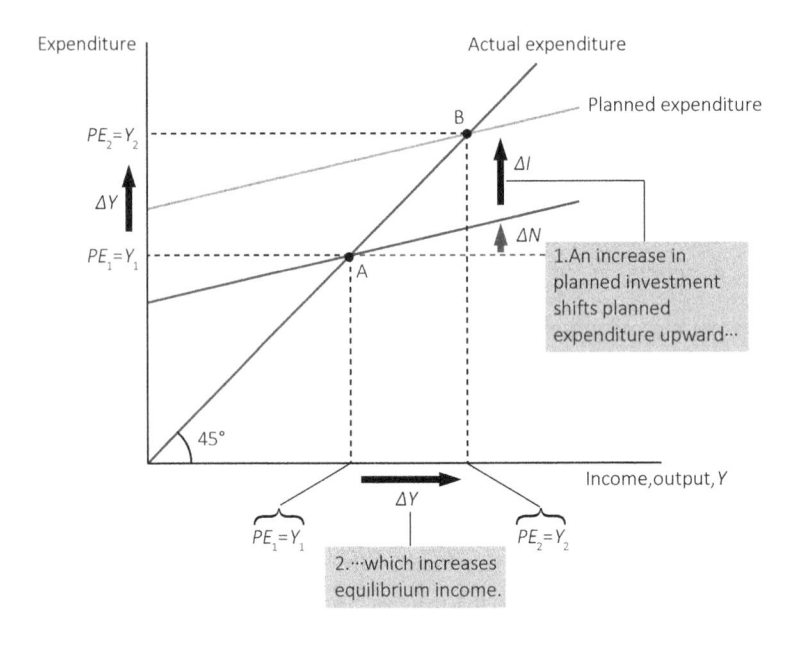

Figure 5-7

The change in induced expenditure is determined by the change in real GDP and the slope of the AE curve, because of

$$\text{Slope of AE curve} = \frac{\Delta N}{\Delta Y}$$

So,

$$\Delta N = \text{Slope of AE curve} \times \Delta Y$$

Now, use this equation to replace ΔN in $\Delta Y = \Delta N + \Delta I$,

$$\Delta Y = \text{Slope of AE curve} \times \Delta Y + \Delta I$$

Now, solve for ΔY as

$$\Delta Y = \Delta I / (1 - \text{Slope of AE curve})$$

Finally, divide both sides of the equation by ΔI to give

$$\text{Multiplier} = \frac{\Delta Y}{\Delta I} = \frac{1}{1 - \text{Slope of AE curve}}$$

For the simple multiplier, where the slope of AE is MPC. So,

$$\text{Multiplier} = \frac{\Delta Y}{\Delta I} = \frac{1}{1-MPC}$$

However, this format is not robust as the slope of AE is not MPC. In the exercise below (Exercise 4) the slope of AE is not equal to MPC.

5.6.3 Other multipliers

We can obtain other multipliers using the similar method. In fact, the multiplier is most easily derived using a little calculus. Begin with the equation,

$$Y = \frac{\alpha - \beta \overline{T} + \beta \overline{TR} + \overline{I} + \overline{G} + \overline{NX}}{1-\beta}$$

This is the expression of equilibrium income. If we want to calculate the multipliers of government purchase, then holding other variables fixed, differentiate with respect to G, to obtain:

$$\frac{dY}{dG} = \frac{1}{1-\beta}$$

Similarly, we can obtain the multiplier of NX by differentiating:

$$\frac{dY}{dNX} = \frac{1}{1-\beta}$$

The multiplier of taxes:

$$\frac{dY}{dT} = \frac{-\beta}{1-\beta}$$

The multiplier of TR:

$$\frac{dY}{dTR} = \frac{\beta}{1-\beta}$$

As we see, only the multiplier of taxes is negative. That is an increase in taxes will decline the equilibrium income.

Because of $0<\beta<1$, the multiplier of government purchase is greater than one. That means the increase in government purchase leads to an even greater increase in income.

▶ Exercise 4

In an economy, the Aggregate expenditure (AE) is the sum of the planned amounts of consumption expenditure (C), investment (I), government (G) and net export (NX). Consumption function $C = \alpha + \beta Y_d$, where disposable income Y_d equals real GDP minus net taxes ($Y-T$). The net taxes, T, equal autonomous taxes (that are independent of income), T_0, plus induced taxes (that vary with income), $t \cdot Y$. So, $T = T_0 + t \cdot Y$. Assume that investment, government and net export are exogenous variables in the model and the price level is fixed.

ⅰ) What is the expression of consumption expenditure function which describes consumption expenditure as a function of real GDP?

ⅱ) What is the expression of equilibrium GDP?

ⅲ) What is the multiplier of government purchase?

Answer:

ⅰ) $$Y_d = Y - T \quad \text{and} \quad T = T_0 + t \cdot Y$$

So,
$$Y_d = Y - T_0 - t \cdot Y$$

Use the last equation to replace the Y_d in the consumption function. The consumption function becomes

$$C = \alpha - \beta T_0 + \beta(1-t)Y$$

This equation describes consumption expenditure as a function of real GDP.

ⅱ) Replace C in AE function using the last equation, the AE equation becomes:

$$AE = \alpha - \beta T_0 + \beta(1-t)Y + I + G + NX$$

The equilibrium occurs when $Y = AE$, so,

$$Y = AE = \alpha - \beta T_0 + \beta(1-t)Y + I + G + NX$$

Solve the equation, we get,

$$Y^* = \frac{\alpha - \beta T_0 + I + G + NX}{1 - \beta(1-t)}$$

That is the expression of equilibrium income.

ⅲ) The multiplier of government purchase, $K_G = \dfrac{\Delta Y}{\Delta G}$,

When $G = G_1$, the equilibrium income becomes:

$$Y_1^* = \frac{\alpha - \beta T_0 + I + G_1 + NX}{1 - \beta(1-t)}$$

If G increases by ΔG, the equilibrium income becomes:

$$Y_2^* = \frac{\alpha - \beta T_0 + I + G_1 + \Delta G + NX}{1 - \beta(1-t)}$$

Therefore,

$$\Delta Y = Y_2^* - Y_1^* = \frac{\Delta G}{1-\beta(1-t)}$$

Then,

$$K_G = \frac{\Delta Y}{\Delta G} = \frac{1}{1-\beta(1-t)}$$

As you see, the multiplier of G is not $\frac{1}{1-MPC}$, because in this case, the slope of AE is $\frac{1}{1-\beta(1-t)}$ rather than $\frac{1}{1-MPC}$. Could you calculate the other multipliers in this case, such as the multiplier of NX?

5.6.4 Summarizing the multiplier effect

There are four key points about the multiplier effect:

· The multiplier effect occurs both when autonomous expenditure increases and when it decreases. For example, with an *MPC* of 0.8, a decrease in planned investment of $100 billion will lead to a decrease in equilibrium income of $500 billion.

· The multiplier effect makes the economy more sensitive to changes in autonomous expenditure than it would otherwise be. Because an initial decline in planned investment spending sets off a series of declines in production, income and consumption.

· The larger the MPC, the larger the value of the multiplier. Because the larger the MPC, the more additional consumption takes place after each rise in income during the multiplier process.

· The formula for the multiplier is oversimplified because it ignores real-world complications, such as the effect that increasing GDP can have on imports, inflation, interest rates, and individual income taxes.

5.6.5 The paradox of thrift

As we are growing up, we are told of the virtues of thrift. Those who spend all their income are condemned to end up poor. Those who save are promised a happy life. However, the simple aggregate expenditures analysis in this chapter tells a different and surprising story.

The AE model has shown us that in the short run, if households save more of their income and spend less of it, aggregate expenditure and real GDP will decline. John Maynard Keynes argued that if many households decide at the same time to increase their saving and reduce their spending, they make themselves worse off by causing aggregate expenditure to fall, thereby pushing the economy into a recession. Keynes referred to this outcome as the paradox of thrift.

This analysis suggests that thrift can be a social vice. From the individual's point of view, a dollar saved may be a dollar earned. But from the social point of view, a dollar saved is a dollar not spent and, therefore, causes a decline in someone else's income. Thrift may be worthy from the individual viewpoint but disastrous from the social standpoint because of its undesirable effects on total output and employment.

So, should we forget the virtues of thrift? Should the government tell people to be less thrifty? No. The results of this simple model are of much relevance in the short run. But, when we look at the medium run and the long run, an increase in the saving rate is likely to lead eventually to higher saving and higher income. Please keep in your mind that policies of encouraging saving may be good in medium run and in the long run, but may lead to a recession in the short run.

Case Study

Consumption the primary driver of China's economic growth for 5 years

The 6.6-percent economic growth China maintained in 2018 was not an easy-won achievement especially given the fact that the country's economy has been developing rapidly for 40 years since reform and opening up, said Yang Decai, director of the Department of Economics at Nanjing University. And he further explained that most economies can only maintain rapid growth for one or two decades at most, and to prolong rapid development is very difficult.

In 2018, China's GDP for the first time exceeded 90 trillion yuan, or $ 13.6 trillion as calculated by the annual average exchange rate, ranking the second largest in the world. The country economic growth, which stood at 6.6 percent, was also the highest among the top five economies of the world. Besides, China was the largest contributor to the world's economic growth, accounting for around 30 percent of the global growth.

Yang pointed out what contributed to last year's growth were a healthier and more sustainable development mode, as well as the further optimization of economic structure. In 2018, Consumption contributed 76.2 percent to China's economic growth, 18.6 percent higher than in 2017, and has been the top growth driver in China for five consecutive years. Domestic trade value added stood at 11.7 trillion yuan ($1.75 trillion) in 2018, contributing around 13 percent to the GDP, with the proportion second only to manufacturing.

The total value of retail goods stood at 38.1 trillion yuan in 2018, up 9 percent from the previous year, maintaining steady growth, among which online retail sales of goods and products accounted for 18.4 percent, an increase of 3.4 percent year-on-year. Service consumption took up 44.2 percent of the average consumption of consumers, up 1.6 percent.

Consumption has been a major driver of economic growth in China due to the efforts the Chinese government has made to stimulate consumption, including offering more retail goods and services, expanding channels of e-commerce, boosting consumers' confidence and improving the consumption environment.

On the other hand, we can see that the contributions of export and investment to economic growth decreased. The growth rate of export fell impacted by the external environment. As the scale of import grew significantly in recent years, trade surplus shrunk compared to before. In terms of investment, China stands at a crucial juncture where new growth drivers are taking the place of old ones and industries are undergoing a supply-side structural reform in capacity cuts and deleveraging, which will also influence investment to some extent. It's probable that consumption would contribute more to economic growth in the future.

Sources: People's Daily, http://en.people.cn/n3/2019/0201/c90000-9543497.html; http://en.people.cn/n3/2019/0308/c90000-9553961.html.

Terms and Concepts

· **Aggregate expenditure (AE)**: Total spending in the economy, the sum of consumption, planned investment, government purchases, and net exports.

· **Aggregate expenditure model**: A macroeconomic model that focuses on the short-run relationship between total spending and real GDP, assuming that the price level is constant.

· **Autonomous expenditure**: An expenditure that does not depend on the level of

GDP.

- **Consumption function**: The relationship between consumption spending and disposable income.
- **Inventories**: Goods that have been produced but not yet sold.
- **Marginal propensity to consume (MPC)**: The slope of the consumption function: The amount by which consumption spending changes when disposable income changes.
- **Marginal propensity to save (MPS)**: The amount by which saving changes when disposable income changes.
- **Multiplier**: The increase in equilibrium real GDP divided by the increase in autonomous expenditure.
- **Multiplier effect**: The process by which an increase in autonomous expenditure leads to a larger increase in real GDP.

Problems and Applications

I. True or False

1. The aggregate expenditure model focuses on the relationship between total spending and real GDP in the short run, assuming the price level is constant.

2. On the 45-degree line diagram, for points that lie below the 45-degree line, planned aggregate expenditure is less than GDP.

3. Consumption spending is $ 22 million, planned investment spending is $ 7 million, actual investment spending is $ 7 million, government purchases are $ 9 million, and net export spending is $ 3 million. Based on this information, we can conclude that aggregate expenditure is greater than GDP.

4. The slope of the consumption function is equal to the change in consumption divided by the change in disposable income.

5. When Xiaoming's income increases by $ 5 000, he spends an additional $ 4 000 dollars. This implies that his marginal propensity to consume is 1.25.

6. If firms are more pessimistic and believe that future profits will fall and remain weak for the next few years, then investment spending will fall.

7. An increase in the price level in China will reduce exports and increase imports.

8. The difference between GDP and net taxes is disposable income.

9. Consumption is $5 million, planned investment spending is $8 million, government purchases are $10 million, and net exports are equal to $2 million. If GDP during that same time period is equal to $27 million, there was an unplanned decrease in inventories equal to $2 million.

10. A decrease in taxes will decrease consumption spending, and an increase in transfer payments will increase consumption spending.

II. Choices

1. A movement along the consumption function shows the change in consumption expenditure as a result of a change in _____.

A. disposable income

B. the price levels

C. the interest rates

D. saving

2. Which of the following leads to an increase in real GDP? _____.

A. A decrease in government spending

B. A decrease in the inflation rate in other countries, relative to the inflation in China

C. A decrease in interest rates

D. Households have increasingly pessimistic expectations about future income

3. As disposable income _____, planned consumption expenditure _____ by a _____ amount.

A. increases; increases; smaller

B. decreases; increases; smaller

C. increases; increases; larger

D. decreases; increases; larger

4. Actual investment spending does not include _____.

A. spending on consumer durable goods

B. spending on new capital equipment

C. spending on new houses

D. changes in inventories

5. An increase in the real interest rate will _____.

A. cause consumers to spend more and save less

B. most likely lower consumers' purchases of durable goods

C. most likely lower the reward to savings

D. most likely lower the cost of borrowing

6. If the MPC is 0.5, then a $10 million increase in disposable income will increase consumption by _____.

A. $2 million

B. $5 million

C. $15 million

D. $50 million

7. Which of the following is a true statement about the multiplier? _____.

A. The multiplier rises as the MPC rises

B. The smaller the MPC, the larger the multiplier

C. The multiplier is a value between zero and one

D. The multiplier effect does not occur when autonomous expenditure decreases

8. If the economy is currently in equilibrium at a level of GDP that is below potential GDP, which of the following would move the economy back to potential GDP? _____.

A. An increase in wealth

B. An increase in interest rates

C. A decrease in business confidence

D. An increase in the value of the dollar relative to other currencies

9. When the real interest rate rises, there is _____.

A. an upward movement along the consumption function

B. a downward movement along the consumption function

C. an upward shift of the consumption function

D. a downward shift of the consumption function

10. As real GDP of China increases, China income increases and so _____.

A. China imports decrease

B. China exports decrease

C. China imports increase

D. China exports increase

11. If the consumption function is defined as $C = 5\,500 + 0.9Y$, the value of the multiplier is _____.

A. 0.1

B. 0.9

C. 9

D. 10

12. Total income is always equal to _____ expenditures; but only in equilibrium is it equal to _____ expenditures, producing in equilibrium _____ on income to change.

A. actual; planned; pressure

B. actual; planned; no pressure

C. planned; actual; pressure

D. planned; actual; no pressure

III. Short Answer

1. Into which category of aggregate expenditure would each of the following transactions fall?

i) Xiaoming purchases a new BYD car.

ii) The city of Suzhou buys 5 new garbage trucks.

iii) Your parents buy a newly constructed apartment.

iv) Consumer in Newyork orders a computer from Xiaomi.

v) A company buys 300 new smart phones from Huawei.

2. Explain any differences between actual investment and planned investment. Also, is it possible for actual investment to be greater than planned investment? If so, explain.

3. Assume a two-sector economy, including only households and firms, so, $AE = C + I$, where $C = \$100 + 0.9Y$ and $I = \$50$. Calculate the equilibrium level of output for this hypothetical economy. What would the level of consumption be if the economy were operating at \$1 400? What would be the amount of unplanned investment at this level? In which direction would you expect the economy to move to at \$1 400 and why?

4. In 2000 the Haier television manufacturing company planned to invest \$1 100 000

by building a new factory at a cost of $ 1 000 000 and increasing its inventories by $ 100 000 worth of television sets. However, by the end of the year the actual amount of investment for the company was $ 1 200 000. What could explain this apparent difference between the company's planned investment and actual investment?

5. Explain the difference between induced consumption expenditure and autonomous consumption expenditure. Why isn't all consumption expenditure induced expenditure?

6. Figure 5-8 illustrates the components of aggregate planned expenditure on an Island. The island has no imports or exports, no incomes taxes, and the price level is fixed.

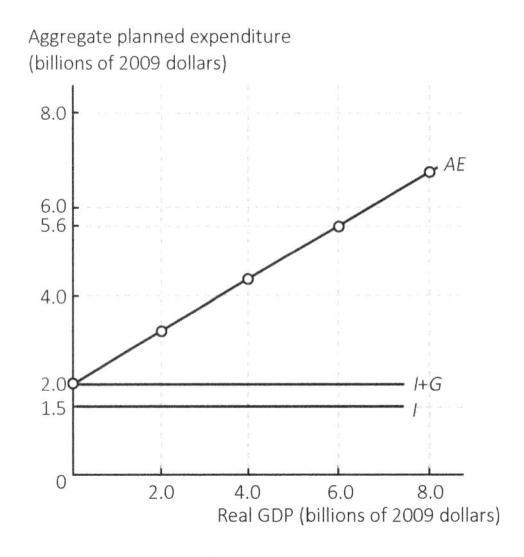

Figure 5-8

i) What is aggregate planned expenditure when real GDP is $ 6 billion?

ii) Calculate autonomous expenditure and the marginal propensity to consume.

iii) If real GDP is $ 4 billion, what is happening to inventories?

iv) If real GDP is $ 6 billion, what is happening to inventories?

7. In an economy, autonomous consumption expenditure is $ 50 billion, investment is $ 200 billion, and government expenditure is $ 250 billion. The marginal propensity to consume is 0.7 and net taxes are $ 250 billion. Exports are $ 500 billion and imports are $ 450 billion. Assume that net taxes and imports are autonomous and the price level is fixed.

i) What is the consumption function?

ii) What is the equation of the AE curve?

iii) Calculate equilibrium expenditure.

iv) Calculate the multiplier.

v) If investment decreases to $ 150 billion, what is the change in equilibrium expenditure?

vi) Describe the process in part v) that moves the economy to its new equilibrium expenditure.

8. Refer to Table 5-4, answer the following questions. The numbers in the table are in billions of dollars.

Table 5-4

Real GDP	Consumption	Planned investment	Government purchases	Net exports
$ 4 000	$ 3 500	$ 350	$ 450	- $ 100
$ 5 000	$ 4 300	$ 350	$ 450	- $ 100
$ 6 000	$ 5 100	$ 350	$ 450	- $ 100
$ 7 000	$ 5 900	$ 350	$ 450	- $ 100

i) What is the equilibrium level of real GDP?

ii) What is the MPC?

iii) If potential GDP is $ 7 000 billion, is the economy at full employment? If not, what is the condition of the economy?

iv) If the economy is not at full employment, by how much should government spending increase so that the economy can move to the full employment level of GDP?

9. Consider the following model of the economy:

$C = 20 + 0.75(Y-T)$,

$I = 380$,

$G = 400$,

$T = 0.2Y$,

$Y = C + I + G$.

i) What is the value of the MPC in this model?

ii) If Y rises by 100, what is the change of consumption?

iii) Compute the equilibrium level of income.

ⅳ) At the equilibrium level of income, what is the value of the government budget surplus?

ⅴ) Increase G by 10 to 410, calculate the government purchases multiplier and explain why it no longer equals $1/(1-MPC)$.

Answers to Problems and Applications

Ⅰ. True or False

1	2	3	4	5	6	7	8	9	10
T	T	F	T	F	T	T	T	F	F

Ⅱ. Choice

1	2	3	4	5	6	7	8	9	10
A	C	A	A	B	B	A	A	D	C
11	12								
D	B								

Ⅲ. Short Answer

1. Answer:

ⅰ) Consumption.

ⅱ) Government purchases.

ⅲ) Planned investment.

ⅳ) Net exports.

ⅴ) Planned investment.

2. Answer: Actual investment represents the amount of investment that takes place during a given period. Actual investment, therefore, also takes into account any unplanned changes in inventories. Planned investment represents those additions to the capital stock that are planned by firms. Yes, it is possible for actual investment to exceed planned investment. For this to occur, production must exceed sales. In this case, firms experience an unplanned increase in inventories that causes actual investment to exceed

planned investment.

3. **Answer**: Equilibrium in a two-sector economy is where $C + I = Y$. In this case that is $100 + 0.9Y + 50 = Y$. Rearranging terms yields $150 = 0.1Y$. Solving for Y results in an equilibrium of $1 500. If the economy is operating at $1 400, the level of unplanned investment is $-$10. Proof: Consumption would be $1 360 ($100 + 0.9\times$ 1 400). With investment of $50, this means aggregate spending is $1 410. This is $10 above the level of aggregate output. With inventories being drawn down the expectation would be that firms would step up production and the economy would expand beyond $1 400.

4. **Answer**: Perhaps the sales of television sets were not as high as they expected. This caused inventories to accumulate to $200 000 instead of the $100 000 they had planned for.

5. **Answer**: Induced consumption expenditure is consumption expenditure that changes when disposable income changes. Autonomous consumption expenditure is consumption expenditure that would occur in the short run even if disposable income was zero. Not all consumption expenditure is induced consumption expenditure because, in the short run, even if someone has no income, they still will have some (autonomous) consumption expenditure, if for nothing else, for food.

6. **Answer**:

ⅰ) Autonomous expenditure is $2 billion. Autonomous expenditure is expenditure that does not depend on real GDP. Autonomous expenditure equals the value of aggregate planned expenditure when real GDP is zero. The marginal propensity to consume is 0.6. When the country has no imports or exports and no income taxes, the slope of the AE curve equals the marginal propensity to consume. When income increases from zero to $6 billion, aggregate planned expenditure increases from $2 billion to $5.6 billion. That is, when real GDP increases by $6 billion, aggregate planned expenditure increases by $3.6 billion. The marginal propensity to consume is $3.6 billion $\div$ $6 billion, which is 0.6.

ⅱ) The figure shows that aggregate planned expenditure is $5.6 billion when real GDP is $6 billion.

ⅲ) Firms' inventories are decreasing. When real GDP is $4 billion, aggregate planned expenditure exceeds real GDP, so firms sell all that they produce and more. As a result, inventories decrease.

iv) Firms are accumulating inventories. That is, unplanned inventory investment is positive. When real GDP is $6 billion, aggregate planned expenditure is less than real GDP. Firms cannot sell all that they produce and inventories pile up.

7. **Answer:**

i) The consumption function is the relationship between consumption expenditure and disposable income, other things remaining the same. In this case the consumption function is $C = 50 + 0.7(Y-250)$ where the "50" is $50 billion and the "250" is $250 billion.

ii) The equation of the AE curve is $AE = 375 + 0.7Y$, where Y is real GDP and the "375" is $375 billion. Aggregate planned expenditure is the sum of consumption expenditure, investment, government purchases, and net exports. Using the symbol AE for aggregate planned expenditure, aggregate planned expenditure is

$AE = 50 + 0.7(Y-250) + 200 + 250 + 50$,

$AE = 50 + 0.7Y - 175 + 200 + 250 + 50$,

$AE = 375 + 0.7Y$.

iii) Equilibrium expenditure is $1 250 billion. Equilibrium expenditure is the level of aggregate expenditure that occurs when aggregate planned expenditure equals real GDP. That is, $AE = 375 + 0.7Y$ and $AE = Y$. Solving these two equations for Y gives equilibrium expenditure of $1 250 billion.

iv) The multiplier equals $1/(1-$ the slope of the AE curve). The equation of the AE curve tells us that the slope of the AE curve is 0.7. So the multiplier is $1/(1-0.7)$, which is 3.333.

v) Equilibrium real expenditure decreases by $166.67 billion. From part iv) the multiplier is 3.333. The change in equilibrium expenditure equals the change in investment, $50 billion, multiplied by 3.333.

vi) When investment decreases by $50 billion, aggregate planned expenditure is less than real GDP. Firms find that their inventories are accumulating above target levels. As a result, they decrease production to reduce inventories. Real GDP decreases. The decrease in real GDP decreases disposable income so that consumption expenditure falls. In turn, the decrease in consumption expenditure leads to a further decrease in aggregate planned expenditure. Real GDP still exceeds aggregate planned expenditure though by less than was initially the case. Nonetheless unwanted inventories are still accumulating and firms continue to cut production, further reducing real GDP. This process continues until eventually real GDP will decrease enough to equal aggregate planned expenditure.

8. Answer:

i) Equilibrium real GDP is determined where aggregate expenditure = real GDP. The values for aggregate expenditure for each level of real GDP are given in Table 5-5. They are found by adding together $C + I + G + NX$. The value where real GDP equals aggregate expenditure is \$ 5 000 billion, and this is equilibrium.

Table 5-5

Real GDP	Aggregate expenditure
\$ 4 000	\$ 4 200
\$ 5 000	\$ 5 000
\$ 6 000	\$ 5 800
\$ 7 000	\$ 6 600

ii) The MPC is found by the formula. In this case, ΔC = \$ 800 billion and ΔY = \$ 1 000 billion, so MPC = \$ 800 billion / \$ 1 000 billion = 0.8.

iii) The economy is not at full employment. Equilibrium GDP is \$ 5 000 billion, which is less than potential GDP. The economy is in recession.

iv) GDP must rise to \$ 7 000 billion to be at full employment. This means that GDP must increase by \$ 2 000 billion. To find the right change in government spending, use the multiplier formula:

$\Delta GDP = M \times \Delta G$. We know the ΔGDP we want to achieve is \$ 2 000 billion. We can find the multiplier since we know the MPC:

Multiplier = 1 / (1−0.8) = 1 / 0.2 = 5. Substituting this into the above equation:

\$ 2 000 billion = 5 × ΔG,

\$ 2 000 billion / 5 = ΔG = \$ 400 billion.

Therefore, government spending must increase by \$ 400 billion to move the economy to full employment.

9. Answer:

i) The value of MPC in this model is 0.75.

ii) When Y rises 100, the taxes rise by 20 according thee equation for taxes. So, the disposable income rises by 80 and consumption rises by $0.75 \times 80 = 60$.

iii) $Y = C + I + G$,

$Y = 20 + 0.75(Y - 0.2Y) + 380 + 400$.

Solve for Y,

Y = 2000.

Therefore, the equilibrium level of income equals 2000.

iv) When $Y = 2000$, $T = 0.2Y = 0.2 \times 2\,000 = 400$,

So the government budget surplus $= T - G = 400 - 400 = 0$.

When G increase to 410, then

$Y = 20 + 0.75(Y - 0.2Y) + 380 + 4\,100$.

Solve for Y,

$Y = 2025$.

The increase in the level of equilibrium Y equals $2\,025 - 2\,000 = 25$.

So the government purchases multiplier $= \dfrac{\Delta Y}{\Delta G} = \dfrac{25}{10} = 2.5$, that is not equal to $1/(1 - MPC) = 4$. Such result is due to the taxes increase as the income increases. for example, when government purchases increase by 1, the Y rises immediately by 1 in the first round. But because the taxes depend on the income, the taxes increase by 0.2, the increase in disposable income is 0.8 rather than 1. Therefore, the consumption increases by $0.8 \times 0.75 = 0.6$, then the income increases by 0.6 in the second round, instead of 0.75. Therefore, the government purchases multiplier equals $1/(1 - 0.6) = 2.5$, rather than $1/(1 - 0.75) = 4$.

6 The IS-LM Model

Learning Objective

By the end of this chapter, students should understand:
- what determines national income for a given price level.
- the relationship between investment and real interest rate.
- the definition of IS curve.
- the effect of government purchases and taxes on the IS curve.
- Theory of Liquidity Preference.
- the definition of LM curve.
- the effect of money supply on the LM curve.
- how to use the IS-LM model to analyze the impact of policies and shocks.

Key Points and Exercises

6.1 What is the IS-LM model?

In this chapter and the next, we continue our study of economic fluctuations by looking more closely at aggregate demand. Our goal is to identify the variables that shift the aggregate demand curve, causing fluctuations in national income.

The model of aggregate demand developed in this chapter, called the IS-LM model, is the leading interpretation of Keynes's theory. The goal of the model is to show what determines national income for any given price level.

The Great Depression caused many economists to question the validity of classical economic theory. They believed they needed a new model to explain such a pervasive economic downturn. In 1936, John Maynard Keynes wrote The General Theory of Employment, Interest, and Money. In it, he proposed a new way to analyze the economy, which he presented as an alternative to the classical theory.

Keynes proposed that low aggregate demand was responsible for the low income and high unemployment that characterized economic downturns. He criticized the notion that aggregate supply alone determines national income. The Keynesian model implies that output is determined by demand and that production or supply adjusts passively to shifts in aggregate demand. The Keynesian model can be viewed as showing what causes the aggregate demand curve to shift. The main idea is that in the short run, when the price level is fixed, shifts in the aggregate demand curve lead to changes in national income, Y, as Figure 6–1 shows: when the aggregate curve shifts to the left or the right, the equilibrium national income will decrease or increase.

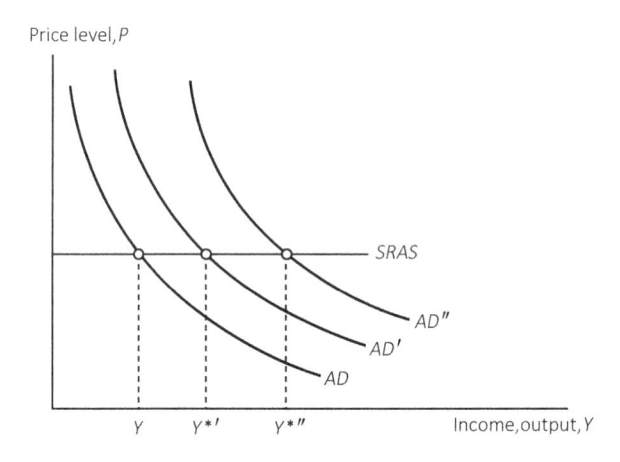

Figure 6–1

The two parts of the IS-LM model are, not surprisingly the IS curve and the LM curve. IS stands for "investment" and "saving," and the IS curve represents what's going on in the market for goods and services. LM stands for "liquidity" and "money" and the LM curve represents what's happening to the supply and demand for money. Because the interest rate influences both investment and money demand, it is the variable that links the two halves of the IS-LM model. The model shows how interactions between the goods and money markets determine the position and slope of the aggregate demand curve and, therefore, the level of national income in the short run.

6.2 The simple aggregate expenditure model

6.2.1 The simple aggregate expenditure model

Aggregate expenditure model: A macroeconomic model that focuses on the short-run relationship between total spending and real GDP, assuming that the price level is constant. We have talked the AE model in Chapter 5. Because the IS curve is based on the simple AE model, let's firstly recall the equilibrium of the AE model.

6.2.2 The algebra of macroeconomic equilibrium

In the simple model, equilibrium in the economy occurs when spending on output is equal to the value of output produced. The total spending includes four components, consumption, planned investment, government purchase and net exports. We can write:

Aggregate expenditure = Consumption + Planned Investment
+ Government purchases + Net exports

or

$$AE = C + I + G + NX$$

In the model, we suppose the aggregate consumption is the function of disposable income, and the other three variables ($I, G,$ and NX) are exogenous variables.

Suppose the consumption function as the following:

$$C = \alpha + \beta Y_d$$

α is autonomous consumption. β is MPC and Y_d is the disposable income, which equals $Y-T+TR$. T stands for taxes and TR stands for transfer payment.

$$I = \bar{I}$$
$$G = \bar{G}$$
$$NX = \overline{NX}$$
$$T = \bar{T}$$
$$TR = \overline{TR}$$

The equilibrium condition is:

$$Y = AE = C + I + G + NX$$

or

$$Y = \alpha + \beta(Y - \bar{T} + \overline{TR}) + \bar{I} + \bar{G} + \overline{NX}$$

or

$$Y-\beta Y=\alpha-\beta\overline{T}+\beta\overline{TR}+\overline{I}+\overline{G}+\overline{NX}$$

or

$$Y=\frac{\alpha-\beta\overline{T}+\beta\overline{TR}+\overline{I}+\overline{G}+\overline{NX}}{1-\beta}$$

Therefore, we derive the expression of equilibrium Y.

6.3 The goods market and the IS curve

In this section we will derive the IS curve. The IS curve shows the relationship between the interest rate and the level of income that arises in the market for goods and services. The definition of IS curve: a graph of all combinations of interest rate (r) and the levels of income (Y) that result in goods market equilibrium, planned aggregate expenditure equals aggregate income. The IS curve is derived in two steps: First, we explain why investment depends on interest rates. Second, we insert the investment function in the aggregate expenditure identity, just as we did with the consumption function in Chapter 5, and find the combinations of income and interest rates that keep the goods market in equilibrium.

6.3.1 The interest rate and investment

The aggregate expenditure model is only a stepping-stone on our path to the IS-LM model. The aggregate expenditure model makes the simplifying assumption that the level of planned investment I is exogenous. In this chapter, investment spending becomes endogenous. It depends on the interest rate, which measures the cost of the funds used to finance investment. Typically, firms borrow to purchase investment goods. For an investment project to be profitable, its return (the revenue from increased future production of goods and services) must exceed its cost (the payments for borrowed funds). The interest rate is the cost of borrowing to finance investment projects. If the interest rate rises, fewer investment projects are profitable, and the quantity of investment demanded falls. Conversely, firms will want to borrow and invest more when interest rate are lower. We can summarize this discussion with an equation relating investment I to the real interest rate r:

$$I=I(r)$$

Figure 6-2 shows the investment function. It slopes downward, because as this interest rate rises, the quantity of investment demanded falls.

Real interest rate, r

Investment function, i(r)

Quantity of investment, I

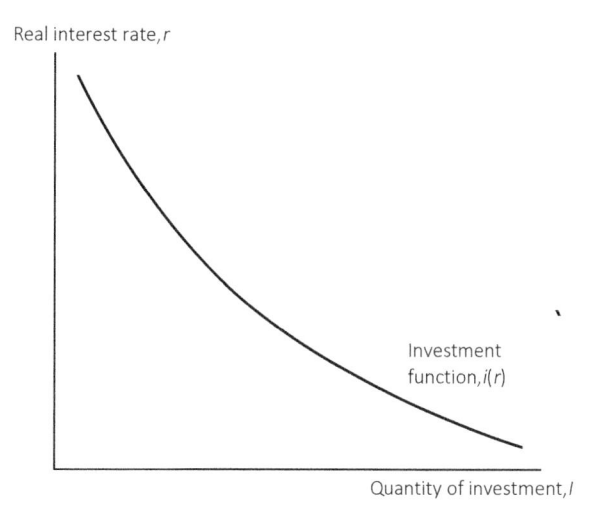

Figure 6-2

We specify an investment spending function of the form:

$$I = e - dr \quad d > 0$$

Where r is the rate of interest and the coefficient d measures the responsiveness of investment spending to the interest rates. If d is large, then relatively small increase in the interest rate generates a large drop in investment spending. e denotes autonomous investment spending, which is independent of both income and the rate of interest.

6.3.2 The IS curve

To add this relationship between the interest rate and investment to the AE model, we can rewrite the relationship between the equilibrium income and the interest rate as:

$$Y = \frac{\alpha - \beta\overline{T} + \beta\overline{TR} + e - dr + \overline{G} + \overline{NX}}{1 - \beta}$$

Rearrange the equation, we get:

$$Y = \frac{\alpha - \beta\overline{T} + \beta\overline{TR} + e + \overline{G} + \overline{NX}}{1 - \beta} - \frac{dr}{1 - \beta}$$

This is the equation for IS curve. Because of $d > 0$ and $1 - \beta > 0$, we can see the IS curve shows the income Y is inversely related to the interest rate.

We can also determine the IS curve by combining the investment function with the Keynesian-cross diagram. For a given level of interest rate, say, r_1, we can get an investment $I(r_1)$, then for the $I(r_1)$, we can get an equilibrium income Y_1. The pair (r_1, Y_1), in the bottom panel gives us one point on the IS curve. And changing the interest rate can give us another point on the IS curve.

Figure 6-3 shows the investment function, an increase in interest rate from r_1 to r_2 reduces the quantity of investment from $I(r_1)$ to $I(r_2)$.

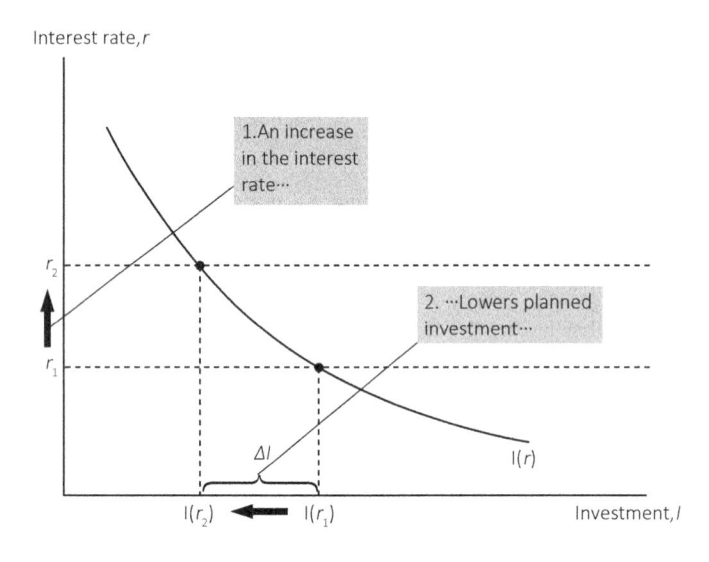

Figure 6-3

The reduction in planned investment, in turn, shifts the planned-expenditure function downward, as Figure 6-4 shows. The shift in the planned-expenditure function causes the level of income to fall from Y_1 to Y_2.

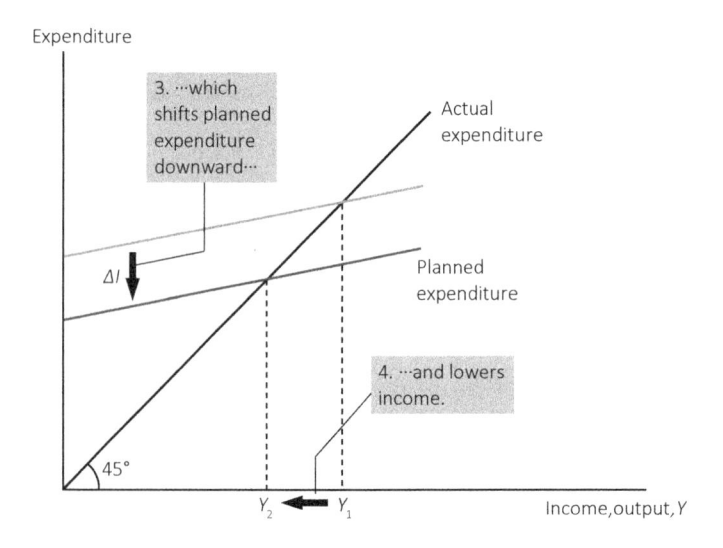

Figure 6-4

Hence, an increase in the interest rate lowers income. The IS curve summarizes these changes in the goods equilibrium, as Figure 6-5 shows. The horizontal axis is income and the vertical axis is interest rate. The higher the interest rate is, the lower the level of income is.

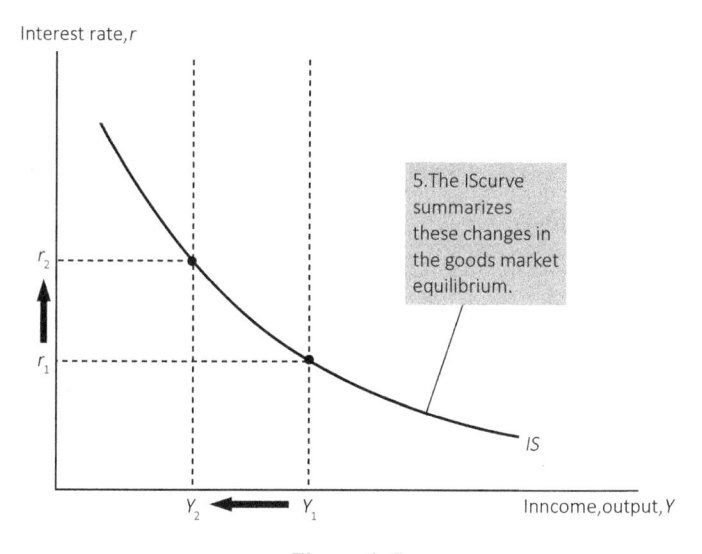

Figure 6-5

Each point on the IS curve represents equilibrium in the goods market, illustrates how the equilibrium level of income depends on interest rate. Because an increase in the interest rate causes planned investment to fall, which in turn causes equilibrium income to fall, the IS curve slopes downward.

▷ Exercise 1

The following equations describe a closed economy.

$Y = C + I + G$,

$C = 100 + 0.8(Y - T)$,

$I = 100 - 4r$,

$G = 50, T = 50$.

i) Identify each of the variables and briefly explain their meaning.

ii) From the above list, derive the IS Curve. Graph the IS curve on an appropriately labeled graph.

Answer:

i) Y stands for the income. Y equals the summer of consumption C, investment I, and government purchase G. T is taxes. r is the real interest rate.

ii) For this economy,

$$Y=C+I+G$$

To plus consumption function and investment function to the AE equation, we can get:

$Y=100+0.8(Y-T)+100-4r+G$.

Substitute $G=50, T=50$ to the equation:

$Y=100+0.8(Y-50)+100-4r+50$.

Rearrange the equation:

$Y=1050-20r$.

This is the equation for the IS curve, which is shown in Figure 6-6.

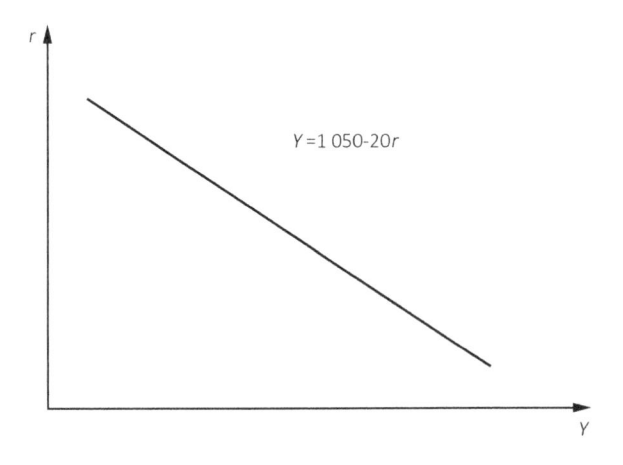

Figure 6-6

6.3.3 The slope of the IS curve

We have already noted that the IS curve is negatively sloped because a higher level of the interest rate reduces investment spending, thereby reducing aggregate demand and thus the equilibrium level of income. From the equation of the IS curve, the steepness of the IS curve depends on how sensitive investment spending is to changes in the interest rate (d) and also depends on the multiplier $\left(\dfrac{1}{1-\beta}\right)$. If d is large, investment spending is very sensitive to the interest rate. Then a given change in the interest rate generates a large change in aggregate demand, and thus shifts the aggregate demand curve by a large amount, thereby a large change in the equilibrium level of income. The IS curve is relatively flat. Correspondingly, if d is small and investment spending is not very sensitive to the interest rate, the IS curve is relatively steep.

Similarly, we can analysis the effect of the multiplier on the steepness of the IS curve. For a given change in interest rate, we can get a given change in investment spending. If the multiplier is large, then the change in investment can produces a large change in the equilibrium level of income. Therefore, the IS curve is relatively flat. The opposite is true.

6.3.4 Shifts of the IS curve

It is important to distinguish shifts of the IS curve with movements along it. This is where the distinction between exogenous and endogenous variables comes to play. The IS curve describes how the two endogenous variables, the real GDP and the interest rate, are combined to achieve equilibrium in the goods market, everything else being held constant. what is "everything else"? this refers to all the variables that we treat as exogenous when we draw the IS curve. Any change in any of these exogenous variables will shift the IS curve. Therefore, the position of the IS curve determined by the exogenous variables. Whenever any of the exogenous variables change, the IS curve shifts. In fact, we can find these exogenous variables in the intercept term of the equation of the IS curve. Change in exogenous variable that raise the aggregate income shift the IS curve to the right. Change in exogenous variable that decline the aggregate income shifts the IS curve to the left.

Fiscal policy is a premier source of shifts in the IS curve. Let's see how the change in government spending G and taxes T shift the IS curve. First, consider an increase in government purchase, from G_1 to G_2, as the following figure shows. At a given interest rate, say r_1, total expenditure increases and the AE curve shifts up. It leads to an increase in equilibrium output, from Y_1 to Y_2. Then the IS curve shifts to the right: at a given interest rate, the equilibrium level of output is higher than it was before.

By how much does the curve shift? the change in income (ΔY) as a result of the change in government spending equals the multiplier $\left(\dfrac{1}{1-MPC}\right)$ times the change in government spending (ΔG). Therefore, the horizontal distance of IS shift equals:

$$\Delta Y = \frac{1}{1-MPC}\Delta G$$

More generally, any factor that, for given interest rate, increases the equilibrium level of output causes the IS curve to shift to the right (as Figure 6-7 shows). Symmetrically, a factor that, for given interest rate, decreases the equilibrium level of output, such as, a decrease in government spending, causes the IS curve to shift to the left (as Figure 6-7 shows).

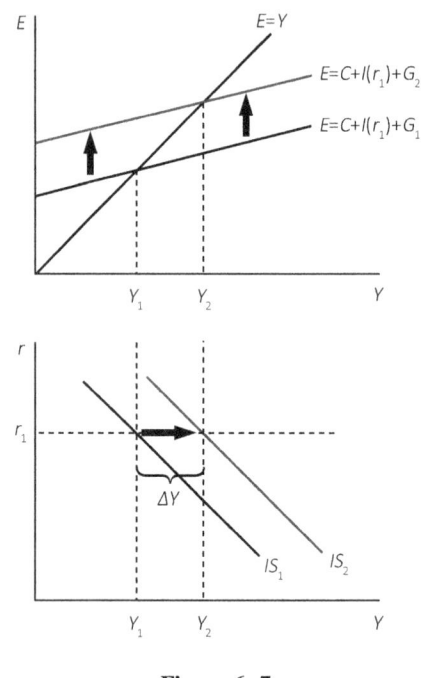

Figure 6-7

As we discussed in Chapter 5, the multiplier of taxes is negative. So, an increase in taxes decrease the equilibrium level of output, causes the IS curve shifts to the left. Conversely, a decrease in taxes causes the IS curve shifts to the right.

Analogously, could you analyze the effect of autonomous consumption and autonomous investment on the position of the IS curve?

Let's summarize:

· the IS curve shows the combinations of the interest rate and the level of income that are consistent with equilibrium in the market for goods and services. The horizontal axis is income and the vertical axis is interest rate.

· The IS curve slopes downward. Because an increase in the interest rate reduces planned investment spending and therefore reduces aggregate demand, thus reducing the equilibrium level of income.

• The more sensitive investment is to changes in the interest rate, and the larger the multiplier, the flatter the IS curve.

• In general, besides r, anything increasing the expenditure will shift the IS curve to the right. anything reducing the demand for goods and services will shift the IS curve to the left.

▶ Exercise 2

The following equations describe an economy.

$Y = C + I + G$,
$C = 100 + 0.8(Y - T)$,
$I = 100 - 4r$,
$G = 50, T = 50$.

i) If G increased by 20%, that is the new G is 60, then what is the equation of IS curve?

ii) Compare to the former one, what is the effect of the change of G on the equilibrium income, for the same r?

iii) If government change the tax, then what is the effect on the equilibrium income?

Answers:

i) $Y = C + I + G = 100 + 0.8(Y - 40) + 100 - 4r + 60$.

Rearrange the equation:

$Y = 1\,100 - 20r$.

ii) For the same r, the equilibrium income increases 50, which equals

$$\frac{1}{1-MPC} \cdot \Delta G = \frac{1}{1-0.8} \times 10 = 50.$$

iii) If government increases the tax, at given interest rate, disposable income decreases, leading to a decrease in consumption, leading in turn to a decrease in the demand for goods and a decrease in equilibrium output.

6.4 The money market and the LM curve

So far, we've derived the IS part of AD, it's now time to complete the model of AD by adding a money market equilibrium schedule, the LM curve. The LM curve plots the relationship between the interest rate and the level of income that arises in the market for money balances. To understand this relationship, we begin by looking at a theory of the interest rate called the theory of liquidity preference.

6.4.1 The theory of liquidity preference

Keynes proposed the theory of liquidity preference in his classic book to explain what factors determine the economy's interest rate. The theory of liquidity preference posits that the interest rate adjusts to balance the supply and demand for the economy's most liquid asset-money. To study equilibrium in the money market, we begin with the supply of real money balances, M/P. M stands for the supply of money and P stands for the price level. The money supply M is an exogenous policy variable chosen by a central bank. The price level P is also exogenous variable in this model. The supply of real money balances is fixed, and does not depend on the interest rate. Therefore, the theory of liquidity preference assumes there is a fixed supply of real money balances. That is,

$$\left(\frac{M}{P}\right)^s = \frac{\overline{M}}{\overline{P}}$$

These assumptions imply that the supply of real money balances is fixed and, in particular, does not depend on the interest rate. Thus, when we plot the supply of real money balances against the interest rate in Figure 6-8, we obtain a vertical supply curve.

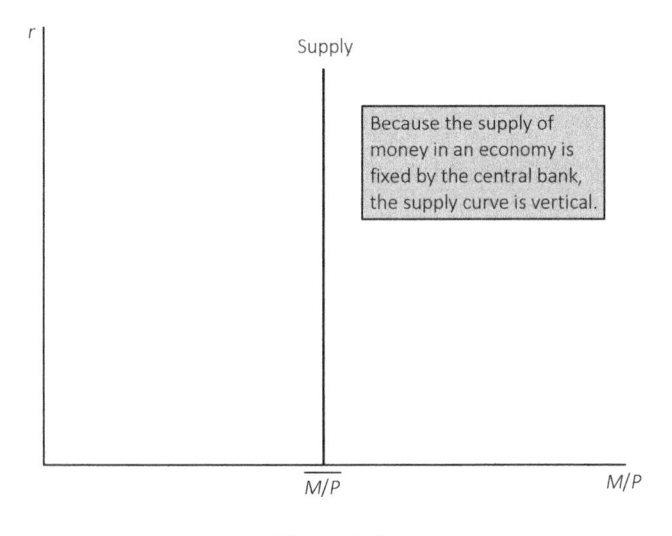

Figure 6-8

Next, let's consider the demand of real money balances. We can think of the demand of money as the demand for liquidity. Any assets' liquidity refers to the ease with which that asset is converted into the economy's medium of exchange. Money is the economy's medium of exchange, so it is by definition the most liquid asset available. People choose to hold money instead of other assets that offer higher rates of return because money can be used to buy goods and service. The amount of money people want to hold — the demand for money-depends on the level of real income and the interest rate.

Since the interest rate is the opportunity cost of holding money, when the interest rate rises, the cost of holding money increases, people want to hold less of their wealth in the form of money. When the interest rate is 1 percent, there is very little benefit from holding bonds rather than money. However, when the interest rate is 10 percent, it is worth some effort not to hold more money than is needed to finance day-to-day transactions. Therefore, the quantity of real money balances demanded is negatively related to the interest rate. Higher interest rates reduce the quantity of real money balances demanded.

When income is high, the expenditure is high, so people engage in more transactions that require the use of money. Thus, greater income implies greater money demand. For example, you like to have coins in your pocket to buy cups of coffee during the day. If a cup costs \$1, you will want to keep about \$1 in coins. But if your income increases, you want to buy two cups of coffee during the day, then you will need \$2 in coins. Therefore, just higher income leads to a greater demand for coffee, higher income also leads to a greater demand for real money balances. Therefore, the quantity of real money balances demanded is positively related to income.

Therefore, the demand for real balances increases with the level of real income and decrease with the interest rate. The demand for real balances is accordingly expressed as:

$$(M/P)^d = L(\underset{(-)}{r}, \underset{(+)}{Y})$$

Where the function shows that the quantity of money demanded depends on the interest rate r and the income Y.

Let's use the following figure to show the demand curve of real money. Let the interest rate be measured on the vertical axis and the real money be measured on the horizontal axis. The income as an independent variable is not at the coordinate axis. Therefore, for each income Y, we can draw a demand curve of real money. An increase in income raises the demand of real money, therefore, the demand curve of real money shifts to the right. As Figure 6-9 shows, when income increases from Y_1 to Y_2, the demand curve shifts to the right. The demand curve of real money slopes downward because the demand of real money is negatively related to the interest rate.

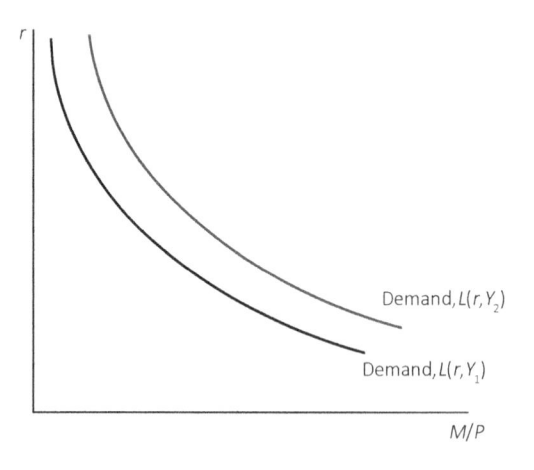

Figure 6-9

According to the theory of liquidity preference, the supply and demand for real money balances determine what interest rate prevails in the economy. That is, the interest rate adjusts to equilibrate the money market. As Figure 6-10 shows, the equilibrium interest rate is r_1, where is the intersection of the demand curve and the supply curve.

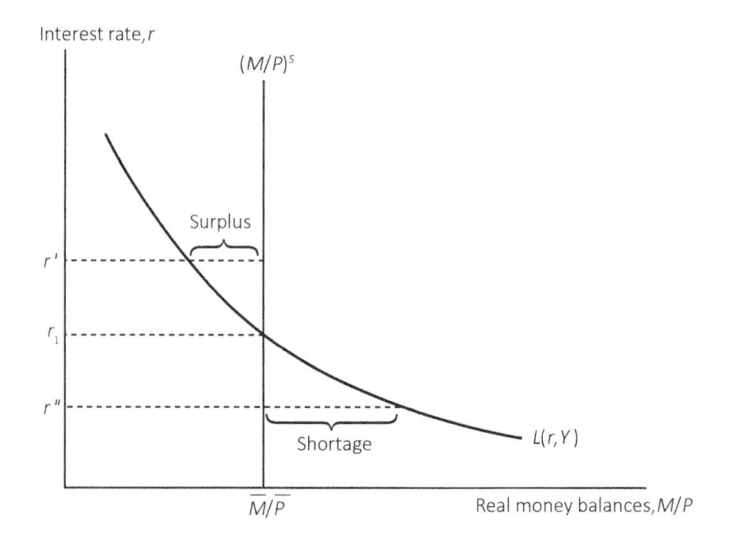

Figure 6-10

How does the interest rate get to this equilibrium of money supply and money demand? Let's consider what happens if a market is not in equilibrium. Suppose the interest rate is above the equilibrium level, say r', as the figure above illustrates, the quantity of real money balances supplied is greater than the quantity demanded. There is a surplus of money in the market. Households holding the excess supply of money try to convert some of their money into bonds. And banks and bond issuers prefer to pay lower interest rates. Then, the interest rate decline until $r=r_1$. Conversely if the interest rate is below the equilibrium level, say r'', so that the quantity of money demanded exceeds the quantity supplied, there is a shortage in the market. Households try to obtain money by selling bonds or making bank withdrawals. To attract now-scarcer funds, banks and bond issuers respond by increasing the interest rates they offer. Eventually the interest rate reaches the equilibrium level, at which people are content with their portfolios of monetary and nonmonetary assets.

6.4.2 Driving the LM curve

Using the theory of liquidity preference, we can figure out what happens to the equilibrium interest rate when the level of income changes. For example, consider what happens in figure below when income increases from Y_1 to Y_2. An increase in income from Y_1 to Y_2 leads people to increase their demand for money at any interest rate. Therefore, As Figure 6-11 illustrates, this increase in income shifts the money demand curve to the right. With the supply of real money balances unchanged, the interest rate must rise from r_1 to r_2 to equilibrate the money market. At r_2, the real money market is again in equilibrium. Therefore, the equilibrium of real money market implies that the higher the level of output, the higher the demand for money, and thereby the higher the equilibrium interest rate.

We can summarize this relationship between the level of income and the interest rate using the LM curve shown in Figure 6-12. Each point on the LM curve represents equilibrium in the money market, and the curve illustrates how the equilibrium interest rate depends on the level of income. The higher the level of income, the higher the demand for real money balances, and the higher the equilibrium interest rate. For this reason, the LM curve slopes upward.

156 | Macroeconomics

Interest rate, r

1. An increase in income raises money demand...

2. ... increasing the interest rate.

$L(r, Y_2)$

$L(r, Y_1)$

$\overline{M/P}$ Real money balances, M/P

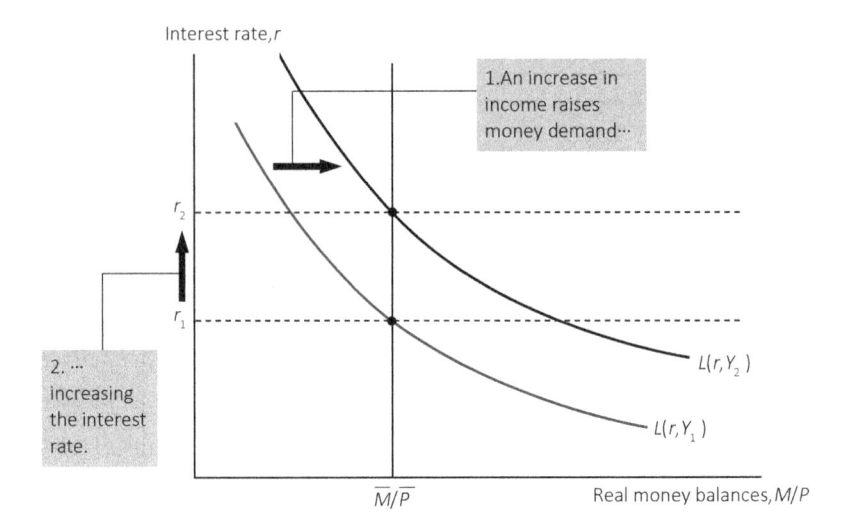

Figure 6–11

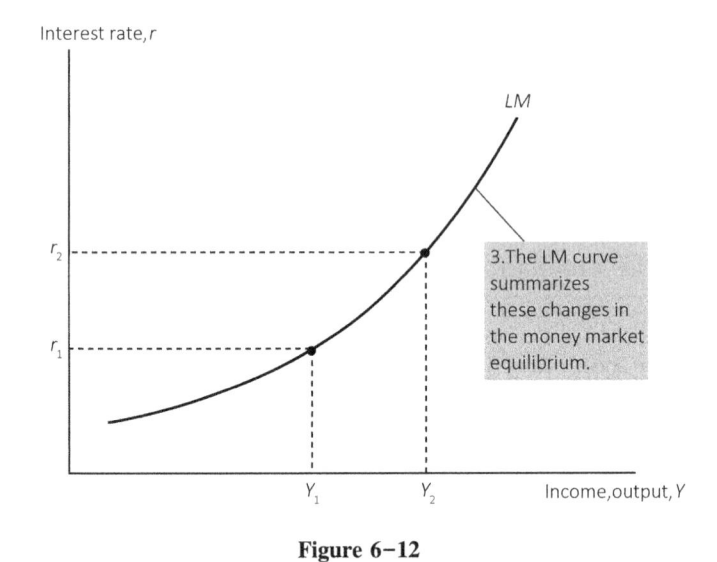

Interest rate, r

LM

3. The LM curve summarizes these changes in the money market equilibrium.

Y_1 Y_2 Income, output, Y

Figure 6–12

6.4.3 The equation for LM curve

The LM curve is a graph of all combinations of r and Y that equate the supply and demand for real money balances. So, we can obtain LM equation from the following equations:

The supply of real money balances:

$$(M/P)^s = \overline{M}/\overline{P}$$

The demand for real money balances:

$$(M/P)^d = L(r, Y)$$

The equilibrium condition of money market:

$$(M/P)^d = (M/P)^s$$

Then the equation for the LM curve is:

$$\overline{M/P} = L(r, Y)$$

Let's suppose the money demand function is:

$$(M/P)^d = ky - hr \quad k, h > 0$$

The parameters k and h reflect the sensitivity of the demand for the real money balances to the level of income and the interest rate, respectively. This demand equation for real balances implies that for a given level of income, the quantity demanded of money is a decreasing function of the rate of interest.

And suppose the money supply is M, and $P = 1$, so the real money supply $m = M$, then the equation for the LM curve is:

$$m = ky - hr$$

Rearrange the equation as:

$$y = \frac{hr}{k} + \frac{m}{k}$$

or

$$r = \frac{ky}{h} - \frac{m}{h}$$

because we measure real income on the horizontal axis and the interest rate on the vertical axis, the slope of LM curve is $\frac{k}{h}$ and it is positive.

▶ Exercise 3

Suppose that the following equation describes the supply of real money balances:

$$\left(\frac{M}{P}\right)^s = \frac{\overline{M}}{P} = \frac{2\,000}{2} = 1\,000.$$

And the demand for real money balances is described as:

$$\left(\frac{M}{P}\right)^d = L(r, Y) = 0.4Y - 20r.$$

Using the two equations to derive the equation of the LM curve.

Answer:

$$(M/P)^d = (M/P)^s$$

The LM curve shows the combinations of the interest rate and the level of income that are consist with equilibrium in the market for real money balances. So, let the demand for real money balances equals the supply for real money balances:

Then,

$1\ 000 = 0.4Y - 20r$.

Rearrange the equation, we can get the equation for the IM curve:

$Y = 2\ 500 + 50r$.

6.4.4 The slope of the LM curve

From the equation of the LM curve, we know the slope of the LM curve depends on the responsiveness of the demand for money to interest rate, as measured by h, and the responsiveness of the demand for money to income, k. If k is large and h is small, a given change in income, ΔY, has a larger effect on the interest rate. So, the LM curve is relatively steeper. If the demand for money is relatively insensitive to interest rate and thus h is close to zero, the LM curve is nearly vertical. If the demand for money is very sensitive to the interest rate and h is very large, the LM curve is close to horizontal. In that case, a small change in the interest rate must be accompanied by a large change in the level of income in order to maintain money market equilibrium.

6.4.5 Shifts of the LM Curve

The LM curve tells us the interest rate that equilibrates the money market at any level of income. Yet, as we saw earlier, the equilibrium interest rate also depends on the supply of real money balances M/P. This means that the LM curve is drawn for a given supply of real money balances.

If real money balances change, for example, if a central bank alters the money supply, the LM curve shifts. We can use the theory of liquidity preference to understand how monetary policy shifts the LM curve. Suppose that the central bank decreases the money supply from M_1 to M_2, which causes the supply of real money balances to fall from M_1/P to M_2/P. Figure 6-13 shows what happens. Holding constant the amount of income, $\overline{Y}$ and thus the demand curve for real money balances, $L(r, \overline{Y})$. We see that a reduction in the supply of real money balances, shifts the supply curve to the left, thus raises the interest rate that equilibrates the money market. That means, to restore money market equilibrium at the income level $\bar{Y}$, the interest rate has to increase to r_2. This implies that the LM curve shifts the left and up to LM_2 in Figure 6-14.

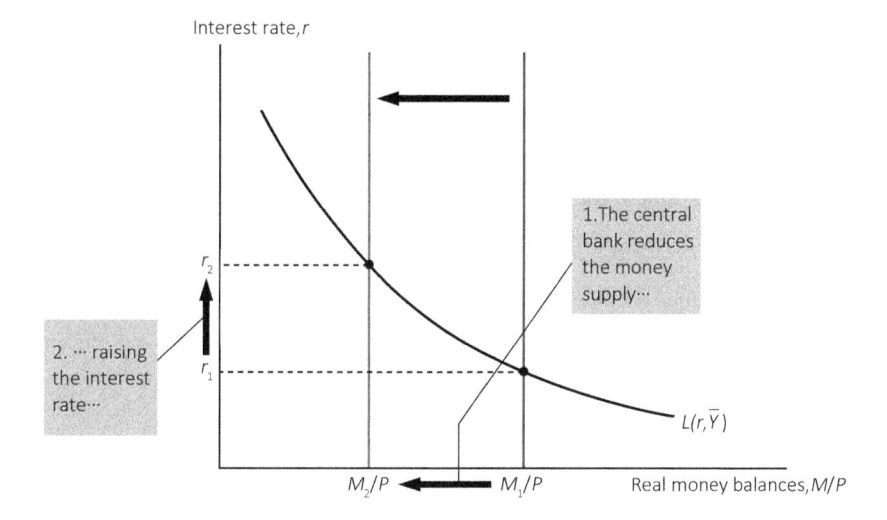

Figure 6-13

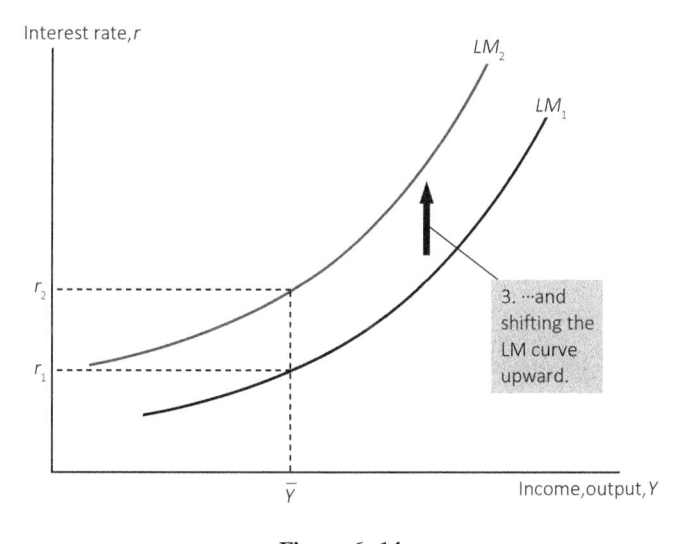

Figure 6-14

Therefore, a decrease in the money supply shifts the LM curve upward (to the left). Symmetrically, an increase in the money supply shifts the LM curve downward (to the right).

Let's summarize:

· The LM curve shows the combinations of the interest rate and the level of income that are consistent with equilibrium in the market for real money balances.

· The LM curve is positively sloped. Given the fixed money supply, an increase in the level of income, which increases the quantity of money demanded, has to be accompanied by an increase in the interest rate. This reduces the quantity of money demanded and thereby maintains money market equilibrium.

· The LM curve is shifted by changes in the money supply. An increase in the money supply shifts the LM curve to the right.

▷ Exercise 4

Suppose that the money demand function is

$$(M/P)^d = 2\,500 - 500r$$

where r is the interest rate in percent. The money supply M is 2 000 and the price level P is 2.

i) Graph the supply and demand for real money balances.

ii) What is the equilibrium interest rate?

iii) Assume that the price level is fixed. What happens to the equilibrium interest rate if the supply of money is decreased from 2 000 to 1 500?

iv) If the central bank wishes to raise the interest rate to 4 percent, what money supply should it set?

Answer:

i) As Figure 6-15 shows:

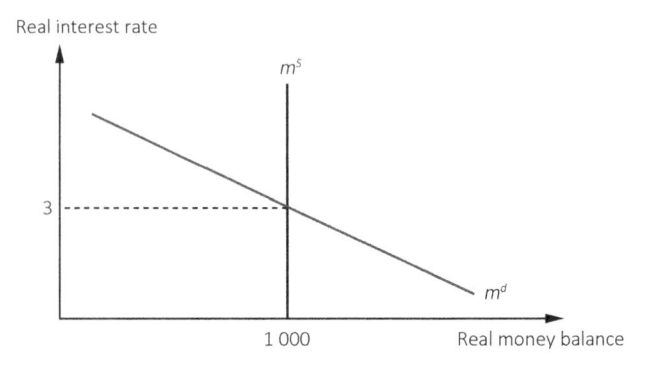

Figure 6-15

ii) Let the supply and demand for real money balances equal, then

$$(M/P)^s = \left(\frac{2\ 000}{2}\right) = (M/P)^d = 2\ 500 - 500r.$$

Solve for r, $r = 3$.

Therefore, the equilibrium interest rate is 3.

iii) Let the new supply of real money equal the demand for real money, then

$$(M/P)^s = \left(\frac{1\ 500}{2}\right) = (M/P)^d = 2\ 500 - 500r.$$

Solve for r, $r = 3.5$.

Therefore, the new equilibrium interest rate will raise to 3.5.

iv) When the interest rate equals 4 percent, then the demand for real money will be 500. Since the price level is 2, to equilibria the market for real money, the money supply should be set 1 000.

6.5 The short-run equilibrium

The IS curve represents the equilibrium in good market which tells us how the interest rate affects output. And the LM curve represents the equilibrium in money market which tells us how output in turn affects the interest rate. Just as no single equation can be solved for two unknowns, neither of the schedules alone can determine both the interest rate and income. Now It's time to determine how these markets are brought into simultaneous equilibrium. for simultaneous equilibrium, interest rates and income levels have to be such that both the goods market and the money market are in equilibrium. Together, the IS curve and the LM curve determine both output and the interest rate.

IS equation: $Y = C(Y-T) + I(r) + G + NX$

LM equation: $\left(\dfrac{M}{P}\right)^s = L(Y, r)$

Figure 6-16 plots both the IS curve and the LM curve on one graph. Any point on the downward sloping IS curve corresponds to equilibrium in the goods market. Any point on the upward-sloping LM curve corresponds to equilibrium in the money market. Only at point E are both equilibrium conditions satisfied. That means point E, with the associated level of output Y and interest rate r, is the overall equilibrium. Therefore, the intersection of the IS curve and the LM curve determines the unique combination of Y and r that satisfies the equilibrium in both markets.

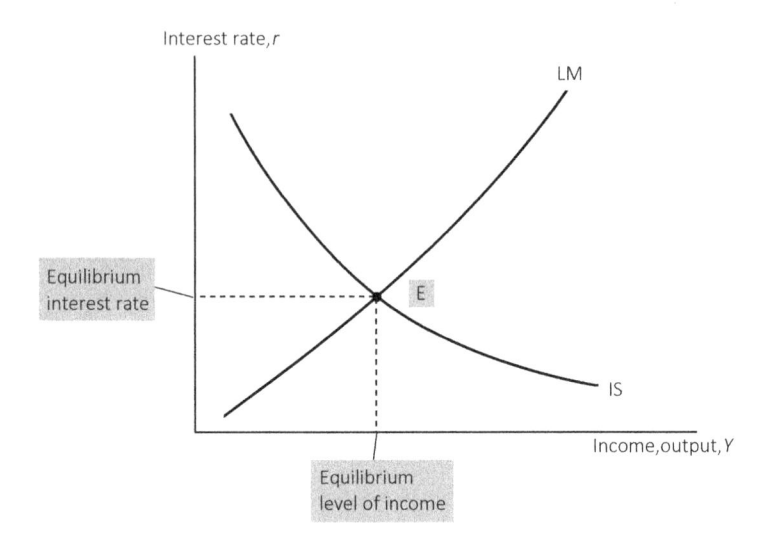

Figure 6-16

The equilibrium of the economy is the point E at which the IS curve and the LM curve cross. This point gives the interest rate r and the level of income Y that satisfy conditions for equilibrium in both the goods market and the money market. In other words, at this intersection, actual expenditure equals planned expenditure, and the demand for real money balances equals the supply.

▶ Exercise 5

The following equations describe an economy.

$Y = C + I + G$,
$C = 100 + 0.8(Y - T)$,
$I = 50 - 5r$,
$G = 50, T = 50$,
$\left(\dfrac{M}{P}\right)^d = Y - 20r$,

$M = 700, P = 2$.

ⅰ) From the above list, derive the IS Curve. Plot the IS curve on an appropriately labeled graph.

ⅱ) From the above list, derive the IM Curve. Plot the LM curve on the same graph you used in part ⅰ).

ⅲ) What is the equilibrium level of income and equilibrium interest rate?

Answer:

i) $Y = C + I + G$,

Substitute the consumption function, investment function and the values of G and T in the equation above.

$Y = 100 + 0.8(Y - 50) + 50 - 5r + 50$.

Rearrange the equation, we can get the equation for IS curve:

$Y = 800 - 25r$.

The IS curve is shown in Figure 6-17.

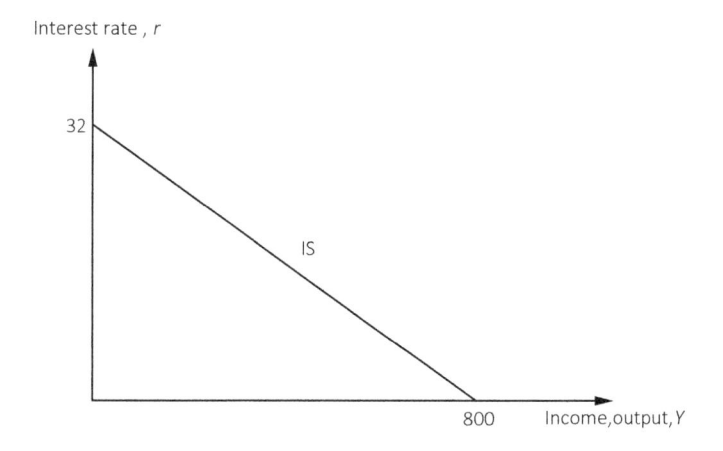

Figure 6-17

ii) Let the supply for real money equal the demand for real money,

$(M/P)^s = \left(\dfrac{700}{2}\right) = (M/P)^d = Y - 20r$.

Rearrange the equation, then we obtain the equation of the LM curve:

$Y = 350 + 20r$.

The LM curve is shown in Figure 6-18.

iii) The intersection of the IS and LM curves in Figure 6-18 corresponds to a situation in which both the IS and LM equations hold. That means the same interest rate and income levels ensure equilibrium in both the goods and money markets. Then we can substitute the Y from IS equation into the LM equation.

$800 - 25r = 350 + 20r$.

Then we can obtain the equilibrium $r = 10$. And Substitute $r = 10$ in the IS equation, then we can obtain the equilibrium $Y = 550$.

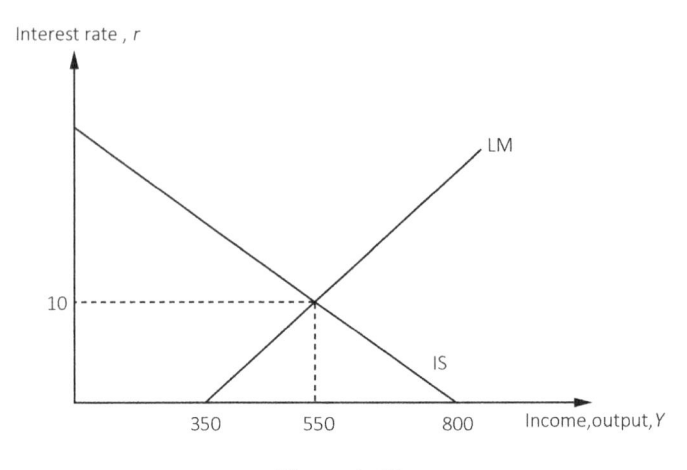

Figure 6-18

6.6 Explaining the fluctuations with the IS-LM model

The ultimate goal of developing the IS-LM model is to analyze short-run fluctuations in economic activity. As we see more fully in the next chapter, the IS-LM model helps explain the position and slope of the aggregate demand curve. The aggregate demand curve, in turn, is a piece of the model of aggregate supply and aggregate demand, which economists use to explain the short-run effects of policy changes and other events on national income.

Monetary policy and fiscal policy are two main macroeconomics policy tools the government can use to keep the economy growing at a reasonable rate, with low inflation. They are also the policy tools that the government uses to try to shorten recessions and to prevent booms. In this chapter, we use the IS-LM model to show how these policy tools can change the short-run equilibrium. First, we should figure out some facts:

• The goods and money market are closely interconnected, both monetary and fiscal policies have effects on the level of both output and interest rates.

• The fiscal policy refers to changes in government purchases and taxes that are intended to achieve macroeconomic policy goals. When recession occurs, the government uses expansionary fiscal policy (government spending increases, taxes reductions, or both) to increase aggregate demand. When demand-pull inflation occurs, contractionary fiscal policy (government spending reductions, tax increases, or both) may help decrease aggregate demand and lower or eliminate inflation. Because fiscal policy has its initial impact in the goods market. And the IS curve represents equilibrium in the goods market. Therefore, for a given price level, expansionary fiscal policy moves the IS curve to the right, raising both income and interest rates. Contractionary fiscal policy moves the IS curve to the left, lowering both income and interest rate.

· Monetary policy refers to the actions the central bank takes to manage the money supply and interest rates to achieve its macroeconomic policy goals. The monetary policy has its initial impact mainly in the money markets. And the LM curve represents equilibrium in the money market. Therefore, expansionary monetary policy moves the LM curve to the right, raising income and lowering interest rates. Contractionary monetary policy moves the LM curve to the left, lowering income and raising interest rates.

Now, let's explain in detail how the policy and shocks can change the short-run equilibrium using the following two examples:

· How fiscal policy shifts the IS curve and changes the short-run equilibrium (changes in government purchases, changes in taxes).

· How monetary policy shifts the LM curve and changes the short-run equilibrium (changes in money supply).

6.6.1 An increase in government purchase in the IS-LM model

Suppose the government decides to reduce the unemployment rate and does so by increasing government purchases of ΔG. Such change in fiscal policy is often called expansionary fiscal policy. What are effects of this fiscal policy on output, on its consumption, and on the interest rate? To answer this kind of questions we always follow the three steps:

· How does it shift the IS curve and/or the LM curves?

· Figure out the effects of these shifts on the intersection of the IS and the LM curve. What does this do to equilibrium output and the equilibrium interest rate?

· Describe the effects in word.

Now, let's start with step 1. Because the fiscal policy has its initial impact in the goods market, it will shift the IS curve rather than the LM curve. And because the increase in government purchases raises the aggregate expenditure that results in the increase in the equilibrium income, the IS curve will shift to the right. The government purchases multiplier in the Keynesian cross tells us that this change in government purchases (ΔG) raises the level of income at any given interest rate by $\Delta G/(1-MPC)$.

Therefore, as figure below shows, the IS curve shifts to the right by this amount.

Step 2: The initial equilibrium is at point A, at the intersection of the initial IS curve (IS_1) and the LM curve. After the increase in government purchase, the IS curve shifts to the right from IS_1 to IS_2. The new equilibrium is at the point B, the intersection of the new IS curve (IS_2) and the unchanged LM curve. The equilibrium of the economy moves from point A to point B. The increase in government purchases raises both income and the interest rate.

Step 3: Describe the process in word. The increase in government purchases leads to raise the aggregate expenditure, which causes an increase in output and income. At the same time, an increase in income raises the demand for money, leading to an increase in the interest rate given that the supply of money is unchanged. Then what happens to consumption? Consumption goes up because of the increase in income. The last question is what happens to investment? According to the function of investment, higher interest rate means lower investment. Thereby, the investment decreases. This result that the investment falls as the government purchase increase is sometimes called crowding out. let's discuss it in detail.

You can see this in Figure 6-19. The horizontal shift in the IS curve equals the rise in equilibrium income $[\Delta G/(1-MPC)]$, when we dealt only with the goods market. However, as Figure 6-19 shows the overall final change in income here is only Y_2-Y_1, which is clearly less than the shift in the IS curve, $[\Delta G/(1-MPC)]$. The difference is explained by the crowding out of investment due to a higher interest rate.

Diagrammatically, it is clear that the explanation is the slope of the LM curve. If the LM curve were horizontal, there would no difference between the extent of the horizontal shift of the IS curve and the changes in income. However, the LM curve slopes up rather than horizontal. When the government increases its purchases of goods and services, the economy's planned expenditure rises. The increase in planned expenditure stimulates the production of goods and services, which causes total income Y to rise. These effects should be familiar from the Keynesian cross. However, an increase in income also increases the demand for money. Because the economy's demand for money depends on income, the rise in total income increases the quantity of money demanded at each interest rate. With the supply of money fixed, the interest rate will rise to ensure that the demand for money stays equal to the fixed money supply. When the interest rate rises, investment

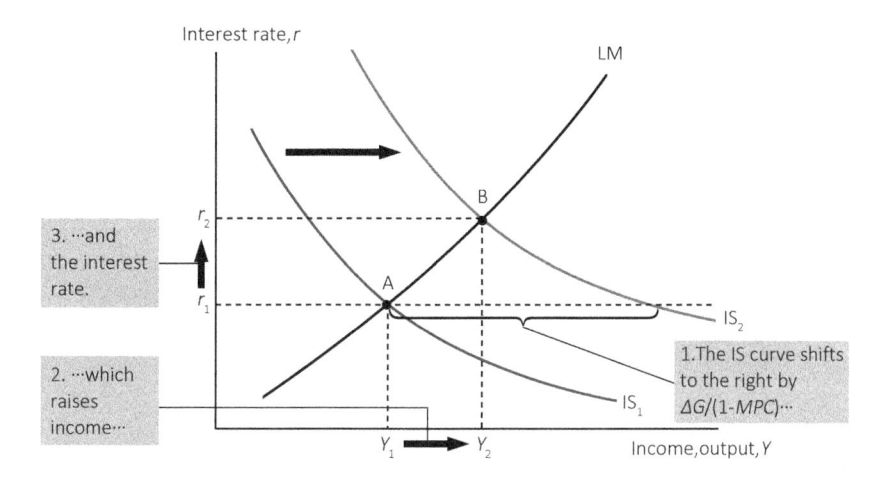

Figure 6-19

spending is reduced because investment is negatively related to the interest rate. This fall in investment partially offsets the expansionary effect of the increase in government purchases. Accordingly, the overall equilibrium change in income is less than the horizontal shift of the IS curve. Thus, the increase in income in response to a fiscal expansion is smaller in the IS-LM model than it is in the Keynesian cross (where investment is assumed to be fixed). This result is called as crowding out: the reduction in investment that results when expansionary fiscal policy raises the interest rate. The expansionary fiscal policies not only include the increase in government purchase but also include the decrease in taxes.

The crowding-out effect implies that equilibrium income will rise by less than the full amount of the horizontal shift in the IS curve. Because of this, the simple autonomous spending multipliers of the Chapter 5, which assumed constant interest rates, are now too large. "Crowding out" is explained and illustrated in Figure 6-20.

6.6.2 An increase in the money supply in IS-LM model

Now, Let's consider an increase in the money supply that is called expansionary monetary policy. Let's take it as an example to talk about what is the effect of monetary policy on the output and investment.

Step 1: A change in M does not directly affect the goods market, but money market. Therefore, an increase in M shifts the LM curve and the IS curve is unchanged. An increase in M leads to an increase in real money balances M/P because the price level

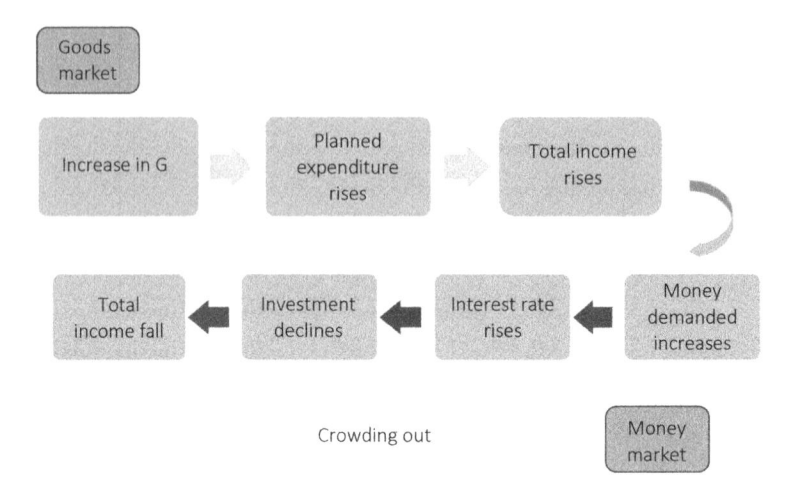

Figure 6-20

P is fixed in the short run. The theory of liquidity preference shows that for any given level of income, an increase in real money balances leads to a lower interest rate. Therefore, the LM curve shifts downward, as Figure 6-21 shows.

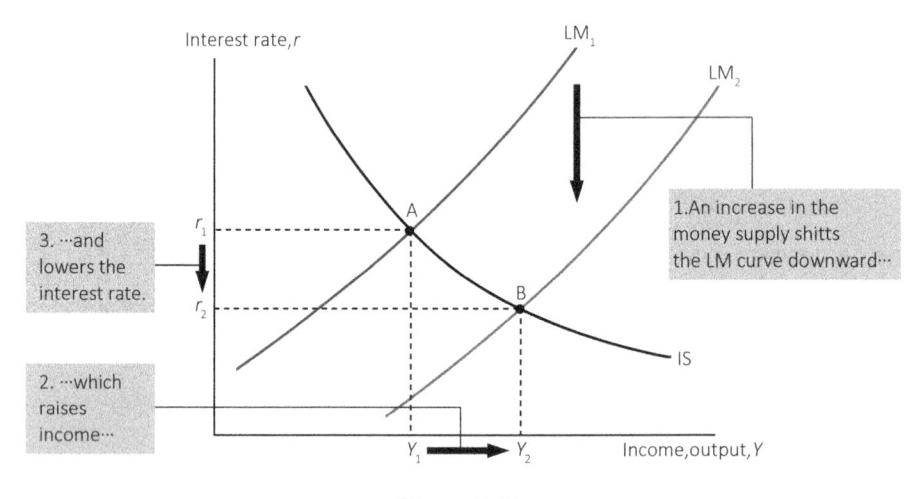

Figure 6-21

Step 2: The equilibrium moves from point A to point B. The increase in the money supply lowers the interest rate and raises the level of income.

Step 3: The central bank increases the supply of money, and people have more money than they want to hold at the prevailing interest rate. As a result, they start depositing this extra money in banks or using it to buy bonds. The interest rate r then falls until people are willing to hold all the extra money that the central bank has created. This brings the money market to a new equilibrium. The lower interest rate, in turn, affects the goods market. A lower interest rate stimulates planned investment, which increases planned expenditure, production, and income Y.

▷ **Exercise 6**

Monetary policy and fiscal policy often change at the same time:

ⅰ) Suppose that the government wants to raise investment but keep output constant. In the IS-LM model, what mix of monetary and fiscal policy will achieve this goal?

ⅱ) In the early 1980s, the U.S. government cut taxes and ran a budget deficit while the Fed pursued a tight monetary policy. What effect should this policy mix have?

Answers:

ⅰ) To raise investment while keeping output constant, the government should adopt a loose (expansionary) monetary policy and a tight (contractionary) fiscal policy, as shown in Figure 6-22. In the new equilibrium at point B, the interest rate is lower, so that investment is higher. The tight fiscal policy — reducing government purchases, for example — offsets the effect of this increase in investment on output.

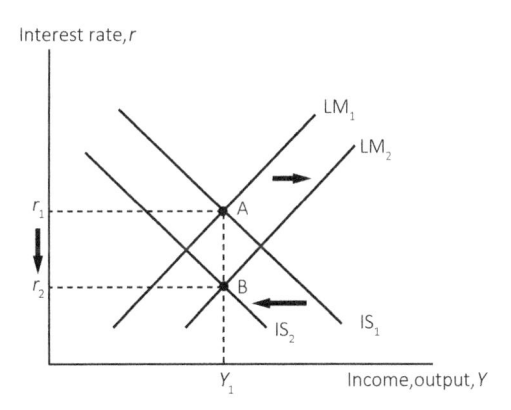

Figure 6-22

ⅱ) Cutting taxes was an expansionary Fiscal policy, while the Fed pursued a tight monetary policy. Such a policy mix shifts the IS curve to the right and the LM curve to the left, as shown in Figure 6-23. The real interest rate rises and investment falls. The policy did an exactly opposite with question ⅰ).

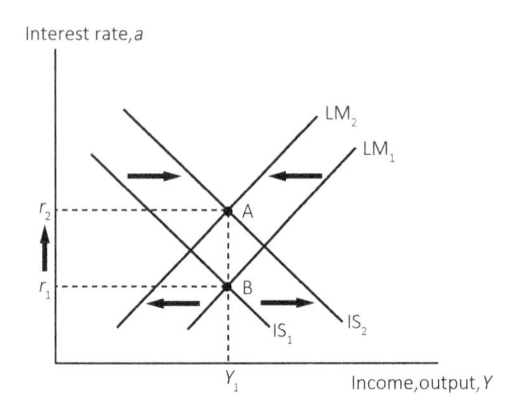

Figure 6-23

6.7 Summary of the IS-LM model

The IS-LM model provides a simple and appropriate framework for analysis the effects of monetary and fiscal policy on the demand for output and on interest rates. The IS-LM model is very important and popular. It is still used today, more than 80 years after it was introduced[①]. But it is material that students often find difficult to master. Therefore, let's summarize the IS-LM model.

· The IS-LM model emphasizes the interaction between the goods market and the money market. The two markets are linked through two variables — interest rate and income.

· In goods market, an increase in the interest rate reduces planned investment spending and therefore reduces aggregate demand, thus reducing the equilibrium level of income. Therefore, interest rate is inversely related to income. This relationship is shown in the IS curve. The IS curve slopes downward.

· In the money market, the supply for real money is fixed. The demand for real money depends on income and interest rate. the quantity demanded is a decreasing function of the interest rate and an increase function of the income. An increase in the interest rate reduces the demand for real money, to keep the equilibrium in money market, income raises to rise the demand for real money. Therefore, interest rate is positively related

---

① British economist John Hicks first introduced the IS-LM model in 1937, just one year after fellow British economist John Maynard Keynes published The General Theory of Employment, Interest, and Money. Hicks's model served as a formalized graphical representation of Keynes's theories.

to income. This relationship is shown in the LM curve. The LM curve is upward-sloping.

· The interaction of the money market (LM) and goods market (IS) determines the interest rate and the level of income.

· The change in fiscal policy shifts the IS curve, such as an increase in government purchase or a decrease in taxes shifts the IS curve to the right.

· The change in monetary policy shifts the LM curve, such as an increase in the supply for real money shifts the LM curve to the right.

Case Study

China's Response to the Global Financial Crisis

China was the first major economy in the world to emerge from the global financial crisis. After a brief sharp downturn in 2008, the Chinese economy recovered and grew by 8.7% in 2009 and by 10.4% in 2010. The robust growth in China helped a host of resource-rich countries avoid the economic downturn. A big factor behind this enviable success was the 4 trillion-yuan ($586 billion) stimulus package program introduced in the fourth quarter of 2008 and implemented through 2009 and 2010.

The CNY 4 trillion "program" refers to the investment component, which was officially announced by former Premier Wen Jiabao on 5 November 2008 as a set of investments totaling CNY 4 trillion, to be spent over 27 months from the fourth quarter of 2008 through 2010. The program focused on seven priority areas:

· Transport and power infrastructure (railroads, roads, airports, electricity grids).
· Earthquake reconstruction.
· Rural village infrastructure.
· Environment, energy efficiency and carbon emission reduction.
· Affordable housing.
· Technological innovation and restructuring.
· Health and education.

The weighting of these components went through some adjustments during the first months of implementation. Their final distribution is presented in Table 6-1.

Table 6-1

Transport and power infra structure (railroads, roads, airports, electricity grids)	37.5%
Post-earthquake reconstruction	25.0%
Rural village infrastructure	9.3%
Environmental investment	5.3%
Affordable housing	10.0%
Technological innovation and structural adjustment	9.3%
Health and education	3.8%

Source: Website of the NDRC (National Development and Reform Commission), China.

For these investments, the central government committed outset to funding at the CNY 1.18 trillion from the budget, with the remaining CNY 2.8 trillion to be financed by local governments, enterprises and banks.

With the investment program, policy makers also adopted some expansionary monetary policies. In September 2008, the central bank reduced the one-year lending rate from 7.47% to 5.58% (China Daily, 2008). In the period from September through December, interest rates were cut five times, with a cut of 108 basis points on 26 November 2008. To give an added boost to the financial sector, in December the State Council released a nine-step plan for financial reform. The package included new credit mechanisms for small to medium-sized enterprises (SMEs), a broader scope for issuing corporate bonds, and new regulations for the creation of real estate investment trust funds (REITs) and private equity (PE) funds. Also, in December 2008, the State Council issued a document authorizing a loan allocation of an additional CNY 100 billion to the policy banks. Commercial banks were urged to increase lending. The credit quota was abolished, and a call was issued to strive for increasing total lending by CNY 4 trillion in 2008 (State Council Office, 2008).

In addition, the government cut taxes, sometimes through accelerating the rollout of some planned reforms. These included: increasing VAT rebates on exports; reducing taxes on small firms by cutting the tax rate from 6% to 3%; and raising the threshold for the tax levy on monthly income from CNY 1 600 to CNY 2 000. The conversion of the value-added tax from an investment-type VAT to a consumption-type VAT, which had been "forthcoming" for much of a decade, was finally rolled out on 1 January 2009.

These effective measures above stimulated china's economic development. One obvious inference to draw from this bold stimulus programs and the economy's quick recovery is that China has a strong, rich and effective public sector. This was indeed the one described by George Soros, who said admiringly at a network meeting of his Soros Foundation-Supported Open Society Institute in mid-2010 that "the Chinese government works better than ours (in the United States)".

This assessment is incontrovertible if the metric used is solely that of economic growth and of how quickly China returned to its high growth path; but the performance through the crisis looks weaker when a broader metric is used. First of all, once unleashed, the stimulus appeared to spin quickly out of control. Investment in fixed assets jumped to 66% of GDP in 2009, and infrastructure investment leaped to more than 18% of GDP, raising immediate concerns about the economy's absorptive capacity and the care with which projects were selected and implemented.

By mid-2009 many policy makers and observers in China had begun to worry about the nature of the growth brought by the stimulus program and its by-products. The big ramp-up in easy credit, for example, helped to fuel an asset bubble that sent prices of land and housing steeply upward, more than doubling in some big cities during 2009. The heavy pace of local investment caused rising local government debt. By early 2010, the government was sufficiently alarmed to call for an immediate freeze and audit of local government investment corporations, and by year-end the urgent problem for macro management had shifted decisively to slowing growth and tamping down inflationary pressures. in mid-2011, controlling inflation was the top priority task for the government this year.

Source: Wong, Christine (2011), "The Fiscal Stimulus Programme and Public Governance Issues in China", *OECD Journal on Budgeting*, Vol. 11/3. http://dx.doi.org/10.1787/budget-11-5kg3nhljqrjl.

Terms and Concepts

· **IS curve**: A graph of all combinations of r and Y that result in goods market equilibrium.

· **LM curve**: A graph plots the relationship between the interest rate and the level of income that arises in the market for money balances.

· **The IS-LM model**: The IS-LM model takes the price level as given and shows what causes income to change. It shows what causes AD to shift.

· **Crowding out** : The reduction in investment that results when expansionary fiscal policy raises the interest rate.

Problems and Applications

I. True or False

1. The IS curve summarizes the relationship between the interest rate and the level of income that arises from equilibrium in the market for goods and services.

2. A decrease in the interest rate shifts IS curve to right.

3. A decrease in taxes T will shift planned expenditure curve to upward, shift IS curve to the right.

4. The LM curve summarizes the relationship between the level of income and the interest rate that arises from equilibrium in the market for real money balances.

5. The LM curve slopes upward, and is drawn for given supply of real money balances.

6. In the IS-LM model, assuming downward sloping IS curve and upward sloping LM curve, reduction in consumers' wealth is going to cause a leftward shift of the IS curve.

7. An increase in government spending stimulates the demand for goods and services, it also causes the interest rate to rise, thereby increases investment spending.

8. An expansionary fiscal policy consists of government spending increases, tax reductions, or both, designed to increase aggregate demand and therefore raise real GDP.

9. An increase in the money supply will decrease the quantity of money held at every interest rate.

10. A decrease in the interest rate causes planned investment to rise.

II. Choices

1. In the simplest Keynesian model of the determination of income, interest rates are assumed to be _____.

   A. exogenous and to gradually change

B. endogenous and to gradually change

C. exogenous and to remain constant

D. endogenous and to remain constant

2. In the development of the IS curve, one variable that turns from exogenous to endogenous is _____.

A. the interest rates

B. consumption

C. saving

D. investment

3. The IS curve shows that higher income levels require _____ interest rates to ensure that income equals _____.

A. higher; planned autonomous spending

B. higher; planned expenditures

C. lower; planned autonomous spending

D. lower; planned expenditures

4. Which of the following leads to the IS curve shifts right? _____.

A. An increase in the money supply

B. An increase in the taxes

C. An increase in the government purchase

D. An increase in the interest rate

5. As income and production rise, the demand for real money balances will _____ and interest rates will _____.

A. fall; fall

B. rise; rise

C. rise; fall

D. fall; rise

6. If spending is NOT responsive to changes in the interest rate, then the _____.

A. LM curve is vertical

B. IS and LM curves are vertical

C. IS curve is vertical

D. IS curve is vertical and the LM curve is horizontal

7. A decrease in real GDP causes _____.

A. movement downward along a money demand schedule

B. movement upward along a money demand schedule

C. a rightward shift of the money demand schedule

D. a leftward shift of the money demand schedule

8. In the IS-LM model, equilibrium income can be affected by _____.

A. fiscal policy alone

B. monetary policy alone

C. both fiscal and monetary policy

D. neither monetary nor fiscal policy

9. If the interest rate were to rise, we expect that _____.

A. autonomous expenditures will rise

B. the supply of money will fall

C. the amount of money people wants to hold will rise

D. the amount of money people wants to hold will fall

10. In deriving LM curves, holding the real money supply constant while raising real GDP causes us to _____.

A. trace up along an LM curve

B. trace down along an LM curve

C. shift the LM curve to the right

D. shift the LM curve to the left

11. How does an increase in the money supply affect the LM curve and the IS curve? _____.

A. It shifts the LM curve upward (left)

B. It shifts the LM curve downward (right)

C. It shifts the IS curve to right

D. It shifts the IS curve to left

12. The intersection of the IS and LM curve represents: _____.

A. Simultaneous equilibrium in the market for goods and services and in the market for real money balances for given values of government spending, taxes and the money supply

B. Actual expenditure equals the planned expenditure

C. The real money supply equals the real money demand

D. All of the above are true

13. A change in the multiplier (k) will change the _____.

A. slope of the IS curve

B. slope and the position of the IS curve

C. slope of the LM curve

D. position of the LM curve

14. When income rises, this increase in income shifts the money demand curve to _____, with the supply of real money balances unchanged, the interest rate must _____ to equilibrate the money market. Therefore, higher income leads to a _____ interest rate.

A. the right; fall; lower

B. the left; fall; lower

C. the right; rise; higher

D. the left; rise; higher

15. "Crowding-out" occurs in the IS-LM model as rising government spending requires a _____ in the interest rate in order to _____ the demand for money at the new equilibrium, thus _____ planned private investment.

A. rise; keep constant; lowering

B. rise; raise; lowering

C. rise; lower; raising

D. fall; keep constant; raising

Ⅲ. Short Answer

1. Consider an economy as the following (the):

$Y = C + I + G$,

$C = 125 + 0.65(Y - T)$,

$I = 200 - 10r$,

$G = \bar{G} = 150$,

$T = \bar{T} = 100$.

ⅰ) From the above list, use the equations to derive the equation of IS curve. Plot the IS curve on an appropriately labeled graph.

ii) If the interest rate is 10, what is the investment? And what is the equilibrium level of income Y?

iii) Suppose that the government purchases are raised from 150 to 160. How does the IS curve shift?

iv) If the interest rate is also 10, what is the new equilibrium level of income Y?

v) If government purchase is still 150, and the taxes T decrease from 100 to 90, How does the IS curve shift? If the interest rate is also 10, what is the new equilibrium level of income Y?

2. Suppose the money demand function is

$(M/P)^d = L(r,Y) = 0.8Y - 16r$

where r is the interest rate in percent. The money supply M is 800 and the price level P is 1.

i) Use the information above to derive the LM curve.

ii) Suppose the central banks decrease the money supply to 640. What is the new equation of LM curve?

iii) The central bank decreases the money supply, the money supply curve shifts to _____ (left or right), holding constant the amount of income, the equilibrium interest rate _____ (rises or falls), so, a decrease in the money supply shifts the LM curve _____ (upward or downward).

3. Suppose the following equations describe an economy (where r is the interest rate in percent, for example, $r = 10$ means $r = 10\%$):

$Y = C + I + G$,

$C = 170 + 0.6(Y-T)$,

$I = 100 - 4r$,

$G = \overline{G} = 350$,

$T = \overline{T} = 200$,

$(M/P)^d = L(r,Y) = 0.75Y - 6r$,

$M^s/P = 735$.

i) What is the equation that describes the IS curve?

ii) What is the equation that describes the LM curve?

iii) What are the equilibrium interest rate and the level of income?

iv) What are the equilibrium consumption and the level of investment?

v) What is government surplus when the economy is in the equilibrium.

4. Using the information given in problem 3, answer the following questions:

i) Compute the value of the multiplier of investment.

ii) Calculate the slope of the IS curve.

iii) Calculate the slope of the LM curve.

iv) If government spending increase by 50. What is the amount of autonomous spending that is crowded out by this expansionary fiscal policy?

v) How much the Fed must increase the money supply if it wants to avoid the crowding out of the expansionary fiscal policy described in question iv). What will be the new value of GDP?

5. Suppose policymakers want to raise investment but keep real GDP constant. use the IS-LM model to describe and illustrate what mix of monetary and fiscal policies would achieve this goal.

Answers to Problems and Applications

I. True or False

1	2	3	4	5	6	7	8	9	10
T	F	T	T	T	T	F	T	F	T

II. Choice

1	2	3	4	5	6	7	8	9	10
C	D	D	C	B	C	D	C	D	A
11	12	13	14	15					
B	D	B	C	A					

III. Short Answer

1. Answer:

i) Total planned expenditure is:

$$AE = C + I + G$$

Plugging in the consumption function and the values for investment, government purchases G, and taxes T given in the question, total planned expenditure AE is

$AE = 125 + 0.75(Y-100) + 200 - 10r + 150$.

Simplify the equation:

$AE = 400 + 0.75Y - 10r$.

When the economy is in equilibrium,

$Y = AE = 400 + 0.75Y - 10r$.

Rearrange the equation, we can obtain the IS equation:

$Y = 1\ 600 - 40r$.

The IS curve is shown in Figure 6-24.

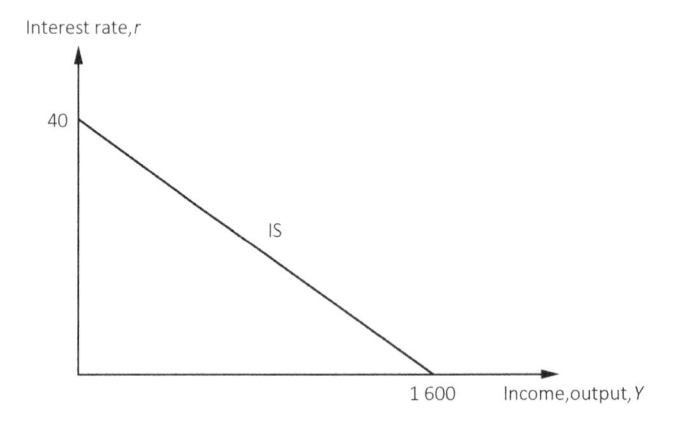

Figure 6-24

ii) When the interest rate equals 10, the investment equals $200 - 10 \times 10 = 100$, the equilibrium Y equals $Y = 1\ 600 - 40 \times 10 = 1\ 200$.

iii) An increase in government purchase leads to the IS curve shifts to right.

iv) When government purchase increases by 10, the new IS curve equation will be

$Y = 1\ 640 - 40r$.

Therefore, the new equilibrium income will be 1 240, when the interest rate is 10.

v) A decrease in taxes can cause the IS curve shifts to right. When the taxes decrease by 10, for the same r, $r = 10$, the equilibrium Y will increase by

$\Delta Y = 10 \times \dfrac{MPC}{1-MPC} = 10 \times \dfrac{0.75}{0.25} = 30$.

Therefore, the new equilibrium Y is 1 230.

2. **Answer:**

i) When the money supply equals the money demand, we can obtain the LM curve:

$$\left(\frac{M}{P}\right)^s = \frac{800}{1} = \left(\frac{M}{P}\right)^d = L(r,Y) = 0.8Y - 16r.$$

So, $800 = 0.8Y - 16r$.

Then the equation of LM curve is: $Y = 1\,000 + 20r$.

ii) When the money supply is 640, so, when real money market is in equilibrium, then

$$\left(\frac{M}{P}\right)^s = \frac{640}{1} = \left(\frac{M}{P}\right)^d = L(r,Y) = 0.8Y - 16r.$$

So, the new equation of LM curve is:

$Y = 800 + 20r$.

iii) The central bank decreases the money supply, the money supply curve shifts to left, holding constant the amount of income, the equilibrium interest rate rises, so, a decrease in the money supply shifts the LM curve upward.

3. Answer:

i) The equation for the IS curve is:

$Y = 1\,250 - 10r$.

ii) The equation for the LM curve is:

$Y = 980 + 8r$.

iii) The equilibrium interest rate is 15 and the equilibrium income is 1 100.

iv) The equilibrium consumption is 710 and the level of investment is 40.

v) The government surplus is −150.

4. Answer:

i) The multiplier equals:

$$\frac{1}{1-MPC} = \frac{1}{1-0.6} = 2.5.$$

Another method to calculate the multiplier is to calculate $\frac{\Delta Y}{\Delta I}$, when investment change is ΔI, we can get the new IS equation using the same method:

$Y = C + I + G = 170 + 0.6(Y-200) + 100 + \Delta I - 4r + 350$.

The equation can be rewritten as:

$0.4Y = 500 + \Delta I - 4r$.

Then, the new IS equation is:

$Y = 1\,250 + \dfrac{1}{0.4}\Delta I - 10r.$

For the same r, we can get:

$\Delta Y = \dfrac{1}{0.4}\Delta I.$

Therefore, multiplier $= \dfrac{\Delta Y}{\Delta I} = \dfrac{1}{0.4} = 2.5.$

ii) The equation for the IS curve is:

$Y = 1\,250 - 10r.$

Rearrange the equation:

$r = 125 - 0.1Y.$

Therefore, the slope of IS curve is 0.1.

iii) The equation for the LM curve is:

$Y = 980 + 8r.$

Rearrange the equation:

$r = \dfrac{1}{8}Y - 125.$

So, the slope of LM curve is $\dfrac{1}{8}$.

iv) If the government spending increase by 50, then for a given interest rate, the IS curve will shift to the right by the amount of $\dfrac{1}{1-MPC} \cdot \Delta G = 2.5 \times 50 = 125$, so the IS equation will become:

$Y = 1\,375 - 10r.$

The LM curve is unchanged:

$Y = 980 + 8r.$

So, we can get the new equilibrium income using the two equations:

$\begin{cases} \text{IS}: Y = 1\,375 - 10r \\ \text{LM}: Y = 980 + 8r \end{cases}$

Solve the system of simultaneous equations, we can obtain the equilibrium income is about 1 156. So, the change in equilibrium is $1\,156 - 1\,100 = 56$. Therefore, the amount of autonomous spending that is crowded out is $125 - 56 = 69$.

v) If the Fed want to avoid the crowding out, then the new equilibrium income will become as 1 100+125 = 1 225. Because the increase in equilibrium is just the amount of 125. From the new IS equation, the equilibrium $r = 15$. The pair of ($Y = 1\ 225, r = 15$) must on the new LM equation. And because the new supply for real money (M_2) should equal the real money demanded:

$M_2 = 0.75Y - 6r.$

Plug $Y = 1\ 225$ and $r = 15$ into the equation, we can obtain the $M_2 = 828.75$, therefore, the fed should increase the real money supply by 93.75 (828.75 − 735).

5. **Answer**: The central bank should increase the money supply, which would shift the LM curve to the right. And the government should shift the IS curve left. Real GDP could remain unchanged, but the reduction in the real interest rate would increase investment.

7 Aggregate Demand and Aggregate Supply Analysis

Learning Objective

By the end of this chapter, students should understand:

· how to identify the determinants of aggregate demand.

· how the aggregate demand curve comes from IS-LM model.

· how to distinguish between a movement along the aggregate demand curve and a shift of the curve.

· what causes the aggregate demand curve to shift.

· how to identify the determinants of aggregate supply.

· what causes the aggregate supply curve to shift.

· how to illustrate the difference between short-run and long-run macroeconomic equilibrium using AD-AS model.

· how to use AD-AS model to analyze the fluctuation in the short-run economy.

· the effect of government policy on the output under the two extreme cases.

· the basic principle of Supply-side economics.

Key Points and Exercises

7.1 Aggregate demand and aggregate supply model

Until now we have modeled long-run economic growth and also how real GDP is determined in the short run. Our new goal in this chapter is to extend the model of the economy in the short run. By doing so, we will be able to understand why real GDP, the level of employment, and the price level fluctuate.

Chapter 5 develops the aggregate expenditures model of the macroeconomy. And Chapter 6 extends the AE model to the IS-LM model by adding the interest rate to the model. Both the AE model and the IS-LM model assume that the general level of prices remains unchanged. These models ignored the fact that changes in real GDP over the business cycle have normally been associated with considerable fluctuations in the price level. Therefore, this chapter aims to develop a variable-price model of the macroeconomy, which allows us to simultaneously analyze changes in real GDP and the price level.

The new model in this chapter is called the aggregate demand and aggregate supply model (AD-AS model); The aggregate demand and aggregate supply model explains short-run fluctuations in real GDP and the price level. To build it up, we must determine how aggregate demand and aggregate supply are each formed. The aggregate demand (AD) curve shows the relationship between the price level and the quantity of real GDP demanded by households, firms, and the government. The short-run aggregate supply (SRAS) curve shows the relationship in the short run between the price level and the quantity of real GDP supplied by firms. In the short run, real GDP and the price level are determined by the interaction of the aggregate demand curve and the short-run aggregate supply curve. In Figure 7-1, real GDP (output, income) is measured on the horizontal axis, and the price level is measured on the vertical axis by the GDP deflator. In this example, the equilibrium real GDP is Y^*, and the equilibrium price level is P^*.

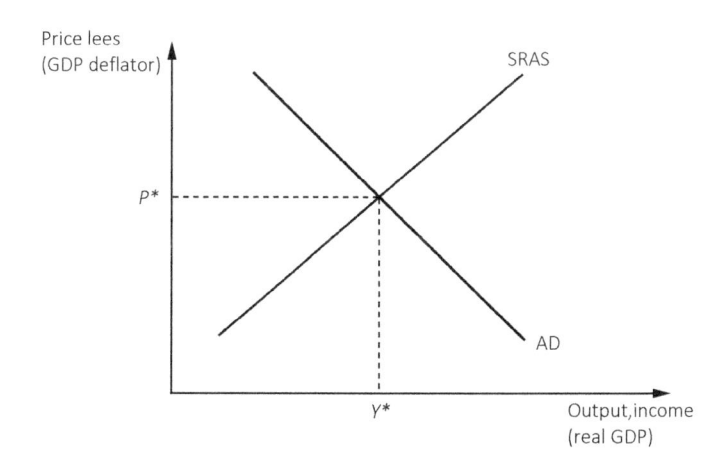

Figure 7-1

Although the aggregate demand and aggregate supply curves look like the single-product demand and supply curves as we discuss in microeconomics, the variables being measured and the underlying rationales for the curves are completely different. In this chapter, our analysis is in terms of aggregates. Therefore, the axes of our diagrams will be the overall price level (CPI or GDP deflator) and real GDP, rather than the price of product X and units of product X. In microeconomics version, price means the ratio at which two goods trade. In contrast, in macroeconomics price means the nominal price level, which is the cost of a basket of all the goods we buy measured in money terms. Therefore, the economics underlying the aggregate demand-aggregate supply diagram is unrelated to the microeconomics version.

7.2 Why is the aggregate demand curve downward sloping?

The aggregate demand curve shows the relationship between the price level and real GDP. As Figure 7-1 shows the aggregate demand curve slopes downwards and to the right. That means other things being equal, the lower the price level, the larger the level of aggregate expenditure will be. Conversely, the higher the price level, the lower the level of aggregate expenditure will be. Why is the aggregate demand curve downward sloping? The reason is not the same as that which applies to the demand for a single product, which is based on income and substitution effects. These explanations fail when we are dealing in terms of aggregates. First, the rationale for the substitution effect is not applicable, because all prices are falling rather than the price of a single product. Second, a demand curve for a single product assumes the consumer's income to be fixed, but the aggregate demand curve implies varying aggregate incomes. For example, a 5 percent increase in the price level increases the income of the resource suppliers by 5 percent at the same time. That means the income will also increase by 5 percent. Therefore, an increase in the price level need not necessarily mean a decline in the aggregate expenditure. However, other reasons will lead to a fall in the total expenditure when the price level rises.

There are three major reasons why there is an inverse relationship between changes in the price level and changes in aggregate expenditure:

· The wealth effect (effect of a change in the level of price on consumption).
· The interest-rate effect (effect of a change in the level of price on investment).

• The international-trade effect (effect of a change in the level of price on net export).

7.2.1 The wealth effect

Current income is the most important variable determining consumption by households. But consumption also depends on wealth. When the price level rises, the real value of household wealth declines and so will consumption. For example, you have 5 000 Yuan in your pocket. If the price level is 100, then you can buy 50 units of goods and services. But if the price level becomes 200, all other things equal, then you can only buy 25 units of goods and services. The real value of the 5000-yuan declines, so, you become poorer than before, and you decide to spend less than before. Conversely, a decline in the price level increases the real value of your wealth and tends to increase spending. The effect of the price level on consumption is called the wealth effect and is one reason why the aggregate demand curve is downward sloping.

7.2.2 The interest-rate effect

The effect of the price level on investment is known as the interest-rate effect and is a second reason why the aggregate demand curve is downward sloping. The interest rate effect suggests that a change in the level of price has impact on interest rates, then affects the consumption and investment. When prices rise, households and firms need more money to finance buying and selling. Therefore, when the price level rises, households and firms will try to increase the amount of money they hold by withdrawing funds from banks, borrowing from banks, or selling assets. These actions drive up the interest rate because the demand for real money increases. A higher price level increases the interest rate and thereby reduces investment spending. It also reduces the quantity of goods and services demanded. Therefore, price level inversely relates to the aggregate demand.

7.2.3 The international-trade effect

If the price level rises in China relative to the price levels in other countries, China exports will become relatively more expensive, and foreign imports will become relatively less expensive. China exports will fall, and China imports will rise, causing net exports to fall. The effect of the price level on net exports is known as the international-trade effect and is a third reason why the aggregate demand curve is downward sloping.

The three reasons are summarized in Figure 7-2.

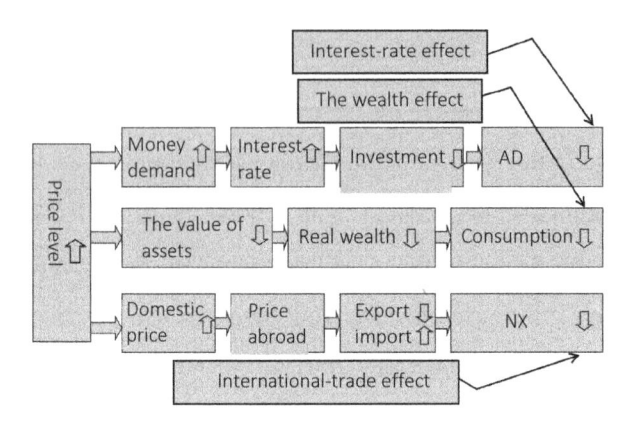

Figure 7-2

7.3 From the IS-LM model to the AD curve

The IS-LM model shows that macroeconomic equilibrium is achieved at the intersection of the IS-LM curves. The model assumes the price level is unchanged. We now use the IS-LM model to derive the aggregate demand curve by examining what happens in the IS-LM model when the price level changes.

For any given money supply M, a higher price level P reduces the supply of real money balances M/P. A lower supply of real money balances shifts the LM curve upward, which raises the equilibrium interest rate and lowers the equilibrium level of income (we have talked about the reason in Chapter 6), as shown in Figure 7-3 (a). When the price level is P_1, the intersection of the IS curve and the LM(P_1) curve gives the level of aggregate demand (Y_1) corresponding to price P_1 and is marked in Figure 7-3 (b) at the point E_1. When the price level rises from P_1 to P_2. The real money supply falls from M/P_1 to M/P_2, then the LM curve will shift upward (to the left), as Figure 7-3 (a) shows, the equilibrium income falls from Y_1 to Y_2. The pair of (P_2, Y_2) is also marked in Figure 7-3 (b). Repeat this operation for a variety of price levels, and connect the points to derive the aggregate demand schedule.

The aggregate demand curve in Figure 7-3 (b) plots this negative relationship between equilibrium income and the price level. In other words, the aggregate demand curve shows the set of equilibrium points that arise in the IS-LM model as we vary the price level and see what happens to income.

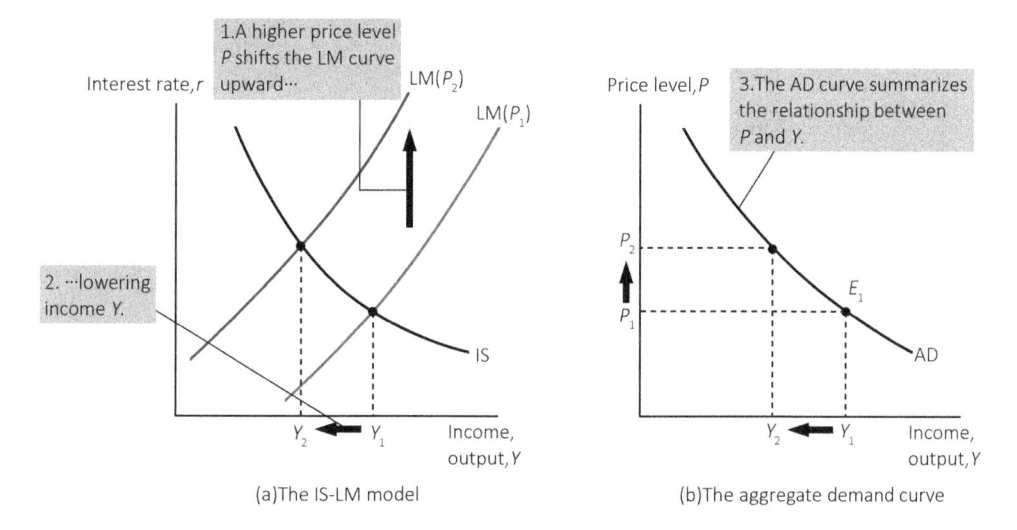

7 Aggregate Demand and Aggregate Supply Analysis | 189

Figure 7-3

(a) The IS-LM model

(b) The aggregate demand curve

1. A higher price level P shifts the LM curve upward…
2. …lowering income Y.
3. The AD curve summarizes the relationship between P and Y.

The algebra of AD:

Now, we can use the equations of the IS curve and the LM curve to drive the equation of aggregation demand.

$$\text{IS: } Y = C(Y-T) + I(r) + G$$
$$\text{LM: } M/P = L(r, Y)$$

These two equations contain three endogenous variables: Y, P, and r. So, we can use them to solve for Y as a function of P, the exogenous variables G, T, and the model's parameters. And the expression shows the equation of the aggregate demand curve. Since the AD curve shows the set of equilibrium points that arise in the IS-LM model, any point in the AD curve satisfies the equilibrium in both markets: the goods market and the money market.

▷ **Exercise 1**

Suppose the equation of IS curve is:

$0.5y + 240r = 3\ 500$.

The equation of LM curve is:

$\dfrac{1\ 000}{p} = 0.5y - 260r$.

So, what is the equation of aggregate demand curve?

Answer:

Solve the two equations for the equation of the aggregate demand curve:

$$\begin{cases} 0.5y+240r=3\,500 \\ \dfrac{1\,000}{p}=0.5y-260r \end{cases}$$

$\Rightarrow y = 3\,640+960/p.$

As you find in the equation, the price level is inversely related to the aggregate expenditure.

7.4 Shifts of the aggregate demand curve vs. movements along it

The aggregate demand curve tells us the relationship between the price level and the quantity of real GDP demanded, holding everything else constant. If the price level changes but other variables that affect the willingness of households, firms, and the government to spend are unchanged, the economy will move up or down a stationary aggregate demand curve, as Figure 7-4 shows: as the price increases from 105 to 110, the equilibrium real GDP falls from 17.2 to 17.0 along the demand curve.

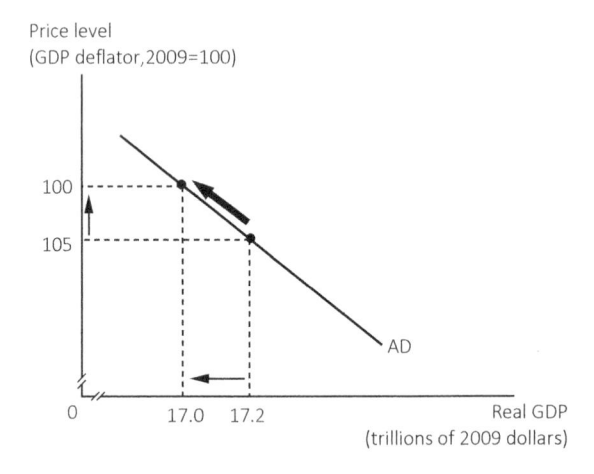

Figure 7-4

If any variable changes other than the price level, the aggregate demand curve will shift. As Figure 7-5 shows, AD curve shifts to the left. When we construct the AD curve, we focused on the effect that change in the price level would have on the real GDP. We assume constant other variables that affect the real GDP, like government purchases. So when government purchases decrease, the real GDP would decrease at each price. This effect can be illustrated by shifting the AD curve to the left.

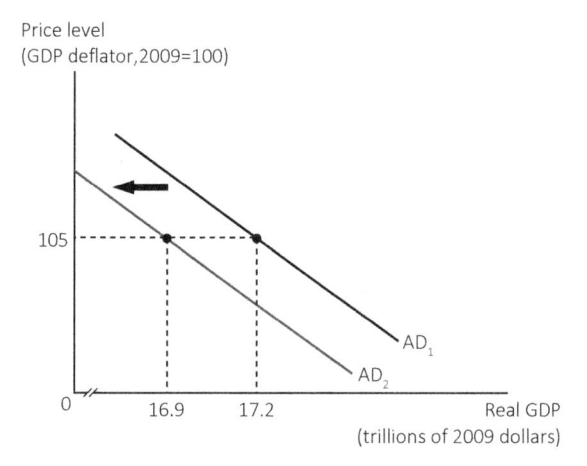

Figure 7-5

In summary, the simplest and most direct approach is to remember that any change in a variable plotted on the two axes (in this case, they are real GDP or price level) will cause a movement along the curve, while any change in the factors affecting the curve but not on either of the axes will shift the curve. Taking AD curve as example, the price level is on the axis, so, a change in the price level will cause a movement along the AD curve. A change in other factors such as government purchases or the money supply which are not on the axes will shift the demand curve.

7.5 What causes the aggregate demand curve to shift?

Because the aggregate demand curve summarizes the results from the IS-LM model, any variables other than the price level that shifts either the IS curve or the LM curve also shifts the aggregate demand curve. For example, an increase in government purchase or a decrease in taxes shifts the IS curve to the right, which raises income for a given price level. Therefore, the aggregate demand curve also shifts to the right. Similarly, an increase in the money supply for any given price level shifts the LM curve to the right, which leads to the increase in the equilibrium income for any given price level. So, the aggregate demand curve shifts to the right. Let us take these main factors as examples to explain how the changes of these factors effect on the position of AD.

7.5.1 AD shifts: changes in government policy

A government policy change could shift the aggregate demand curve. There are two categories of government policies here:

1) Monetary policy

Monetary policy refers to the actions the central bank takes to manage the money supply and interest rates to pursue macroeconomic policy objectives.

If the central bank decreases the money supply and causes interest rates to rise, investment spending will fall which shifts the aggregate demand curve to the left; if it causes interest rates to fall, investment spending will rise which shifts the aggregate demand curve to the right.

2) Fiscal policy

Fiscal policy refers to changes in taxes and government purchases that are intended to achieve macroeconomic policy objectives.

Increasing or decreasing taxes affects disposable income, and hence consumption. The government can also alter its level of government purchases. These changes will shift the aggregate demand curve to the right or the left.

We will talk about the effect of government policies on the aggregate income and prices in the next several chapters in detail.

7.5.2 AD shifts: changes in expectations

If households or firms could become more optimistic about the future, they are likely to increase their current consumption or investment respectively. The increasing in consumption and investment will lead to the aggregate demand curve shifts to the right. Of course, the opposite could also occur.

7.5.3 AD shifts: changes in foreign variables

If foreign incomes rise more slowly than ours, their imports of our goods fall. Then the aggregate demand curve shifts to the left. If ours rise more slowly, our imports fall. Then the aggregate demand curve shifts to the right.

If our exchange rate (the value of the RMB) rises, our exports become more expensive, so foreigners buy less of them (and we buy more imports, also). Then the aggregate demand curve shifts to the left. Of course, the opposite could also occur.

7.5.4 Summary

We can summarize these results as following: A change in income in the IS-LM model resulting from a change in the price level represents a movement along the aggregate demand curve. A change in income in the IS-LM model for a given price level represents a shift in the aggregate demand curve. There are many variables' change to cause the aggregate demand curve to shift as Figure 7-6 shows. Could you explain your classmates the effects that the changes in these factors have on the AD curve?

Figure 7-6

▷ Exercise 2

Explain whether the following case will cause a shift in or a movement along the AD curve.

i) Consumer's optimism strengths and people decide to consume larger portions of their income than before.

ii) Inflation in the country goes down to 2 percent, which is the central bank's target for that variable.

iii) The government decides to build five new public universities in favor of spreading higher education.

Answers:

i) This increase in consumer's optimism will shift the aggregate demand curve to the right.

ii) Inflation has to do with the price level, which is an endogenous variable of the model. If the price level goes down, we witness a movement down along the aggregate demand curve.

iii) An increase in government expenditure will shift the aggregate demand curve to the right.

7.6 The aggregate supply curve

Aggregate supply refers to the quantity of goods and services that firms are willing and able to supply for each given price level. The relationship between this quantity and the price level is different in the long and short run. So, we will develop both a short-run and long-run aggregate supply curve. In the short run the AS curve is sloping upward. In an extreme case, the short-run AS curve is horizontal which is called the Keynesian aggregate supply curve. In the long run the AS curve is vertical which is called the classical aggregate supply curve. The shape of the aggregate supply curve reflects what happens to production costs as the domestic output expands or contracts. First, let us figure out how to define the short run and the long run in Macroeconomics.

7.6.1 Definitions: short run and long run

The short run is a period in which input prices, particularly nominal wage, remain fixed in the present of a change in the price level. In other word, the changes in the price level normally do not immediately change nominal wages in the short run. The possible reason is most employees are hired under conditions of fixed-wage contracts. But in the long run inputs prices, particularly nominal wage, are fully responsive to change in the price level. Given sufficient time, workers become fully informed about price-level changes and learn about the effects on their real wages. More importantly, workers and employers in the long run can negotiate changes in nominal wages. Therefore, the long run is a period in which wages are fully responsive to changes in the price level.

7.6.2 The long-run aggregate supply curve

By definition, nominal wages are assumed to be fully flexible in the long run in response to changes in the price level. So, when the price level rises, workers will discover that their real wages have fallen. As a result, they will demand higher nominal wage to restore their previous real wages. When all prices (including wages and other inputs' prices) increase, the real outputs cannot change. The only change is the price level. Because in the long run, changes in the price level do not affect the number of workers, the capital stock, or technology. Thereby the level of real GDP is also unchanged. Please remember it is assumed that wages are fully responsive to change in the price level in the long run.

The long-run aggregate supply (LRAS) curve shows the relationship in the long run between the price level and the quantity of real GDP supplied. The level of real GDP in the long run is called potential GDP or full-employment GDP. Changes in the price level do not affect the level of aggregate supply in the long run. Therefore, the long-run aggregate supply (LRAS) curve is a vertical line at the potential level of real GDP. The LRAS is also called classical supply curve. We will explain it in detail later.

Because potential GDP increases each year, the long-run aggregate supply curve shifts to the right each year. Figure 7-7 shows the long-run aggregate supply curves for each year. For instance, the price level was 107 in 2013, and potential GDP was $ 16.7 trillion. If the price level had been 117, or if it had been 97, long-run aggregate supply would still have been a constant $ 16.7 trillion. Each year, the long-run aggregate supply curve shifts to the right, as the number of workers in the economy increases, more machinery and equipment are accumulated, and technological change occurs. It is important to note that while potential GDP changes each year, the changes do not depend on the price level. The potential GDP is exogenous with respect to the price level. What's more, because the changes in potential GDP over a short period are usually relatively small, we can draw a single vertical line at potential GDP and call it LRAS in a certain period.

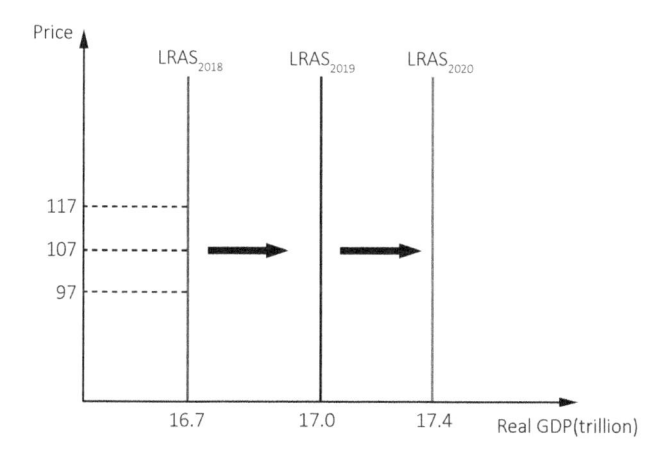

Figure 7-7

7.6.3 Short-Run Aggregate Supply Curve

While the LRAS is vertical, the SRAS is upward sloping. The price level increases, the quantity of goods and services firms are willing to supply increases. Why?

In the short run, input prices such as wages are assumed to be fixed or sticky. An increase in the price level will improve profits and encourage firms to expand real output. Alternatively, a decrease in the price level will reduce profits and real output. Therefore, the short run aggregate supply curve is upward-sloping. The main reason firms behave this way is that as the prices of goods and services rise, prices of inputs rise more slowly. Economists tend to believe that some firms and workers fail to accurately predict changes in the price level. Based on this, there are three potential explanations for why the SRAS curve is upward-sloping:

· Contracts make some wages and prices "sticky."

Prices and wages are said to be "sticky" when they do not respond quickly to changes in demand or supply. Some firms and workers fail to predict price level changes, and hence do not correctly build them into long-term contracts. Therefore, when prices increase, because of the contracts, workers will not adjust their wage demands accordingly.

· Firms are often slow to adjust wages.

Annual salary reviews are "normal", for example. Also, firms dislike cutting wages — it's bad for morale. When the economy enters into a recession, your employer is unlike to reduce your wages because lower wages reduce productivity and morale. Therefore, your employer only decreases production when prices fall.

· Menu costs, the costs to firms of changing prices, make some prices sticky.

Altering prices is sometimes costly in itself. Firms have menu costs when they change prices, for example, print new catalogs. A small "optimal" change in price may not be worth the hassle for a firm to perform. As the price level rises, some firms will be reluctant to raise their prices because of menu cost. Their prices are lower comparatively, then sales at those firms will increase, and their output will increase. This creates the possibility that an increase in the price level will increase output. More menu costs can make the short-run aggregate supply curve flatter.

An extreme case of the short-run AS curve is horizontal (the Keynesian aggregate supply curve), indicating that firms will supply whatever amount of goods is demanded at the existing price level. The idea underlying the Keynesian aggregate supply curve is that because there is unemployment, firms can obtain as much labor as they want at the current wage. During the Great Depression the output could expand endlessly without increasing prices, by putting idle capital and labor to work. In the short run, firms are reluctant, or unable, to changes prices when demand shifts, instead, at least for a little while, they increase or decrease output. As a result, the aggregate supply curve is quite flat in the short run as Figure 7-8 shows.

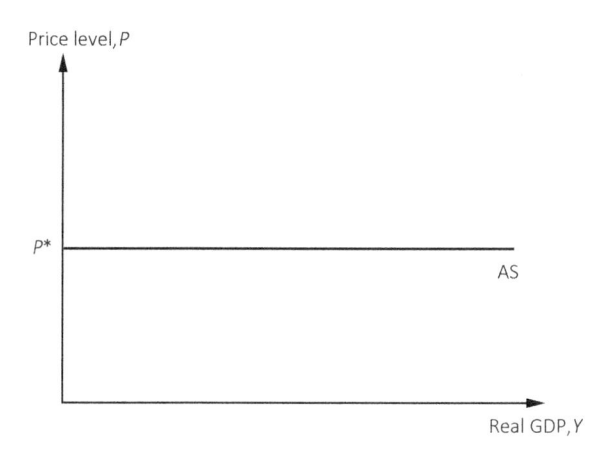

Figure 7-8

7.6.4 Shifts of the SRAS Curve vs. Movements along It

The short-run aggregate supply curve describes the relationship between the price level and the quantity of goods and services firms are willing to supply, holding constant all other variables that affect the willingness of firms to supply goods and services. A change in the price level results in a movement along a stationary SRAS curve. But some factors that would affect short-run aggregate supply cause the SRAS curve to shift. The most important variables that cause the short-run aggregate supply curve to shift are:

1) Increases in the labor force and in the capital stock

An increase in the availability of the factors of production, like labor and capital, allows more production at any price level, which shifts the SRAS curve to the right. And a decrease in the availability of these factors reduces the aggregate supply, which shifts the SRAS curve to the left.

2) Technological change

Improvements in technology allow productivity to improve, and hence the level of production at any given price level, which shifts the SRAS to the right.

3) Expected changes in the future price level

If workers and firms believe the price level will rise by a certain amount, they will try to adjust their wages and prices accordingly. For example, if the firms and workers expect that the price level will increase by 3 percent, from 110.0 to 113.3, they will adjust their wages and prices by that amount. Holding constant all other variables that affect aggregate supply, the short-run aggregate supply curve will shift to the left. Figure 7-9 shows the situation. Each output will response to a higher price than before. On the contrary, if workers and firms expect that the price level will be lower in the future, the short-run aggregate supply curve will shift to the right.

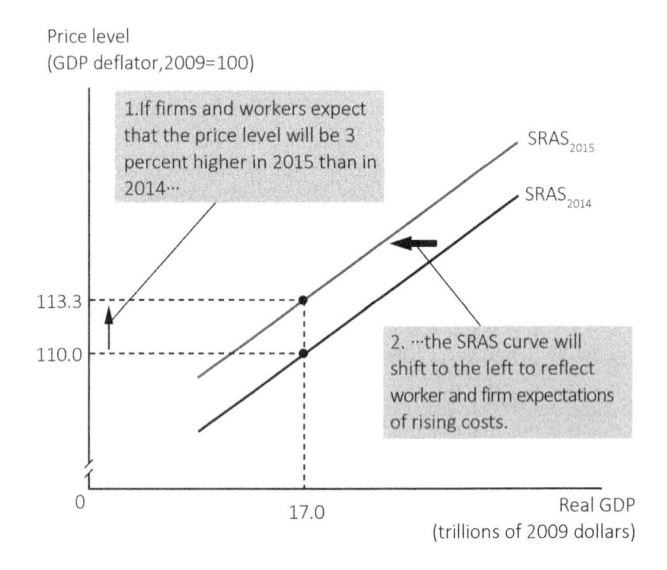

Figure 7-9

4) Adjustments of workers and firms to errors in past expectations about the price level

Workers and firms sometimes make incorrect predictions about the price level. As time passes, they will attempt to compensate for these errors. Suppose everyone failed to predict an increase in the price level. Prices rise, therefore so does output. Then once firms and workers notice the rising prices, they update their expectations and increase their price demands, decreasing short-run aggregate supply. Therefore, the ARAS shifts to the left.

5) Unexpected changes in the price of an important natural resource

A supply shock is an unexpected event that causes the short-run aggregate supply curve to shift. For example: Oil prices increase suddenly. Firms immediately anticipate rising input prices, and as a consequence will produce the same amount of output only if their own prices rise. In other words, at a given level of output, the prices increase. Therefore, the SRAS curve shifts to the left.

▶ Exercise 3

Explain how each of the following events would affect the short-run aggregate supply curve:

ⅰ) An increase in the price level.

ⅱ) An increase in what the price level is expected to be in the future.

ⅲ) A price level that is currently higher than expected.

ⅳ) An unexpected increase in the price of an important raw material.

ⅴ) An increase in the labor force participation rate.

Answer:

ⅰ) A higher price level would cause a movement up along the short-run aggregate supply curve.

ⅱ) An increase in what the price level is expected to be in the future would cause the short-run aggregate supply curve to shift to the left.

ⅲ) A price level currently higher than expected would lead workers and firms to increase wages and prices, causing the short-run aggregate supply curve to shift to the left.

ⅳ) An unexpected increase in the price of an important raw material would cause the short-run aggregate supply curve to shift to the left.

ⅴ) An increase in the labor force participation rate would cause the short-run aggregate supply curve to shift to the right.

7.7 Macroeconomic equilibrium in the long run and the short run

We can use the aggregate demand and aggregate supply model to analyze changes in real GDP and the price level. Macroeconomic equilibrium occurs when the quantity of real GDP demanded equals the quantity of real GDP supplied at the point of intersection of the AD curve and the AS curve. We have two kinds of equilibrium, the short run equilibrium and the long run equilibrium.

In the long run, the short-run aggregate supply curve and the aggregate demand curve intersect at a point on the long-run aggregate supply curve, and the economy produces its potential level of real GDP. At this point, firms are operating at their normal level of capacity, and everyone who wants a job will have one, except the structurally and frictionally unemployed. As the following figure shows, both point A and point C are in the long-run equilibrium. We know, however, that the economy is often not in the long-run macroeconomic equilibrium.

In the short run, the equilibrium occurs at the intersection of aggregate demand curve and the short-run aggregate supply curve. There are three types of short-run macroeconomic equilibrium.

· A full employment equilibrium occurs when equilibrium real GDP equals potential GDP. The point A and point C in Figure 7-10 indicate the full employment equilibrium.

· A recessionary gap (or below full employment equilibrium) occurs when real GDP is less than potential GDP and that brings a falling price level. A recessionary gap occurs when the AS curve and the AD curve intersect to the left of the potential GDP line, as illustrated at point B in Figure 7-10. The potential GDP is Y_1, but the actual GDP is Y_2. In a recessionary gap, there is a surplus of labor and firms can hire new workers at a lower wage rate.

· An inflationary gap (or above full employment equilibrium) occurs when real GDP exceeds potential GDP and that brings a rising price level. An inflationary gap occurs when the AS curve and the AD curve intersect to the right of the potential GDP line, as illustrated at point D in Figure 7-10. The potential GDP is Y_1, but the actual GDP is Y_3. In an inflationary gap, there is a shortage of labor and firms must offer higher wage rates to hire the labor they demand.

The long-run macroeconomic equilibrium cannot occur at any other level of output. Because of automatic mechanism: A process of adjustment back to potential GDP occurs without any actions by the government. For example, suppose the economy begins at point C with GDP at Y_1. If there is a decline in wealth, then the decline in wealth shifts the aggregate demand curve to the left from AD_1 to AD_2. The new short-run equilibrium occurs at point B. As a result, prices fall and output declines. Unemployment also rises as the economy falls below potential GDP (Y_1). The slowing economy causes workers

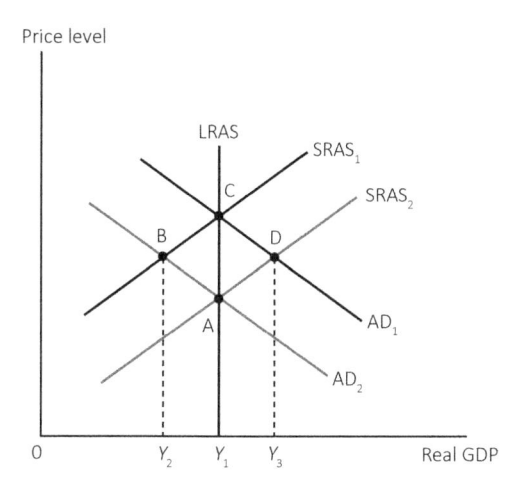

Figure 7-10

and firms to adjust their expectations about wages and prices downward. Eventually this will cause them to accept lower wages and prices, which will shift the short-run aggregate supply curve to the right from $SRAS_1$ to $SRAS_2$. Eventually, the economy moves to point A, with real GDP restored back to potential GDP at Y_1 and prices even lower. The unemployment rate will return to the natural level.

Conversely, suppose the initial equilibrium at point A and there is an increase in wealth, then the AD curve shifts to the right. The new short-run equilibrium occurs at point D. Both the price level and output will increase. In the long run, workers will discover that their real wage have fallen as a result of this increase in the price level. Therefore, they will respond, most likely, by demanding higher nominal wages to keep their real wages unchanged. The short-run aggregate supply curve will shift to the left, which will move the economy from point D to point C. Real output will fall to its potential level and the unemployment rate will return to its natural rate. Economists refer to this adjustment process as an automatic mechanism because it occurs without any actions by the government.

Next, we will examine the short-run and long-run effects of recession, expansions and supply shocks, which will help us to understand the fluctuation in the short-run economy.

For simplicity, assume:

· No inflation; the current and expected-future price level is 100.

- No long-run growth; i. e. the LRAS curve is not moving.

Though unrealistic, these assumptions allow us to understand the key ideas of the aggregate demand and aggregate supply model.

7.7.1 Recession

Suppose the initial long-run equilibrium occurs at point A, as the following figure shows. Assume that rising interest rates reduces investment and causes the aggregate demand curve to shift to the left from AD_1 to AD_2, resulting in a recession (at point B). The recession will eventually end because there are forces that push the economy back to potential GDP in the long run. The shift in aggregate demand lowers the price level. Workers will be willing to accept lower wages, and firms will be willing to accept lower prices. This causes the SRAS curve to shift to the right from $SRAS_1$ to $SRAS_2$. It may take the economy several years to return to potential GDP (at point C). The adjustment process is illustrated by Figure 7–11, which is an automatic mechanism because it occurs without any actions by the government.

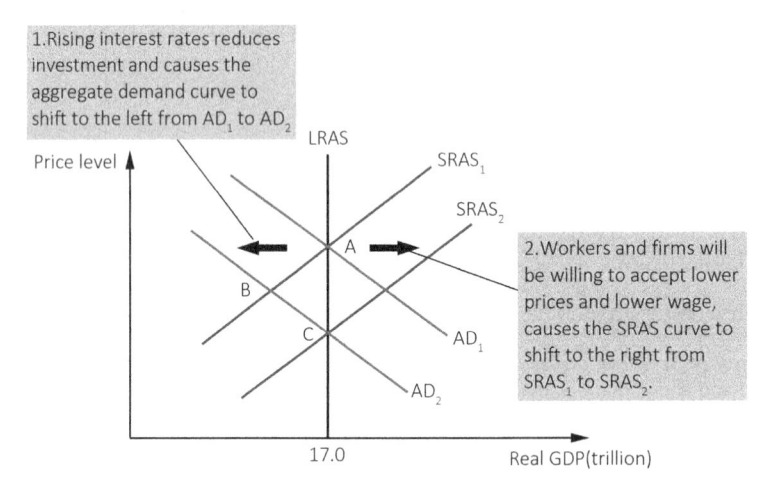

Figure 7–11

An alternative to waiting for the automatic mechanism to work is for the government to use monetary and fiscal policy to shift the AD curve to the right and restore potential GDP more quickly. For example, the government can increase government purchases which causes the AD curve to shift to the right from AD_2 to AD_1. As a result, the economy restores back to point A.

7.7.2 Expansion

Suppose the initial long-run equilibrium occurs at point A, as Figure 7-12 shows. If many firms become more optimistic about the future profitability of new investment, the resulting increase in investment shifts the AD curve to the right from AD_1 to AD_2. The new equilibrium occurs at point B. Firms will operate beyond their normal capacity, and some workers who would ordinarily be structurally or frictionally unemployed are employed. An automatic mechanism will bring the economy back from a short-run equilibrium beyond potential GDP. Workers will push for higher wages, and firms will charge higher prices. As a result, the SRAS curve will shift to the left from the $SRAS_1$ to the $SRAS_2$. Eventually, the equilibrium occurs at the point C. The process of returning to potential GDP may last more than a year. Similarly, government can adopt some contractionary policies to make the economy go back to the long-run equilibrium, such as reducing the government purchases.

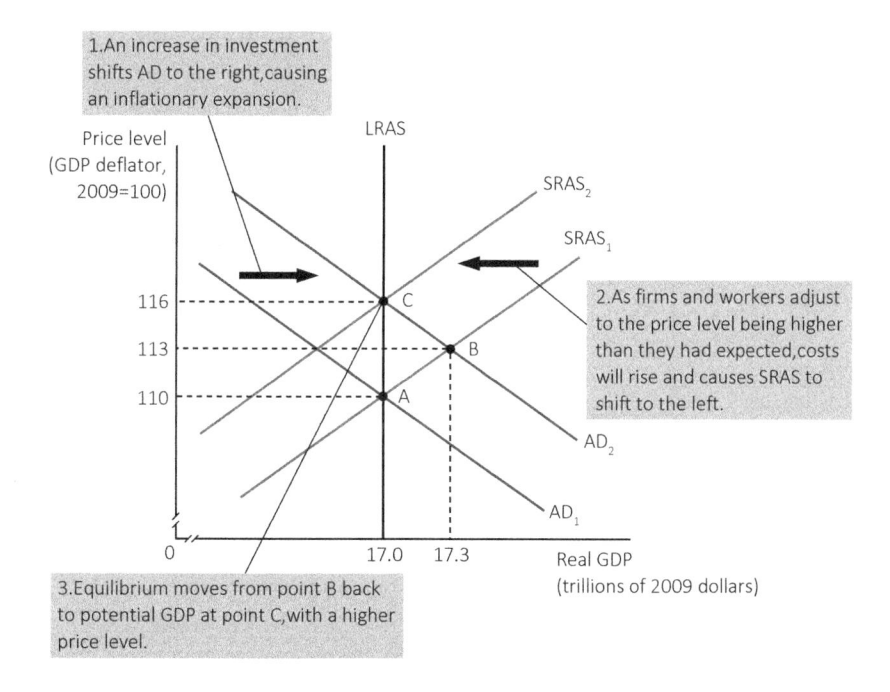

Figure 7-12

7.7.3 Supply Shock

If oil prices were to increase substantially, this would increase many firms' costs and cause the SRAS curve to shift to the left. As Figure 7-13 shows, the price level is higher in short-run equilibrium but real GDP is lower. This result is called stagflation, a combination of inflation and recession, usually resulting from a supply shock. The recession eventually results in workers accepting lower wages and firms accepting lower prices. As this occurs, the SRAS curve will shift to the right. The economy returns to potential GDP at the original price level, is illustrated at point A. It may take the economy several years for this process to be completed. Alternatively, the government can use monetary and fiscal policy to restore potential GDP more quickly. For example, the government can increase government purchases such as building up infrastructure, which rises the aggregate demand and shifts the AD curve to the right. Then the economy returns to the long run equilibrium. But this would result in a permanently higher price level.

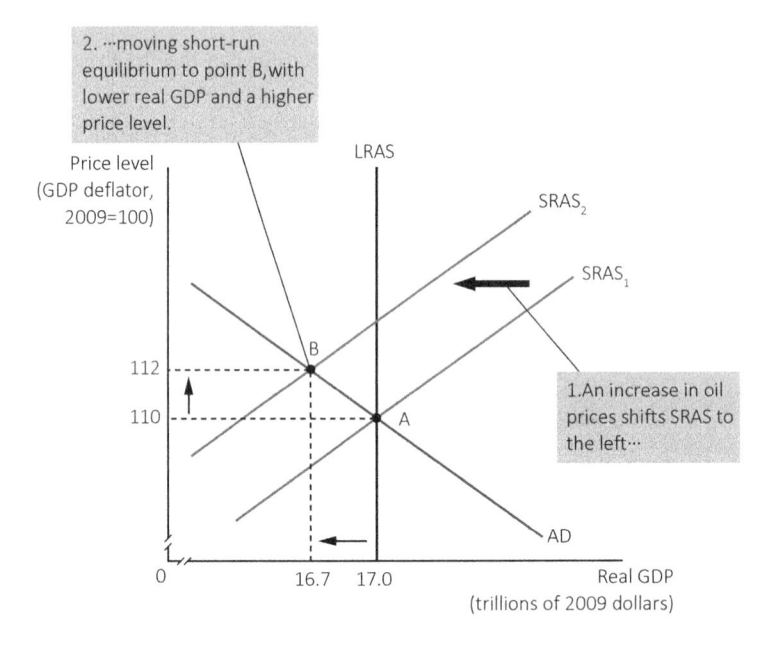

Figure 7-13

▷ Exercise 4

Figure 7-14 illustrates an economy in long-run equilibrium at a price level of 120 and real GDP of $ 17.0 trillion. Assume that an increase in real estate prices raises household wealth.

ⅰ) What two assumptions are used when the economy is said to be in initial long-run equilibrium at a price level of 120 and real GDP equals to $ 17.0 trillion?

ⅱ) Use a graph to describe the changes in aggregate demand and aggregate supply

Price level (GDP deflator, 2009=100)

LRAS, SRAS₁, AD₁

120 at Real GDP 17.0 (trillions of 2009 dollars)

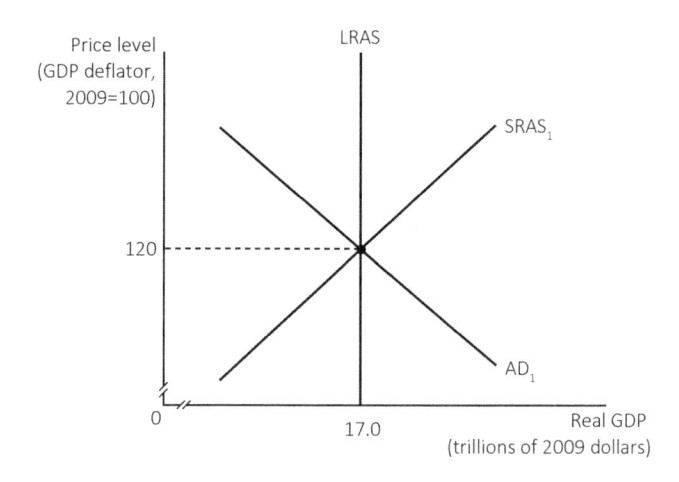

Figure 7-14

that result in a short-run and a long-run equilibrium following the increase in household wealth.

Answer:

ⅰ) The first assumption is that the economy has not been experiencing any inflation because the price level is 120 and is expected to remain at this level. The second assumption is that potential GDP equals 17.0 trillion and will remain at this level.

ⅱ) The increase in wealth will increase consumption. As Figure 7-15 shows, this increase will cause a shift in aggregate demand to the right from AD_1 to AD_2. The economy will reach short-run equilibrium (point B) at a higher real GDP ($17.3 trillion) and a higher price level (122). Workers and firms will eventually adjust to the price level being higher than they had expected. Workers will push for higher wages — because each dollar of wages will buy fewer goods and services — and firms will charge higher prices. In addition, the low levels of unemployment resulting from the expansion will make it easier for workers to negotiate for higher wages, and the increase in demand will make it easier for firms to charge higher prices. As a result, the SRAS curve will shift to the left from $SRAS_1$ to $SRAS_2$. At this point (C), the economy will be back in long-run equilibrium. The economy's new long-run equilibrium will have a higher price level, but the same level of real GDP as before the increase in wealth occurred.

206 | Macroeconomics

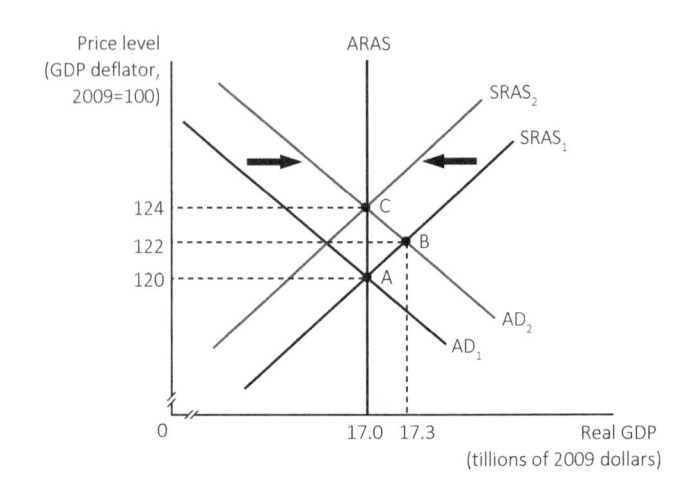

```
Price level                    ARAS
(GDP deflator,
2009=100)                            SRAS₂
                                     SRAS₁
              →          ←
   124 -------------●C
   122 -------------●B
   120 -------------●A
                                AD₂
                            AD₁
    0        17.0  17.3          Real GDP
                            (tillions of 2009 dollars)
```

Figure 7−15

7. 8 Two extreme supply cases — Keynesian and classical

Macroeconomics became a separate field of economics in 1936, with the publication of John Maynard Keynes's book *"The General Theory of Employment, Interest and Money"*. The Keynesian revolution is the name given to the widespread acceptance during the 1930s and 1940s of John Maynard Keynes's macroeconomic model. The aggregate demand and aggregate supply model developed by Keynes remains the most widely accepted approach to analyzing macroeconomic issues. We have talked the aggregate supply and demand curves together determine the equilibrium level of output and prices in the economy. Now we use the AD-AS model to study the effects of monetary and fiscal policy in the two extreme supply cases-Keynesian and classical.

7. 8. 1 The Keynesian case

The Keynesian aggregate supply curve is a horizontal AS curve, as Figure 7−16 shows. The initial equilibrium is the intersection of AS and AD_1. At that point the goods and assets markets are in equilibrium. Consider an increase in aggregate demand — such as an increase in the money supply, increased government purchases, or a cut in taxes — which shifts the AD curve to the right, from AD_1 to AD_2. At the new equilibrium, output has increased to Y_2. Because firms are willing to supply any amount of output at the level of price P^*, there is no effect on prices. The only effect is an increase in output and employment. Therefore, when the AS curve is horizontal, perfectly elastic supply, an expansionary fiscal expansion will increase output, but leave the equilibrium price level unchanged.

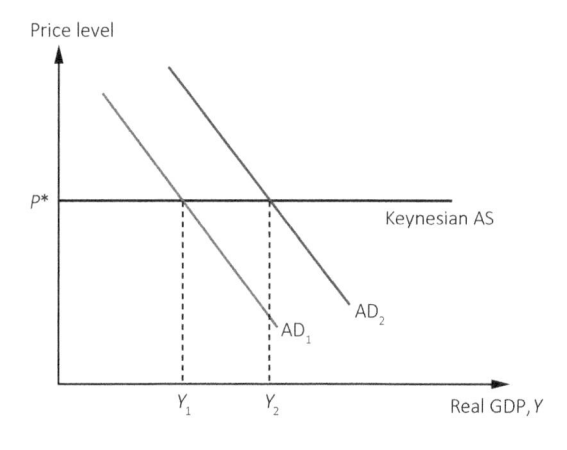

Figure 7-16

7.8.2 The classical case

In the classical case, the aggregate supply curve is vertical at the full-employment level of output. Firms will supply the level of output whatever the price level. Under this supply assumption we obtain results very different from those reached using the Keynesian supply curve. In Figure 7-17 we study the effect of expansionary policies under classical supply assumptions.

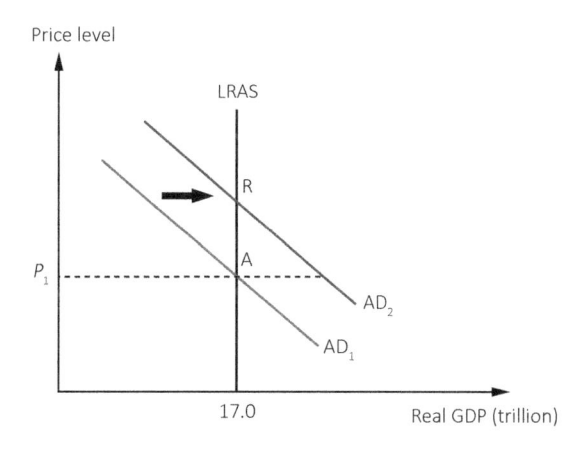

Figure 7-17

As Figure 7-17 shows, the initial equilibrium is at point A. The expansion in demand shifts the aggregate demand curve shift to the right. At the price level P_1, the demand for goods has risen. But, because at the point A there is full employment, firms cannot obtain extra labor to produce more output, and output supply cannot respond to the increased demand. As firms try to hire more workers, they have to raise wages and their costs of production, so they must charge higher prices for their output. The increase in the demand for goods therefore leads only to higher prices and not to higher output. The expansionary policies have no effect on the output. It is inefficiency in the long run.

7.9 Supply-side economics

Like most economic theories, supply-side economics tries to explain both macroeconomic phenomena and — based on these explanations — offer policy prescriptions for stable economic growth. In contrast to Keynesian theory, which includes ideas that demand determines the equilibrium income and the government should intervene with fiscal and monetary stimuli, supply-side economics focuses on the incentive effects of taxation, regulation and social policy affecting the supply side of the economy. A pure Keynesian believes that consumers and their demand for goods and services are key economic drivers, while a supply-sider believes that producers and their willingness to create goods and services set the pace of economic growth. As we talked before, when the supply curve is vertical, fiscal and monetary policies have no effect on the output. But, an increase in the supply can raise output and lower prices. Therefore, supply-siders think only supply-side policies can permanently increase output and demand management policies are useful only for short-term results.

All economists are in favor of policies that move the aggregate supply curve to the right by increasing potential GDP. Supply-side policies such as removing unnecessary regulation, maintaining an efficient legal system and encouraging technological progress are all desirable. However, there is a group of politicians and pundits who use the term supply-side economics in reference to the idea that cutting tax rates will increase aggregate supply enormously-so much, in fact, that tax collections will rise, rather than fall. Then, what happens when tax rates are cut?

Cutting tax rates has effects on both aggregate supply and aggregate demand. First, the aggregate demand curve shifts to the right, because cutting tax rates can encourage households' consumption and firms' investment. Second, the aggregate supply curve also shifts to the right, because lower tax rates increase the incentive to work. However, economists have known for a long time that the effect of such incentive is quite small. As a result, the GDP increase, but only by a very small amount, and prices are permanently higher as the point C at Figure 7-18 shows.

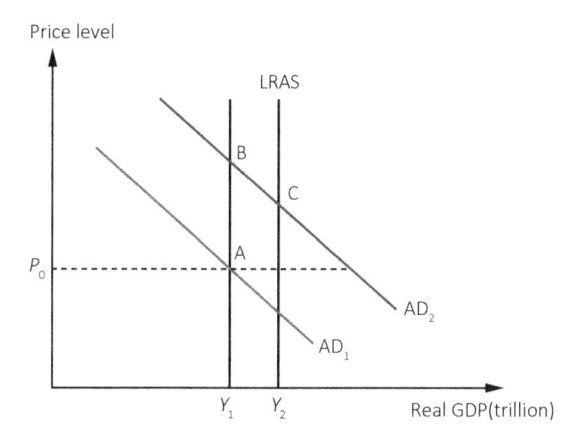

Figure 7-18

The results were demonstrated by the United States' experiment. Between 1998 and 2001, the United states had been running budget surpluses. In 2001, President George W. Bush and the US congress enacted major tax cuts in the United States in an attempt to stimulate the economy and counter the recession. Despite helping to stimulate the economy, the tax cuts again contributed to the emergence of large, sustained budget deficit.

Not all supply-side policies are misguided. Many economists strongly favor supply-side policies, but they just don't believe in the magic of cutting tax rates. As to whether cutting tax rate have a positive effect on the government budget, please refer to the resources about the Laffer curve.

Case Study

Supply-Side Structural Reforms and China's Economic Growth

China's growth miracle since the early 1980s has significantly raised the standards of living in China. It has also made China an increasingly important contributor to world economic growth and a large and growing market for U.S. exports. The rapid growth was driven primarily by productivity gains and capital investment. The recent growth slowdown has raised the concern that China's growth miracle could be ending and China might be falling into a pattern commonly referred to as the "middle-income trap".

Under such a complex situation as an ageing population, overcapacity and pollution, coupled with flagging international demand, the 11th Session of the Central Financial and Economic Steering Group identified the strategy of supply-side structural reforms in November 2015. The supply-side structural reforms refer to measures taken at the supply and production side to deregulate, improve production, reduce transaction costs and give better play to market mechanisms to unlock total factor productivity (TFP) and enhance the efficiency, competitiveness and sustainability of growth. Intrinsically, supply-side structural reforms have the following features:

First, supply-side structural reforms aim to enhance the effectiveness of the allocation of resources to match the needs of supply and demand by addressing the issues of production structure, industrial structure, income gaps and regional imbalances.

Second, supply-side structural reforms are intended to reshape existing systems and restructuring so as to create new systems of social security, government administration, socialist market economy, and a pro-growth institutional environment.

Third, supply-side structural reforms reflect the shift of mid-and long-term economic momentum. Under the new normal of China's economy, the demand pulling approach of growth is losing steam. It is imperative to seek out new forms of economic growth. According to many economic theories, economic growth is dependent on the efficient supply of labor, capital and TFP in the long run. Among them, TFP plays a critical role in growth. By putting focus on the quality and efficiency of growth as well as the increase of TFP through technological progress, institutional innovation and structural improvement, with supply-side structural reforms providing enduring and stable growth momentum to the economy. In this sense, supply-side structural reforms will unleash the unremitting potential of China's economy in the medium and long term.

Fourth, supply-side reforms represent an earnest requirement of China's development stage and basic national conditions. Although China's GDP aggregate ranks the second in the world. However, in terms of per capita GDP, China still are far behind that of developed countries. Many parts of China remain underdeveloped and many social needs remain unaddressed. The key issue facing China's economy remains long-term development rather than short-term macro regulation. From a long-term perspective, efficient supply is a fundamental assurance for economic development and prosperity. As shown by world history, an economy grows rapidly only when supply efficiency increases with the most rapidity. Without rising TFP, prosperity will be unsustainable and eventually stagnate. In the post-crisis era of the world economy, major nations all agreed to promote the innovation of science and technology and the effective supply of real economy.

However, it should be noted that supply-side structural reforms are not the withdrawal of demand-side management. Supply side and demand side are two sides of the same coin and must be coordinated with each other. Demand side management aims to moderately expand aggregate demand to maintain economic growth within a reasonable range and create a favorable macro environment for supply-side structural reforms. Supply-side structural reforms must enhance effective supply, create new sources of supply, improve the quality of supply and foster new market demand, enhance the endogenous momentum and vitality of the economy, and foster an environment for sustained and healthy growth in the medium and long run. The subsystems of demand-side and supply side factors must form a synergy to spur growth in an efficient and quality manner.

In recent years, China's economic growth rates maintain at about 6%. Although this rate is still quite remarkable by international standards, it is significantly lower than the 10% average recorded in the previous three decades. Historically, fast-growing countries have often fallen into such a trap, in which growth slows sharply as income reaches a threshold level and wages rise sufficiently to erode a country's comparative advantage. However, some countries have successfully avoided the middle-income trap and moved to high-income status. For example, in the 1960s, Japan had per capita real GDP of about $ 6 000 and an average growth rate of over 10%. In subsequent decades, however, Japan's GDP per capita rose and its growth slowed. By 2011, Japan's GDP reached over $ 30 000 per capita and growth slowed to about 1.25%. Therefore, a growth slow-down might be a necessary progress in the economic development and might be a chance to solve the current issues in the economy. If these supply-side structure reforms can be successfully implemented, then China should be able to avoid the middle-income trap and sustain long-term growth at a reasonable pace. In the transition process, however, structural reforms may contribute to a slowdown in economic growth.

Source: Li Ping and Lou Feng, "Supply-Side Structural Reforms and China's Potential Economic

Growth Rate", http://www.sohu.com/a/157320042_673573.

Terms and Concepts

· **Aggregate demand (AD) curve**: A curve that shows the relationship between the price level and the quantity of real GDP demanded by households, firms, and the government.

· **Long-run aggregate supply (LRAS) curve**: A curve that shows the relationship in the long run between the price level and the quantity of real GDP supplied.

· **Short-run aggregate supply (SRAS) curve**: A curve that shows the relationship in the short run between the price level and the quantity of real GDP supplied by firms.

· **Stagflation**: A combination of inflation and recession, usually resulting from a supply shock.

· **Supply shock**: An unexpected event that causes the short-run aggregate supply curve to shift.

· **Menu costs**: The costs to firms of changing prices.

Problems and Applications

I. True or False

1. The basic aggregate demand and aggregate supply curve model helps explain short-term fluctuations in real GDP and the price level.

2. Wealth effect is when the price level falls, the real value of household wealth rises and so will consumption and the demand for goods and services.

3. In the interest-rate effect, an increase in the price level raises interest rates, which increases investment spending and consumption spending, particularly on durable goods.

4. Potential GDP or full-employment GDP refers to the level of real GDP in the long run.

5. On the long-run aggregate supply curve, a decrease in the price level decreases the aggregate quantity of GDP supplied.

6. An increase in the price level will shift the short-run aggregate supply curve to the right.

7. Suppose there has been an increase in investment. As a result, real GDP will increase in the short run, and increase further in the long run.

8. The process of an economy adjusting from a recession back to potential GDP in the long run without any government intervention is known as an automatic mechanism.

9. A decrease in imports would cause net exports to be greater, causing the aggregate demand curve to shift to the right.

10. Technological change would cause the long-run aggregate supply curve to shift to the right.

II. Choices

1. A combination of recession and inflation is called _____.

A. an expansion

B. stagflation

C. a business cycle

D. depression

2. The recession of 2007-2009 made many consumers pessimistic about their future incomes. How does this increased pessimism affect the aggregate demand curve? _____.

A. This will move the economy up along a stationary aggregate demand curve

B. This will move the economy down along a stationary aggregate demand curve

C. This will shift the aggregate demand curve to the left

D. This will shift the aggregate demand curve to the right

3. All of the following are reasons why the wages of workers and the prices of inputs rise more slowly than the prices of final goods and services except _____.

A. unions are successful in pushing up wages

B. firms are often slow to adjust wages

C. contracts make prices and wages "sticky"

D. menu costs make some prices sticky

4. Which of the points in Figure 7-19 are possible long-run equilibrium? _____.

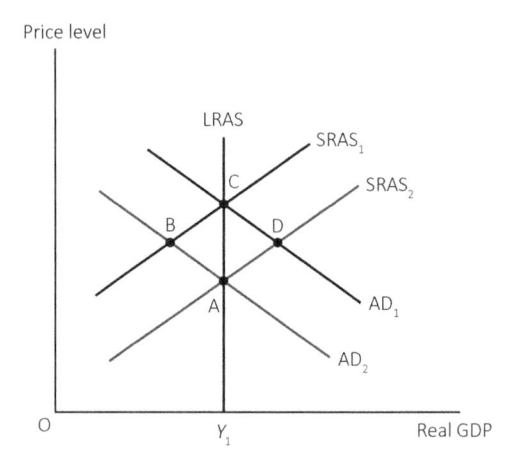

Price level graph with LRAS vertical line, SRAS₁ and SRAS₂ upward sloping curves, AD₁ and AD₂ downward sloping curves. Points labeled: C at intersection of LRAS, SRAS₁, and AD₁; B on SRAS₁ to the left of C; D on SRAS₂ to the right of C; A on LRAS below C at Y₁.

Figure 7–19

A. A and B

B. A and C

C. A and D

D. B and D

5. Which of the points in Figure 7–19 are possible short-run equilibrium but not long-run equilibrium? Assume that Y_1 represents potential GDP. _____.

A. A and B

B. A and C

C. C and D

D. B and D

6. Suppose the economy is at point A in Figure 7–19. If investment spending increases in the economy, where will the eventual long-run equilibrium be? _____.

A. A

B. B

C. C

D. D

7. Suppose the economy is at point C in Figure 7–19. If government spending decreases in the economy, where will the eventual long-run equilibrium be? _____.

A. A

B. B

C. C

D. D

8. Suppose the economy is at point A in Figure 7-19. If the economy experiences a supply shock, where will the short-run equilibrium be? _____.

A. A

B. B

C. C

D. D

9. Which of the points in in Figure 7-19 are possible short-run equilibria? _____.

A. A and B

B. A and C

C. A and D

D. A, B, C, and D

10. Potential GDP _____.

A. increases as the price level increases because firms supply more goods and services

B. decreases as the price level increases because people demand fewer goods and services

C. might either increase or decrease as the price level increases, depending on whether aggregate demand increases or decreases

D. is independent of the price level

11. A fall in the real wage rate _____ firms' profits and leads to _____ in the quantity supplied.

A. raises; an increase

B. raises; a decrease

C. lowers; an increase

D. lowers; a decrease

12. The AD curve will shift to the _____.

A. right if the price level falls and the quantity of money is held constant

B. right if the price level rises and the quantity of money is held constant

C. right if the price level is held constant and the quantity of money rises

D. right if the price level is held constant and the quantity of money falls

13. If the price level rises but the money wage rate does not, then firms will hire

_____ labor and the quantity of real GDP supplied will _____.

A. more; increase

B. the same amount of; not change

C. less; decrease

D. more; not change

14. Which of the following changes aggregate supply and shifts the aggregate supply curve? _____.

i) changes in the price level

ii) change in potential GDP

iii) change in the real wage rate

A. i) only

B. ii) only

C. iii) only

D. ii) and iii)

15. Which of the following does NOT shift the aggregate supply curve? _____.

A. An increase in energy prices

B. An increase in the nominal wage rate

C. An increase in the price level

D. A decrease in the capital stock

16. In the short run, a rise in the price level brings a _____ in the real interest rate that _____ investment, bringing _____ in the quantity of real GDP demanded.

A. rise; decreases; a decrease

B. fall; decreases; a decrease

C. fall; increases; an increase

D. rise; increases; an increase

17. When the domestic price level increases, exports decrease and imports increase. Other things the same, this change is illustrated by a _____.

A. movement upward along the aggregate demand curve

B. movement downward along the aggregate demand curve

C. rightward shift of the aggregate demand curve

D. leftward shift of the aggregate demand curve

18. Aggregate demand _____ if the expected inflation rate increases because _____.

A. increases; people expect to receive cost of living raises as the inflation begins

B. decreases; people wait for the exchange rates to change before making purchases

C. does not change; inflation does not affect the aggregate demand curve

D. increases; people want to make purchases now before the price of goods and services begin to increase

19. If a country is trying to recover from a recent recession, it is unlikely their government officials will decide to _____ because it would _____.

A. lower interest rates; decrease aggregate demand

B. raise interest rates; decrease aggregate demand

C. raise interest rates; increase aggregate demand

D. institute a tax cut; increase aggregate demand

20. If the aggregate demand curve and the aggregate supply curve intersect at a level of real GDP less than potential GDP, there is _____.

A. a recessionary gap

B. an inflationary gap

C. a rising price level

D. a falling real GDP

III. Short Answer

1. How does an increase in the price level affect the aggregate quantity of goods and services demanded?

2. How does a rise in the foreign exchange rate affect aggregate demand in China? Explain your answer.

3. Explain how each of the following events would affect the aggregate demand curve.

i) Lower interest rates.

ii) A decrease in net exports.

iii) A decrease in the price level.

iv) Slower income growth in other countries.

v) A decrease in imports.

4. Explain how each of the following events would affect the long-run aggregate supply curve.

ⅰ) A lower price level.

ⅱ) A decrease in the labor force.

ⅲ) A decrease in the quantity of capital goods.

ⅳ) Technological change.

5. What is the current equilibrium price level and real GDP for the economy illustrated in Figure 7-20? Does this economy have an inflationary gap, a recessionary gap, or neither? As it adjusts toward full employment, which curve shifts? What is the equilibrium real GDP and price level that the economy will ultimately reach?

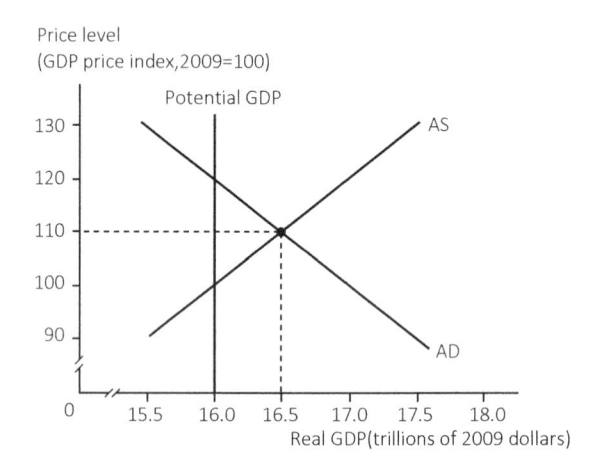

Figure 7-20

6. The economy is at full employment and then aggregate demand increases. Describe what happens as an immediate result of the increase in aggregate demand. Describe how the economy adjusts back to full employment.

Answers to Problems and Applications

Ⅰ. True or False

1	2	3	4	5	6	7	8	9	10
T	T	F	T	F	F	F	T	T	T

Ⅱ. Choice

1	2	3	4	5	6	7	8	9	10
B	C	A	B	D	C	A	B	D	D
11	12	13	14	15	16	17	18	19	20
A	C	A	D	C	A	A	D	B	A

Ⅲ. Short Answer

1. **Answer**: An increase in the price level decreases the aggregate quantity of goods and services demanded for three reasons. First, it decreases the buying power of money. As a result, people decrease their demand for goods and services. Second, it raises the real interest rate. The real interest rate rises because an increase in the price level increases the demand for money, which raises the nominal interest rate, which, in the short run, raises the real interest rate. When the real interest rate rises, people and businesses delay plans for investment and purchases of big-ticket items. Finally, an increase in the price level makes domestically produced goods and services more expensive relative to foreign-produced goods and services. As a result, people and firms buy more foreign produced and fewer domestically produced goods and services, which decreases the quantity demanded of domestically produced goods and services.

2. **Answer**: An increase in the yuan exchange rate increases China's aggregate demand. The yuan's exchange rate against the U.S. dollar is the amount of the renminbi that a U.S. dollar can buy. If the yuan's exchange rate rises, a dollar buys more yuan. As a result, chinses goods and services become cheaper to foreigners because foreigners need to spend fewer dollars to buy China-produced goods and services. Simultaneously, China-produced goods and services become cheaper to foreigners. As a result, China's imports decrease and China's exports increase, both of which increase China's aggregate demand.

3. **Answer**:

ⅰ) Lower interest rates would increase investment spending and consumer spending, particularly on durable goods, which would cause the aggregate demand curve to shift to the right.

ii) A decrease in net exports would cause the aggregate demand curve to shift to the left.

iii) A decrease in the price level would cause a movement along the aggregate demand curve.

iv) Slower income growth in other countries would decrease China's exports, which would cause the aggregate demand curve to shift to the left.

v) A decrease in imports would cause net exports to be greater, causing the aggregate demand curve to shift to the right.

4. **Answer:**

i) A lower price level would cause a movement along the long-run aggregate supply curve.

ii) A decrease in the labor force would cause the long-run aggregate supply curve to shift to the left.

iii) A decrease in the quantity of capital goods would cause the long-run aggregate supply curve to shift to the left.

iv) Technological change would cause the long-run aggregate supply curve to shift to the right.

5. **Answer:** The equilibrium is where the aggregate demand and aggregate supply curves intersect. Thus, the equilibrium price level is 110 and equilibrium real GDP is $16.5 trillion. Real GDP exceeds potential GDP, so the economy has an inflationary gap. The aggregate supply curve will shift leftward as the economy adjusts to full employment. Ultimately the aggregate supply curve will shift so that it intersects the aggregate demand curve where the aggregate demand curve crosses the potential GDP line. Thus, ultimately equilibrium real GDP equals potential GDP, $16.0 trillion, and the price level is 120.

6. **Answer:** The immediate effect of an increase in aggregate demand is to increase both the price level and real GDP. The money wage rate does not change, so with the higher price level the real wage rate falls. Eventually, however, workers demand a higher (money) wage rate to compensate for the higher price level. As firms pay the higher money wage rate, aggregate supply decreases. The decrease in aggregate supply means that the price level rises and real GDP decreases. Workers continue to demand a higher money wage rate and aggregate supply continues to decrease until finally the economy

returns to full employment. At that point, the money wage rate has increased enough so that the real wage rate is back to its initial level. Real GDP once again equals potential GDP, so the changes in real GDP were only temporary. The price level, though, is higher than its initial level, so the increase in the price level is permanent.

8 Monetary System and Money Growth

Learning Objective

By the end of this chapter, students should understand:
- the meaning of money and its functions.
- the definitions of money supply and the function of banks.
- the central bank's tools of monetary control.
- what the quantity theory of money is.

Key Points and Exercises

8.1 The meaning of money

Money refers to the assets that people are regularly willing to use in exchange for goods and services, roughly speaking, the RMB, Pounds, or dollars and so on, which makes up the nation's stock of money. People can buy food or T-shirts with their cash. But, if you owned a company, as Zhengfei Ren does, you would be very wealthy, but this is not considered as money. In terms of economists' definition, money includes only those that are generally accepted by sellers and buyer in exchange for goods and services.

8.1.1 The invention of money

Before the invention of money, if a person wanted to buy something, he would have to barter, which means exchange goods directly for other goods from somebody else. This requires each person must want what the other one has at the same time, which is called as a double coincidence of wants. Money eliminates the need for barter because people can buy goods with it directly instead of exchange from goods to goods. In the history, there are commodity money such as shell, animal skins, silver, gold and other precious metals. Commodity money is a good used as money but also has value independent of its use as money. Money makes trading easier, and allows for specialization and higher productivity.

8.1.2 The functions of money

Money should bear the following three functions:

1) Medium of exchange

Sellers are generally willing to accept it in exchange for goods or services. When you walk into a bookstore to buy a book, the seller gives you the book, and you give the seller your money. Thus, transactions take place as money transfers from buyers to sellers. And you are confident that the sellers will accept your money to exchange the items they have because money you hold is the commonly accepted medium of exchange.

2) Unit of account

This means that money is a method of an agreed-upon measuring value in a standard manner. When you go shopping, you may find that a book costs ¥30 and a bottle of water costs ¥3. Although the price of the book is 10 bottles of water, prices are never quoted in such way. That means goods and services are quoted in RMB instead of other goods or services. When we need to measure economic value of any item, we use money as the unit of account.

3) Store of value

People can hold money and defer consumption till a later date. That is, people transfer their purchasing power to the future by money. If you earn ¥200 today, you can hold the ¥200 and spend it any time you want, next week or next month. Money is not a perfect way of storing value. If there is inflation, the purchasing power of same money is reducing. But we are still liking to hold money because of its value storing.

There are other assets to store value, too, for example, stocks and bonds. They may be a better store of value, but these kinds of wealth are not as good at providing liquidity, such as house. Liquidity is the ease of conversion of an asset into a medium of exchange. Money works particular well at liquidity.

8.1.3 Money today

A medium of exchange should have 5 characteristics, which are acceptable to most people, having standardized quality, durable, divisible and valuable relative to its weight.

Commodity money, such as silver and gold, their value depends on the purity. The higher the purity, the higher their value. The problem is that it is difficult to control the supply because the discovery of gold or silver fields is unpredictable. So, silver and gold cannot meet above requirements, and cannot serve as money.

In modern economies, paper money is issued by a central bank, which is run by the government. Fiat money refers to any money, such as paper currency (RMB in China, Dollar in United States) that is authorized by a central bank or governmental body, and that does not have to be exchanged by the central bank for gold or some other commodity money. The law decrees them to be money. Paper currency (and coin) is authorized as money without intrinsic value, so it's not a commodity money, either.

Central banks are flexible in creating money. But there is a problem in fiat money. Only if people have confidence in it, they will hold them to exchange for other items. Otherwise, people will stop keeping them. That means fiat money becomes useless.

8.2 How to measure money

It is not so easy to determine which assets should be included in the money, so there is more than one measure available. But the most common measures for studying the impacts of money on the economy are M1 and M2.

· M1: A narrow definition of the money supply. It shows money's role as the medium of exchange.

M1 consists of currency in circulation, demand deposits, traveler's checks, and other checkable deposits.

· M2: A broader definition of money.

M2 consists of M1 plus savings deposits, small time deposits, balances in money market deposit accounts in banks, and noninstitutional money market fund shares. M2 is much larger than M1.

8.3 Money supply

Money Supply refers to the quantity of money available in an economy. In a system of commodity money, the quantity of commodity money is the money supply. In today's economies, fiat money is used in most country. The government controls money supply by monetary policy. In many countries, including China, monetary policy is entrusted to central bank. The central bank of China is The People's Bank of China. If you look at a Chinese RMB bill, you can see there is ZHONGGUO RENMIN YINHANG on it.

The primary way of money policy is open-market operations — purchase and sale of government bonds. When the central bank wants to increase money supply, central bank buys government bonds from the public, thus these RMB enter into the hands of the public and the market. This open-market purchasing of government bonds increases the quantity of money in circulation, thus increases money supply. On the contrary, when the central bank wants to decrease money supply, it sells government bonds to the public. This open-market sale of bonds takes RMB from the hands of the public and, so decreases the quantity of money in circulation. Open market operations are easy to carry out and can effectively control the money supply. It is very important to control the money supply because it affects economy.

In order to control money supply, we need to know how to measure it first. So, it is necessary to make it clear what it includes.

- Currency, the paper money and coins held by the public in China.
- Demand deposits, balances in bank accounts that can be converted into currency.

Credit cards are not money — they are methods of deferring payment that allow short-term loan from the bank issuing the card. Debit cards and checks are not money. They represent instructions to transfer money from one person to another, but the checking account balance is money.

Money supply consisting of currency and demand deposits (checking account deposits) is its narrowest definition. Balances in bank account are included in the money supply, so we can see that banks play an important role in the money supply.

8.4 The role of banks

8.4.1 Chinese banking system

Chinese banking system consists of central banks, regulatory agencies, self-regulatory organizations and financial institutions.

- The People's Bank of China is the central bank. Under the leadership of the

State Council, it is responsible for formulating and implementing monetary policies, preventing and resolving financial risks and maintaining financial stability.

• China Banking and Insurance Regulatory Commission is responsible for the supervision of the country's banking financial institutions and their business activities.

• China Banking Association (CBA) is a national non-profit social organization registered with the Ministry of Civil Affairs and a self-regulatory organization, including six committees with different functions.

• Banking financial institutions include policy banks (China Development Bank, Export-Import Bank of China, Agricultural Development Bank of China), large commercial banks (Industrial and Commercial Bank of China, Bank of China, Agricultural Bank of China, China Construction Bank, Bank of Communications), small and medium-sized commercial banks, rural financial institutions, and Postal Savings Bank of China and foreign banks. Non-bank financial intermediaries regulated by the CBRC include financial Asset Management Corporation, trust companies, conglomerate finance companies, financial leasing companies, auto finance companies and currency brokerage companies.

8.4.2 Banks and money supply

As we know that the public can hold their money as currency or demand deposit. Because of these deposits in banks, bank's behavior can impact the money supply.

There are 2 situations, 100-percent-reserve banking and fractional-reserve banking, in which banks affect the money supply as per banks making loans or not, and accept deposits and make loans are the key roles banks play in the economy.

8.4.3 100-percent-reserve banking

Reserves are deposits that a bank receives and keeps as cash without loaning out. 100-percent-reserve banking means banks are only safety places to store money without loaning out the deposits.

On a bank's balance sheet, the main assets are its reserves, loans, and holdings of securities (such as Treasury bills). A largest liability is deposits, which include checking accounts, savings accounts, certificates of deposit, and so on. Assets are listed on the left of the balance sheet, and liabilities are listed on the right. The left and right sides must add up to the same amount. A more realistic balance sheet is shown as Table 8-1.

Table 8-1

Assets		Liabilities	
Reserves	100	Deposits	1 000
Loans	900	Others	400
Others	400		
Total assets	1 400	Total liabilities	1 400

If the public deposits ¥100 of currency in Bank A, balance sheets of Bank A should record changes in it. The balance sheet is shown as Table 8-2.

Table 8-2   Bank A

Assets		Liabilities	
Reserves	¥ 100	Deposits	¥ 100

Bank A has assets of ¥100 because there are cash reserves of ¥100 in its vault. Deposit of ¥100 is its liabilities, because it shows bank A owes of ¥100 to the depositor. The amount of money held by the public was reduced by ¥100 and deposits held by the public have increased by ¥100. Thus, we find Bank A does not affect the money supply at all. Adopting 100-percent-reserve banking, banks will have no any influence on the money supply.

8.4.4 Fractional-reserve banking

Lots of people deposit currency in banks, but few people ask for back of their deposit on any given day. So, banks don't need to hold all their deposit as cash reserves. They can lend some of their deposits and keep the rest on reserve. This is fractional-reserve banking. The fraction of deposits held as reserves is the reserve ratio. The minimum fraction of deposits banks is required by law to keep as reserves is called the Required Reserve Ratio, RR for short. If banks hold reserves over the legal requirement, it is called Excess Reserves. Suppose the Reserve Ratio is 10% for Bank A, so Bank A keeps 10 percent of deposits on reserve, and the remainder can be lent out. If you deposit ¥100 of currency in Bank A, Table 8-3 shows the balance sheets of Bank A.

Table 8-3 Bank A

Assets		Liabilities	
Reserves	¥100	Deposits	¥100

With the Reserve Ratio of 10%, Bank A keeps 10% of the deposit as reserves, the other 90%, that is ¥90, is lent out, creating a ¥90 checking account deposit. As Table 8-4 shows, Bank A has increased money supply by ¥90 because it still holds a ¥100 of deposit, and the borrower's checking account increases ¥90.

Table 8-4 Bank A

Assets		Liabilities	
Reserves	¥100	Deposits	¥100
Loan	¥90	Deposits	¥90

But this is not over. The people, who borrows the ¥90, spends it and the receiver, who gets the borrower's ¥90, deposits it in Bank B again. We assume Bank B has a same reserve ratio, that is 10%, then balance sheets of Bank B is as shown in Table 8-5.

Table 8-5 Bank B

Assets		Liabilities	
Reserves	¥90	Deposits	¥90

Now, Bank A's T-account becomes as shown in Table 8-6.

Table 8-6 Bank A

Assets		Liabilities	
Reserves	¥10	Deposits	¥100
Loan	¥90		

As we see in these balance sheets of banks, the total deposits in the bank system have increased by ¥190 (¥100+¥90) until now. If this process lasts, the total amount of money generated by the banking system from the original deposit of ¥100 is:

¥100 + ¥90 + ¥81 + ¥72.9 + ⋯
= ¥100 + ¥100×(1−10%) + ¥100×(1−10%)² + ¥100×(1−10%)³ + ⋯
= ¥100×(1/10%)
= ¥1 000

10% is the reserve ratio.

This is the way that the banking system increases the volume of checking account balances and the money supply by making new loans.

8.4.5 The simple deposit multiplier

The simple deposit multiplier is the ratio of the number of deposits created by banks to the number of new reserves. In this case, the number of deposits created by banks is ¥1 000. And we can get the number of new reserves by the following calculation:

As the reserve ratio is 10%, the reserves in bank A will increase by ¥10 (¥100 ×10%). And the reserves in bank B will increase by ¥90×10%, because the deposits in bank B increase by ¥90, Bank B should keep at least ¥90×10% as reserves. If the process lasts, the reserves in the bank system will increase by:

¥100×10% + ¥100×(1−10%)×10% + ¥100×(1−10%)²×10% + ¥100×(1−10%)³×10% + ⋯
= ¥100×10%×[1+(1−10%)+(1−10%)²+(1−10%)³+⋯]
= ¥100×10%×(1/10%)
= ¥100

We can find it is geometric progression summation. So, the sum of the data in the parentheses is:

$$\frac{1}{1-(1-10\%)} = \frac{1}{10\%}.$$

So, the total increase in reserves from the deposits of ¥100 is ¥100.

Your initial deposit of ¥100 increase the reserves of the banking system by ¥100, and led to a total increase in checking account deposits of ¥1 000. Therefore, the simple deposit multiplier in this case is $\frac{1\ 000}{100} = 10$.

Notice that the 10 is equal to the reserve ratio's reciprocal. So, the simple deposit multiplier actually equal:

$$\text{Simple deposit multiplier} = \frac{1}{\text{RR}}$$

Where RR is the required reserve ratio.

If simple deposit multiplier multiplies the total increase in bank reserves, we can get the total increase in checking account deposits and the money supply.

$$\text{Change in checking account deposits} = \text{Change in bank reserves} \times \frac{1}{\text{RR}}$$

The greater the required reserve ratio, the smaller the loan amount for the same number of reserves, and the smaller the simple deposit multiplier. Fractional-reserve banking system enlarges money supply, but does not create net wealth. Because when a bank loans its received reserves, it creates money, but it also creates an equal amount of debt. This is why in the banks' balance sheets; the left assets are always equal to the right liabilities.

▷ Exercise 1

If you want to withdraw ¥100 in cash from your checking account in China Construction Bank. Draw a T-account showing the changes on your bank's balance sheet?

Answer:

China Construction Bank

Assets		Liabilities	
Reserves	−¥100	Deposits	−¥100

8.4.6 The simple deposit multiplier vs. the real-world deposit multiplier

From above discussion, we got the Simple Deposit Multiplier from Mathematical inference. But the process to get the results has been simplified in two ways. First, we assume that banks don't keep any excess reserves. In reality, banks do not loan out all their excess reserves. Banks like to keep some excess reserves on hand in case withdrawals are higher than the bank might typically expect. If this is the case, then the amount of money that is available to loan out in the next round is a bit smaller. This will shrink the amount of money expansion. Second, we assume that the whole amount of every check is deposited in a bank. But not all the amount of money that is loaned out in the money expansion process is put back into the banking system. Some of it leaks out in the form of currency and does not get entirely redeposited. Both of these actions make the money expansion smaller. Therefore, the real-world multiplier is smaller than the deposit multiplier, 1/RR. The impacts of these two assumptions reduce the real-world multiplier to about 1.6.

We draw two important conclusions:

· Whenever banks receive reserves, they make new loans and the money supply expands.

· Whenever banks loss reserves, they reduce loans and money supply contracts.

8.5 How does the central banks manage the money supply?

A bank run refers to many depositors go to the bank to withdraw money at the same time. Bank panic refers to many banks experience bank runs at the same time. One bank may be to handle bank run by borrowing from other banks. But banks cannot handle bank panic by themselves. A central bank can help stop a bank panic by make loans to banks. Banks can use these loans to pay off depositors.

The central banks can control the money supply indirectly by adjusting the required reserve ratio. Money multiplier is the reciprocal of reserve ratio. This is one way to control the money supply. Normally, the central banks influence the money supply through monetary policy.

Monetary policy is defined as the actions the central banks take to control the money supply and interest rates to pursue macroeconomic policy objectives. There are three kinds of monetary policy tools:

· Open market operations.

· Discount policy.

· Reserve requirements.

Open market operations refer to the purchase of government bonds by the central bank to buying government bonds from the public or sell the government bonds to the public in order to control the money supply. If a central bank buys government bonds from the public, the money for the bonds goes to the market, thus increase the money supply in the economy. If a central bank sells government bonds to the public, the central bank collects the money for the bonds from the public, thus decrease the money supply in the economy.

By cutting down the discount rate, which means central banks change on discount loans, the central banks can encourage banks to make additional loans and increase their reserves. Raising the discount rate would have the reversed effect.

When the central banks lower the required reserve ratio, it converts required reserves into excess reserves. If the central banks enhance the reserve requirement, it would have the opposite effect.

These policy tools are designed to influence the reserves of banks as a means of changing the amount of money deposited in checking accounts. Why do the central banks prefer open market operations? There are three reasons.

· The central banks control the timing and the volume of open market operations totally.

· Buying government Treasury and selling are opposite. It is easily reversible.

· There is no requirement for any changes in relative regulations, so open market operations can be implemented quickly, without administrative delay, which is important for the economy.

8.6 The quantity theory of money

8.6.1 The Quantity Equation: The classical dichotomy and monetary neutrality

The quantity equation shows the relationship between money and prices. The equation of exchange states that the quantity of money (M) multiplied by the velocity of money (V) equals the price level (P) multiplied by real GDP (Y).

$$M \cdot V = P \cdot Y$$

The velocity of money is the speed of circulation, which is the average number of times in a year the average Renminbi in the money supply is used to buy goods and services included in GDP. The left side of this equation must equal the right side. If the quantity of money increases, P or Y must rise, or V must fall.

If the circulation velocity of money is assumed constant, the quantity theory of money shows the connection between money and prices.

Rearranging the equation by dividing both sides by M, we get:

$$V = P \cdot Y/M$$

where:

- M1 for M (money supply).
- the GDP deflator for P (price level).
- real GDP for Y (the level of real output).

We know that $P \cdot Y$ equals nominal GDP. If nominal output is ￥800 (800 items at ￥1 each) and M is ￥200, then $V=4$. That means, in order for ￥200 to accommodate ￥800 of purchases and sales, each Yuan must be spent 4 times on average.

8.6.2 The quantity theory explanation of inflation

As a mathematical rule states that an equation where variables are multiplied together is equal to an equation where the growth rates of the variables are added together. In rates of growth, the quantity equation is transformed to:

Growth rate of the money supply+Growth rate of velocity

=Growth rate of the price level + Growth rate of real output

In previous chapter, we know that the inflation rate is the growth rate of the price level. We rearrange the quantity equation to get,

Inflation rate=Growth rate of the money supply+Growth rate of velocity

−Growth rate of real output

If velocity is constant, then the growth rate of velocity is zero. We rearrange the equation again as,

Inflation rate = Growth in the money supply−Growth rate of real output

From the above equation, we can predict the inflation as follows:

- If the money supply grows faster than real GDP, there will be inflation.
- If the money supply grows slower than real GDP, there will be deflation.
- If the money supply grows at the same rate as real GDP, the price level will be stable, so there will be no inflation or deflation.

In the long run, inflation is the result of the money supply growing faster than real GDP.

8.6.3 Accuracy of the quantity theory for estimates of inflation

We use growth in the money supply minus growth rate of real output to get inflation rate. But there is an assumption that velocity is constant. Actually, velocity may move erratically in the short run, the quantity equation can't make good inflation forecasting. But in the long run, there is a strong link between changes in the money supply and inflation.

8.6.4 High rates of inflation

Hyperinflation is caused by central banks increasing the money supply at a rate far faster than the growth rate of real GDP. A high rate of inflation causes money to lose its value so rapidly that households and firms avoid holding it. Economies suffering from high inflation usually also suffer from very slow growth, if not severe recession. The economy, which is affected by high inflation, also typically suffers a severe recession or very slow growth.

▷ Exercise 2

Suppose that during a particular year, the money supply grows at a rate of 10 percent, velocity grows at a rate of 4 percent, and real GDP grows at a rate of 3 percent. Calculate the resulting inflation rate.

Answer:

This problem is about the link between increases in the money supply and the inflation rate. We can get the following relationship between the inflation rate and the other variables given by rewriting the quantity equation:

Inflation rate = Growth rate of the money supply + Growth rate of velocity
　　　　　　　　－Growth rate of real output

Substituting the numbers from the question into the equation above, we have:

Inflation rate = 10% + 4%－3% = 11%.

Therefore, the inflation rate is 11%.

Case Study

The History of Chinese Money: From Shells to Silver

The earliest form of Chinese money was shells (hence the use of the shell character in many other characters related to value, money and wealth). Money shells were later bronzed. In the period of rival states (770－221 B.C.) different shapes of money were used by different states: knife-shaped, spade shaped, and ant-nose-shaped.

When Qin Shihuang, the First Emperor, united China in 221 B.C. round coins with a square hole in the middle were introduced and this form of currency was used until around 1890. This is the form of the currency in the nation's popular imagination, and representations of it can be seen in the modern day as symbols of wealth and prosperity.

For higher level transactions, ingots of silver were commonly used. These ingots resemble in their form the classic origami boat children enjoy folding out of paper, and it may be seen on souvenir stalls as the item held aloft in some representations of the Buddha, a symbol of prosperity.

The early-modern era

Chinese banking started almost by accident in the 1820s when a successful dyer with a branch office in Beijing was asked by a friend if he might give him some money in Pingyao, his home town, collecting the same amount from the dyer's office in Beijing. This enabled the friend to avoid bandits. Others caught on to this idea and so that hometown, the attractive and well-preserved walled town of Pingyao in Shanxi province, became for a while the financial center of all China.

The end of the imperial era and the turbulent time that followed saw first local mints, then high inflation and financial instability. It was not until the Communist era began in 1949 that a stable currency was established, using mostly notes, and coins for denominations of 1 yuan and lower.

Chinese money today

Money forms a big part of the everyday lives of Chinese. Electronic transactions are becoming increasingly common, so expect the frustrations in supermarket queues as everywhere else in the world when someone ahead of you has a handful of items and chooses to pay with a bank card. Checks are rarely used. Cash is still the preferred means of transaction, so notes of various denominations are changing hands all day long, even for quite large amounts.

Source: https://www.chinahighlights.com/travelguide/money.htm.

The Transformation of China's Currency Control Mode in the Stage of High-Quality Economic Development

Chinese economy has become the high-quality development stage from the high growth period, which means the financial policy should de-emphasize the quality targets and measures to fully play the role of the price leverage in financial resources allocation. With the interest rate liberalization reform was preliminary accomplished, due to financial innovation and disintermediation as well as the more sophisticated financial market and products, it is urgent to transform China's monetary policy from the quantity-based mode to the price-based mode, which is also the necessary step to achieve the high-quality economic development. We first elaborately review the theory of monetary policy and practices in the advanced economies. We find out that the quantity and price are the two sides of one coin and it is equivalent of the quantity based monetary policy and the price based monetary policy in theory. The quantity policy takes effects directly but is prone to contort the price mechanism and individual behaviors. The price policy takes effects with the adjustment of the individuals which needs a good financial market and interest policy transmission. The development of financial market and monetary policy channel play an important role for the monetary policy mode. The retrospect of monetary policy in China shows that the necessary conditions for monetary policy transformation have been satisfied, but we also point out that the practice of monetary policy in modern sense lasts for only around twenty years, after abandoning the direct controls on credit behavior and turning to the quantity indirect policy with the money supply as the intermediate target in 1998. Central bank in China is always confronting the impetus of investment and credit expansion due the traditional growth-led economic mode. Because of the governmental preference to a higher growth rate, there are soft budget constraint sectors such as the local government vehicles, stated owned firms and housing industry enterprises. The supervisory affaires of the central bank in China were separated. While, due to the industry development dominance of the supervisory ideology, there are race to the bottom in the financial supervision, which promote the rapid growth of the shadow banking in recent years and financial risks are accumulated heavily. Although there is enough market breadth of the financial market, there are still too strict regulations and the market depth is relatively low. The monetary markets and bond markets are still separated, the admittance of the market, esp. the derivative markets are sill strictly controlled, the financial products are immature and there are still implicit dual interest track. The exchange rate is still lack of edacity. So, with the problems above, monetary policy in China still needs quantity measures and we should do lots of preparations to fulfill the sufficient conditions for the monetary policy transformation. The crucial point is the development of the financial market system, including mature financial micro foundations, good guards of financial institutions and well functional financial product markets. Financial markets developments also promote the interest policy transmission and will ensure the success of the monetary policy transformation. With the deepening of the supply-side reform and reform in the difficult areas of hedge risks, esp. the improvements of the governmental debts and supervisory systems, we should vigorously promote price-based monetary policy transformation, with which to enhance economic and financial high quality development.

Source: Xu Zhong, http://www.pbc.gov.cn/yanjiuju/124427/133100/3487653/3559889/index.html.

February 2019 Financial Statistics Interpreted

At end-February, M2 and the stock of aggregate financing to the real economy (AFRE) maintained stable growth, increasing by 8% and 10.1% year-on-year, respectively. In the first two months, new RMB loans increased by RMB 374.8 billion year-on-year to RMB 4.1 trillion while AFRE expanded by RMB 5.3 trillion, RMB 1.05 trillion more than the growth in the same period last year. The year-on-year AFRE growth was higher than end-2018 for two consecutive months, indicating initial success of moves to curb its continuous slide, and providing support for the start of economic and financial work in 2019. Overall, this was mainly attributable to stepped-up countercyclical adjustment in macro regulation and marginal improvement achieved in monetary policy transmission, which showed the cumulative effect of prudent monetary policy.

M2 maintained the growth of around 8% while the M1 growth picked up

At end-February, the M2 growth was 8% year-on-year. We can rightly say that the sustained stable growth of M2 this year reflected the cumulative effect of preceding monetary policy adopted. At the same time, commercial banks stepped up fund use so that on-balance-sheet credit, bond investment, as well as equities and other investments posted large increases, contributing to the maintenance of stable M2 growth. In the first two months, on-balance-sheet credit, bond investment, and equities and other investments rose by RMB 4.1 trillion, 872.7 billion and 832.9 billion, respectively, up by RMB 374.8 billion, 771.5 billion and 370.2 billion year-on-year, respectively.

At end-February, M1 recorded a year-on-year growth rate of 2%, up by 1.6 percentage points from a month earlier. As we can see, the slow M1 growth in January was mainly caused by the sharp fall in corporate demand deposits for the month as the end of January this year was the peak period for salary and bonus payments right before the

Spring Festival. Then the situation improved much in February. Generally speaking, the M1 slowdown was mainly a reflection of structural changes in all-system liquidity rather than changes in aggregate liquidity.

The year-on-year AFRE growth was higher than end-2018 for two consecutive months

At end-February, outstanding AFRE posted a year-on-year growth rate of 10.1%, outpacing the growth at end-2018 for two consecutive months. Major contributing factors for the pickup of AFRE growth this year included the sizable year-on-year increase in lending, the substantial rise in bond financing, and the smaller fall in entrusted loans.

First, lending increased considerably year-on-year. At end-February, the outstanding balance of loans issued to the real economy stood at RMB 139 trillion, up by 13.3% year-on-year, 0.2 percentage point higher than a year earlier; outstanding RMB loans accounted for 67.6% of outstanding AFRE, up by 1.9 percentage points from a year earlier. The first two months saw an increase of RMB 4.3 trillion in outstanding RMB loans, RMB 625.9 billion more than the growth in the same period a year earlier.

Second, bond financing rose significantly. The growth of bond financing had started to rise since Q2 2018. Entering 2019, corporate bond financing picked up markedly, with the amount outstanding posting RMB 20.5 trillion at end-February, up by 10.7% year-on-year, the same pace as the previous month and the fastest since April 2017. At end-February, outstanding bonds accounted for 10% of outstanding AFRE, up by 0.1 percentage point from a year earlier. In the first two months, net financing via local government special bonds reached RMB 285.9 billion, up by RMB 275.1 billion from a year earlier.

Third, the decline in entrusted loans moderated continuously, a structural feature newly observed of AFRE this year. In the first two months, entrusted loans fell by RMB 120.8 billion, RMB 25.1 billion less than the decrease a year earlier. Entrusted loans dipped by RMB 69.9 billion in January and posted a smaller fall of RMB 50.8 billion in February.

Overall, the rebound of AFRE growth in the first two months was largely attributable to stepped-up countercyclical adjustment in macro regulation and marginal improvement achieved in monetary policy transmission.

One thing to note is that seasonal factors should be taken into consideration in the observation of AFRE. January and February data, or rather data for even longer periods, should be viewed as a whole while attention should not be overly focused on data for a single month. Judging from January and February data combined, AFRE has seen stable growth, and the full-year AFRE growth is projected to be in line with nominal GDP growth.

The decline in the three off-balance-sheet financing items of AFRE narrowed down markedly

In the first two months, the three off-balance-sheet financing items of AFRE declined by a total of RMB 21. 7 billion, indicating significant improvement compared with the average monthly fall of RMB 209. 2 billion in Q4 2018. Specifically, entrusted loans dropped by RMB 120. 8 billion, narrowing down markedly compared with the average monthly fall of RMB 149 billion in Q4 2018; trust loans and undiscounted bankers' acceptances both stopped falling and started to rise, increasing by RMB 30. 8 billion and 68. 3 billion, respectively, in the first two months.

The improvement in off-balance-sheet financing resulted from concerted efforts. First, work has been done to strengthen forward-looking pre-emptive adjustment and fine-tuning of monetary policy, and to enhance coordination with financial regulation policy. Second, financial institutions have been gradually adapting to new regulations on asset management and dealing with off-balance-sheet asset holdings. Third, the amount of off-balance-sheet financing with concentrated maturity dates has been decreasing while off-balance-sheet businesses compliant with regulations maintain sound growth.

Overall, the slide of off-balance-sheet financing in AFRE will stabilize so that better services will be provided to meet financing needs of the real economy.

Bills grew at normal pace excluding seasonal factors

Bankers' acceptances include discounted and undiscounted ones. The so-called discounting occurs when a holder sells the bill before maturity to a bank. Discounted bills thereby become the bank's on-balance-sheet loans called bill financing. Undiscounted bankers' acceptances, classified as off-balance-sheet financing, are a form of banks' credit support for enterprises.

In January 2019, outstanding bankers' acceptances grew by RMB 894. 6 billion, with bill financing and undiscounted bankers' acceptances increasing by RMB 516 billion and 378. 6 billion, respectively. Things were reversed in February when outstanding bankers' acceptances declined by RMB 140.8 billion. Specifically, bill financing grew by RMB 169.5 billion whereas undiscounted bankers' acceptances fell by RMB 310.3 billion.

The dramatic growth of both bill financing and undiscounted bankers' acceptances in January can be explained by the following. First, enterprises were motivated to use bills by falling interest rates in the bill market. Second, as more settlements took place between enterprises before the Spring Festival, seasonal factors contributed to the growth of bills. Third, as loan quotas were relatively sufficient, some banks stepped up the promotion of bills. Besides, there were cases of arbitrage arising in the market.

The rapid fall in the volume of bill business in February was mainly attributable to seasonal factors. As the Spring Festival holiday this year fell in February, there were fewer working days in the month, leading to fewer settlements and therefore less demand from enterprises for bill issuance. Also, February is traditionally a "minor month" for AFRE growth. Furthermore, the driving forces behind the growth of bankers' acceptances in January were tapering off.

Accordingly, the observation of the bill business should not be based on data for a single month. January and February data combined, outstanding bankers' acceptances increased by RMB 753.8 billion, with bill financing and undiscounted bankers' acceptances rising by RMB 685.5 billion and 68.3 billion, respectively. Overall, the bill business has played a bigger role in supporting the real economy this year.

Compared with other means of financing, bills have the apparent advantages of shorter maturity, more convenience, better liquidity, and lower financing cost, which particularly benefit micro and small enterprises as well as private enterprises. As bill financing and undiscounted bankers' acceptances can both support the growth of the real economy effectively, the financial authorities readily encourage the development of bill business with authentic trade background, but are intolerant of arbitrage through bill financing. More work needs to done in the future to smooth the transmission mechanism of monetary policy and improve the efficiency and performance of the financial sector to support the real economy.

Source: http://www.pbc.gov.cn/en/3688247/3688978/3732405/3787823/index.html.

Terms and Concepts

- **Bank run**: Many depositors go to the bank to withdraw money at the same time.
- **Bank panic**: Many banks experience bank runs at the same time.
- **Commodity money**: A good used as money but also has value independent of its use as money.
- **Excess reserves**: If banks hold reserves over the legal requirement, it is called Excess Reserves.
- **Fiat money**: Any money, such as paper currency (RMB in China, Dollar in United States) that is authorized by a central bank or governmental body, and that does not have to be exchanged by the central bank for gold or some other commodity money.
- **100-percent-reserve banking**: Deposits that a bank receives and keeps as cash without loaning out.
- **M1**: A narrow definition of the money supply. It shows money's role as the medium of exchange.
- **M2**: A broader definition of money. M2 consists of M1 plus savings deposits, small time deposits, balances in money market deposit accounts in banks, and noninstitutional money market fund shares.
- **Monetary policy**: The actions the central banks take to control the money supply and interest rates to pursue macroeconomic policy objectives.
- **Open market operations**: Refers to the purchase of government bonds by the central bank to buying government bonds from the public or sell the government bonds to the public in order to control the money supply.
- **Quantity theory of money**: Shows the connection between money and prices.
- **Required reserve ratio**: The minimum fraction of deposits banks are required by law to keep as reserves.
- **Simple deposit multiplier**: The ratio of the amount of deposits created by banks to the amount of new reserves.
- **Velocity of money**: The speed of circulation, that is the average number of times in a year the average money in the money supply is used to buy goods and services included in GDP.

Problems and Applications

I. True or False

1. An economy without money would have no exchanges of goods and services.

2. The Fed has complete control over the money supply.

3. If banks receive a greater amount of reserves and do not hold all of these reserves as excess reserves, the money supply expands.

4. The real-world money multiplier is greater than the simple money multiplier.

5. If banks receive a greater amount of reserves and do not hold all of these reserves as excess reserves, the money supply expands.

6. Money will fail to serve as a medium of exchange if it ceases to be a store of value.

7. The amount of national income in an economy equals the money supply in an economy.

8. Consider the following T-account for a bank:

Assets		Liabilities	
Reserves	$ 1 000	Deposits	$ 5 000
Loans	$ 4 000		

If the required reserve ratio is 20 percent and the bank is holding no excess reserves, the bank at this point can make no more loans.

9. If the rate of growth in real GDP exceeds the rate of growth in the money supply, the quantity theory of money predicts a price deflation.

10. For the purchasing power of money to increase, the price level has to fall.

II. Short Answer

Suppose the People's Bank of China purchases a government security from you for ¥ 10 000.

i) What is the name of The People's Bank of China's action?

ii) Suppose you deposit the ¥ 10 000 in Bank A. Show this transaction on Bank

A's T-account.

iii) Suppose the required reserve ratio is 10 percent. Show Bank A's T-account if they make the maximum loan.

iv) At this time, how much money has been created from The People's Bank of China's policy action?

v) What is the value of the Simple Deposit Multiplier?

vi) What is the maximum increase in the money supply from The People's Bank of China's policy action?

vii) If some people keep extra money and don't deposit all their receipts in the process of depositing and lending, will there be more or less money created from the People's Bank of China's policy actions than you calculate in vi)? And why?

viii) If some banks fail to loan the maximum amount of reserves allowed and have to keep excess reserves in the process of depositing and lending, will there be more or less money created from The People's Bank of China's policy actions than you calculate in 6? And why?

Answers to Problems and Applications

I. True or False

1	2	3	4	5	6	7	8	9	10
F	F	T	F	T	T	F	T	T	T

II. Short Answer

Answer:

i) Open-market operations.

ii)

Bank A

Assets		Liabilities	
Reserves	¥10 000	Deposits	¥10 000

iii)   **Bank A**

Assets		Liabilities	
Reserves	￥1 000	Deposits	￥10 000
Loans	￥9 000		

iv) ￥10 000+￥9 000=￥19 000.

v) 1/0.1=10.

vi) ￥10 000×10=￥100 000.

vii) Less. Some people keep extra money and don't deposit all their receipts, this will result in a smaller amount of loan to be redeposited available to be loaned again.

viii) Less. Some banks fail to loan the maximum amount of reserves allowed and have to keep excess reserves, this will result in a smaller amount of deposit to be loaned out available to be deposited again.

9 Monetary Policy

Learning Objective

By the end of this chapter, students should understand:
- what is monetary policy and what are the monetary policy objectives.
- monetary policy targets and its equilibrium.
- how monetary policies affect the interest rate.
- how monetary policy influences aggregate demand.

Key Points and Exercises

9.1 What is monetary policy?

Monetary policy refers to the actions taken by central banks to manage the money supply and interest rates to achieve macroeconomic policy goals.

The Objectives of Monetary Policy

There are four monetary policy goals aiming at promoting a well-functioning economy (as Figure 9-1 shows).

- Price stability. Since rising prices erode the value of money as a medium of exchange and a store of value, policymakers in most countries pursue price stability as a primary goal.
- Maximum employment /or a low rate of unemployment.
- Economic growth. In the long-run, monetary policy cannot influence real variables — such as output and employment. A country's economic growth is determined by real factors such as investment in capital and the level of technology, not by monetary

Figure 9-1

policy. But In the short run, monetary policy can affect output and employment, and at least smooth business cycles. For example, Monetary policy can stimulate economic growth and employment by providing incentive for saving to encourage a large pool of investment funds.

· Financial stability. Financial markets and institutions operate normally to allocate capital resources and risk. This is essential to economy growth.

9.2 The money market and its equilibrium

9.2.1 Monetary policy targets

Money supply and interest rate are two main monetary policy targets to keep the low unemployment rate and low inflation rate. The Fed has generally focused more on the interest rate than on the money supply. There are many interest rates in the economy. For purposes of monetary policy, the Fed has targeted the interest rate known as the federal funds rate. The federal funds rate is the interest rate banks charge each other for overnight loans. The Fed does not legally set the federal funds rate. Instead, the federal funds rate is determined by the supply of reserves relative to the demand for them. The FOMC announces a target for the federal funds rate after each meeting. No households or firms, except banks, can borrow or lend in the federal funds market. However, changes in the federal funds rate usually result in changes in interest rates on other short-term financial assets, such as Treasury bills, and changes in interest rates on long-term financial assets, such as corporate bonds and mortgages.

9.2.2　Money demand (MD) curve

The money demand curve is downward as lower interest rate cause the public to change financial assets (Treasury bills) to money. Because the opportunity cost of holding money is the interests, and it is low when interest rates on financial assets are low. So, the public would prefer holding money. The demand for money will be high. The MD curve is shown in Figure 9-2.

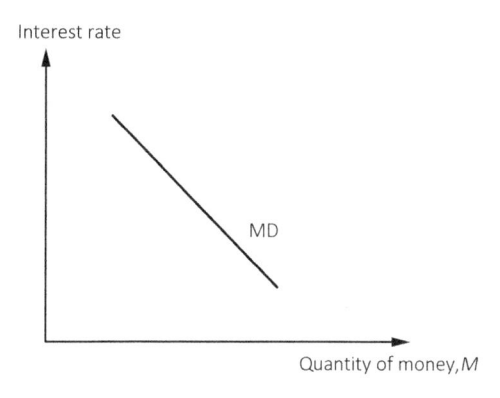

Figure 9-2

9.2.3　Shifts in the MD curve

What could cause the money demand curve to shift and how does it shift? The two important reasons are real GDP and the price level. When there is an increase in real GDP, it means the amount of buying and selling has increased. This will raise demand for money whatever the interest rate, so MD curve shifts to the right. MD_1 shifts to MD_3 as shown in the following figure. When there is a decrease in real GDP, it means the amount of buying and selling has decreased. This will reduce demand for money whatever the interest rate, so MD curve shifts to the left. MD_1 shifts to MD_2 as shown in the following figure.

If there is an increase in the price level, money for each transaction is increased, so the demand for money will be higher. MD curve shifts to the right. MD_1 shifts to MD_3 as shown in the following figure. If there is a decrease in the price level, money for each transaction is decreased, so the demand for money will be lower. MD curve is shifted to the left. MD_1 moved to MD_2 as shown in Figure 9-3.

9.2.4　Governments (central banks) manage the money supply (MS)

Different central banks have different ways and rules to manage the money supply.

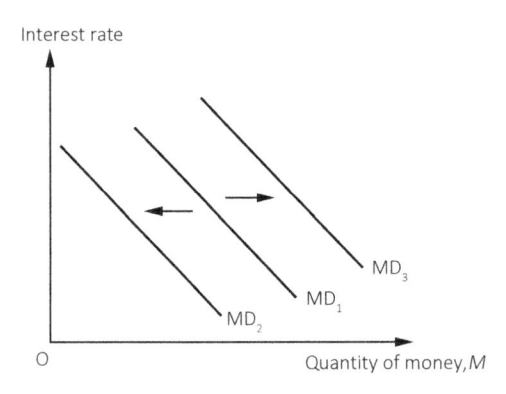

Figure 9-3

But normally, central banks control money supply by selling and buying government securities. Central banks buy securities from the public, and the public deposit the money from the central banks in their checking account. So, banks get more reserves and can make more loan, thus money supply is expanded. Instead, Central banks sell securities, to decrease the money supply.

9.2.5 Equilibrium in the money market: the intersection of MD and MS

Equilibrium in the money market means money demand equals money supply. In order to facilitate the analysis, we assume central banks can control and fix the money supply. So, quantity of money supplied cannot affected by changes in the interest rate. MS is a vertical line. Equilibrium occurs where the MD curve crosses the MS curve. When central banks increase the money supply, MS1 moves to MS2, as shown in Figure 9-4, so equilibrium point moves from A to B and the equilibrium interest rate decrease from r_1 to r_2. Because when central banks increase the money supply, the public hold more money initially than they want. They will make deposit or buy securities. This increased demand causes banks and securities sellers to lower interest rates on these financial assets. At last, interest rates fall until the public are willing to hold the additional money.

Alternatively, central banks decrease the money supply, and MS_1 moves to MS_3, as shown in Figure 9-4. So, equilibrium point moves from A to C and the equilibrium interest rate increases from r_1 to r_3.

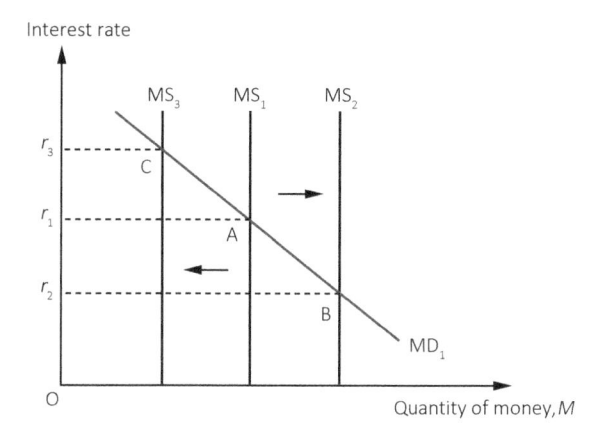

Figure 9-4

9.2.6 Two interest rates, in the loanable funds model and the money-market model

We have learned two models of the interest rate. One is the loanable funds model and the other is the money-market model. The loanable funds model is concerned with long-term real rate of interest relevant for long-term investors. The money-market model is concerned with the short-term nominal rate of interest relevant for conducting monetary policy. But these two interest rates are closely related, and an increase in one usually results in increasing in the other.

9.3 How monetary policy influences aggregate demand

The aggregate-demand (AD) curve shows the relationship between quantity of goods and services and the price level. We learnt that because of the wealth effect, the interest-rate effect, and the exchange-rate effect, AD curve slopes downward. And the interest rate is a key determinant factor in aggregate demand.

9.3.1 How interest rates affect aggregate demand

Changes in interest rates have impacts on aggregate demand through affecting consumption, investment, and net exports, as shown in Figure 9-5.

1) Consumption

Lower interest rates lower the return on saving and increase expenditures on durables. So, households always choose to spend more and save less.

2) Investment

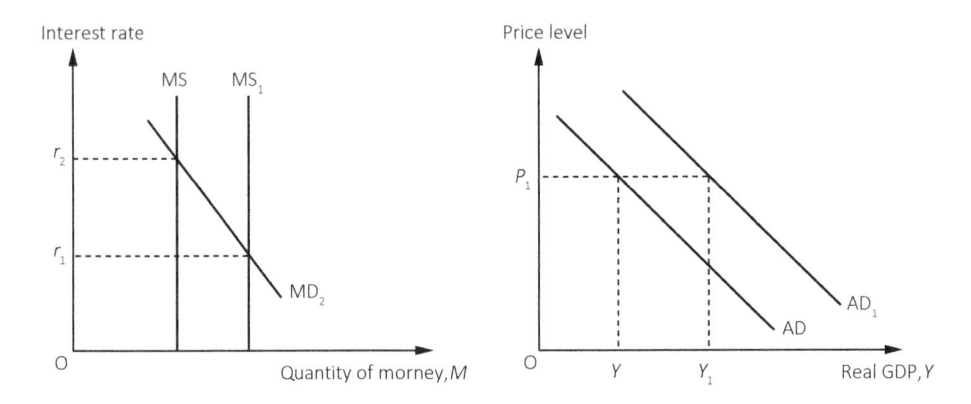

Figure 9-5

Lower interest rates costs less for firms to borrow and make investment. This leads them to invest more. For households, lower interest rates can also increase their investment on durables, such as houses, too.

3) Net exports

If interest rates decline in China relative to interest rates in other countries, the value of RENMINBI will fall, and net exports will rise.

9.3.2 The effects of monetary policy on AD curve

Expansionary monetary policy is the Federal Reserve's policy of decreasing interest rates to increase real GDP. Contractionary monetary policy is the Federal Reserve's policy of increasing interest rates to reduce inflation. The Fed can use monetary policy to affect the price level and, in the short run, the level of real GDP.

If central banks take expansionary monetary policy to buy government bonds, the money supply will shift to the right, from MS_1 to MS_2 as Figure 9-6 shows. So, the interest rate falls from r_1 to r_2. As we know, this will reduce investment cost of borrowing. Demands for goods and services are increased, and AD shifts to the right. As shown in Figure 9-6, the short-run equilibrium is at point A, with real GDP of Y_1 and a price level of P_1. An expansionary monetary policy causes aggregate demand to shift to the right, from AD_1 to AD_2, increasing real GDP from Y_1 to Y_2 (potential income) and the price level from P_1 to P_2 (point B). With real GDP back at its potential level, the central bank can meet its goal of high employment.

On the contrary, when the economy is producing above potential GDP, the central bank will perform contractionary monetary policy, which will increase interest rate, and

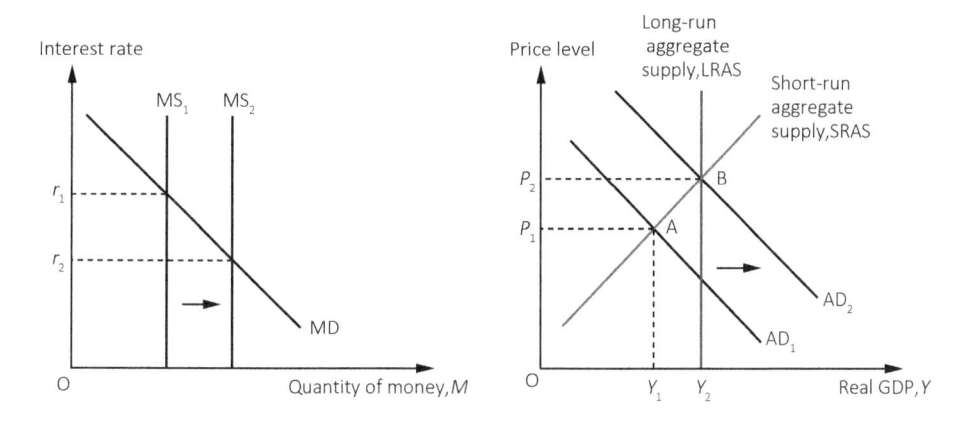

Figure 9-6

AD shifts to the left, causing real GDP to decline. Because real GDP cannot continue to remain above potential GDP. To keep real GDP above potential GDP would lead to rising inflation. A central bank needs to carry out a contractionary monetary policy to intentionally cause real GDP to decline. A central bank is mostly concerned with long-run growth. If it determines that inflation is a danger to long-run growth, it can contract the money supply in order to discourage inflation, i. e., encouraging price stability.

As Figure 9-6 shows, an expansionary monetary policy can bring real GDP back to potential GDP. In fact, monetary policy is much harder to get right than the figures make it appear. In practice, the central bank is hard to quickly recognize the need for a change in monetary policy. There is typically a delay between a policy change and its effect on real GDP, employment and prices. Therefore, the best a central bank can do is keep recession shorter and milder than they would otherwise be.

In summary, when the economy is in a recession, an expansionary monetary policy causes aggregate demand to shift to the right, which increases real GDP and the price level. With real GDP back at its potential level, the central bank can meet its goal of high employment. On the contrary, when real GDP is greater than potential GDP, the economy experiences rising wages and prices, a contractionary monetary policy causes aggregate demand to shift to the left, which causes real GDP to decrease and the price level to fall. With real GDP back at its potential level, the central bank can meet its goal of price stability.

9.4 The Taylor rule

Most economists believe that an interest rate is the best monetary policy target. But some economists argue that rather than using an interest rate as its monetary policy target, the Fed should use the money supply. Milton Friedman and other monetarists prefer replacing monetary policy with a monetary growth rule. A monetary growth rule is a plan for increasing the money supply at a constant rate that does not change in response to economic conditions. During the 1970s, some economists pressured the Fed to adopt a monetary growth rule. But support for this proposal declined after 1980, because the relationship between movements in the money supply and movements in real GDP and the price level weakened. In 1990s, the economist John Taylor analyzed the factors involved in Fed decision making and developed a rule of thumb, the Taylor rule which roughly matched the actual policy of Fed over many time periods.

The Taylor rule assumes that the federal funds rate is equal to the sum of the inflation rate, the equilibrium real federal funds rate, and two additional terms: the inflation gap and the output gap. The inflation gap is the difference between current inflation and a target rate. And the output gap is the percentage difference between real GDP and potential real GDP. The inflation gap and output gap are each given "weights" that reflect their influence on the federal funds target rate. With weights of 1/2 for both gaps, we have the following Taylor rule:

Federal funds target rate=Current inflation rate+Equilibrium real federal funds rate+ [(1/2) × Inflation gap + (1/2) × Output gap]

For example, if the equilibrium real federal funds rate is 3%, and the target rate of inflation is 2%, the current inflation rate is 4%, the real GDP is 1% below potential GDP. Then the inflation gap equals 2% (4%−2%) and the output gap is −1%. Inserting these values in the Taylor rule, we can compute the predicted value for the federal funds target rate:

$$\text{Federal funds target rate} = 4\% + 3\% + \left[\left(\frac{1}{2}\right) \times 2\%\right] + \left[\left(\frac{1}{2}\right) \times (-1\%)\right] = 7.5\%.$$

According to the Taylor rule, if the real GDP is above potential GDP and inflation is above the target rate of inflation, the Fed should raise the federal funds target rate in responds to the increase in both factors.

Case Study

China's Monetary Policy Is Complex and Shifting. Here's What You Need to Know.

Key points:

· China's central bank, the People's Bank of China, doesn't have a single primary monetary policy tool like the U.S. Federal Reserve.

· The PBOC instead uses multiple methods to control money supply and interest rates in the world's second-largest economy.

· Those tools include open markets operations, the reserve requirement ratio and various types of PBOC loans to Chinese banks.

Investors have for years watched the U.S. Federal Reserve for information about where global markets are headed: The decisions made by the American central bank influence assets around the world.

Increasingly, however, markets are also focusing on changes out of the world's second-largest economy, attempting to analyze its policy decisions to understand how vast flows of Chinese funds will react.

But the Federal Reserve system is quite unlike China's economic policy regime.

When it comes to where money is headed within the U.S. economy, investors watch for changes that the Fed makes to its target for the "federal funds rate" — the interest benchmark that influences borrowing costs, asset prices and exchange rates in the American economy. In China, such a signal is less clear because the country doesn't have a single representative policy rate like the Fed's.

Instead, the central bank uses multiple tools to control interest rates and the amount of money in the Chinese economy. So, interpreting what China wants to achieve can sometimes be a confusing affair.

Chinese policymakers also frequently add new tools or retire older ones as they modernize their country's system into something more aligned with those in developed countries. Keeping track of those changes can add to the difficulty of reading the central bank's signals.

What is China's central bank?

China's central bank is called the People's Bank of China, or PBOC for short. Like its counterparts in the advanced economies, the PBOC has the dual mandate of maintaining price stability and promoting growth through the management of monetary policies.

Monetary policy refers to the ways central banks manage the supply of money and interest rates in their economies. Those policies are adjusted according to the economic conditions that a country is facing.

For example, when central banks want to boost growth during a downturn, they cut interest rates. Doing so lowers borrowing costs, which encourages businesses and individuals to take out loans to invest and make purchases to stimulate the economy.

How does China manage its monetary policy?

The PBOC's website lists seven tools that it uses to make adjustments to its monetary policy. They are:

· Open market operations, OMO

In China, open market operations mostly involve two processes called repurchase or reverse repurchase agreements. The former term, as it is used in China, means removing liquidity from the system when the PBOC sells short-term bonds to some commercial banks.

It also does the opposite for a "reverse" repurchase agreement, buying up those contracts, so banks have more cash on hand.

Those operations allow the PBOC to control money supply and interest rates on a short-term basis — the assets are normally offered on time frames ranging from seven to 28 days.

· Reserve requirement ratio, RRR

The reserve requirement ratio refers to the amount of money that banks must hold in their coffers as a proportion of their total deposits. Lowering the required amount will increase the supply of money that banks can lend to businesses and individuals, and therefore cutting borrowing costs.

Increasing the ratio of what banks need to keep in reserve achieves the opposite result.

· Benchmark interest rates

The PBOC controls the benchmark one-year lending and deposit rates, which affects the borrowing costs for banks, businesses and individuals.

It last adjusted those rates in October 2015 and now allows commercial banks some leeway to go above or below the official level in determining the interest rates that they charge.

· Rediscounting

The PBOC offers an option to banks to "rediscount" the loans that they extend to their customers.

The monetary policy tool involves the central bank buying up existing loans from commercial lenders, giving them some extra liquidity. It's a complicated concept, so here's an example to illustrate the process:

A consumer takes a loan of $ 10 000 from a bank, with a promise to re-pay $ 12 500 at a later date. That loan agreement is said to be bought by the bank at a price of $ 10 000, which is a discount to the $ 12 500 it will ultimately receive in return. Subsequently, the bank sells that agreement to the PBOC for $ 11 000, which is another discount — or "rediscount" — of the contract's paper value of $ 12 500.

The PBOC charges an interest rate on those funds it lend to the banks, which would influence other borrowing costs in the banking system.

· Standing lending facility, SLF

Standing lending facility is also a type of PBOC lending to commercial banks. Introduced in 2013, such loans have a maturity period of one to three months — longer than funding options such as the open market operations.

To receive money through this framework, banks must guarantee assets with high credit ratings as collateral. That means such funds are usually only available to the larger lenders.

· Medium-term lending facility, MLF

Chinese banks get funds with even longer maturities — typically three months to a year — from the PBOC through the medium-term lending facility. The funding channel, introduced in 2014, allows the central bank to inject liquidity into the banking system and influence interest rates for longer-term loans.

Like the standing lending facility, banks must put up collateral to receive funds. Unlike the SLF, however, a wider range of collateral is accepted under the medium-term version. That includes government bonds and notes, local government debt and highly rated loans of small companies.

· Pledged supplementary lending, PSL

As one of the newest monetary policy tools in China, pledged supplementary lending was introduced to guide long-term interest rates and money supply. Such funds are injected into selected banks so that they can provide loans to specific sectors such as agriculture, small businesses and shantytown re-development. The banks that have received those particular funds are the three Chinese "policy" lenders: China Development Bank, Agricultural Development Bank of China and the Export-Import Bank of China.

· How has China's monetary policy evolved?

In the past, the PBOC has mostly focused on managing the quantity of money in its economy and setting quotas on how much banks can lend. That took a definitive turn in 2018 when the central bank stopped setting those specific targets.

Instead, China is seeking to establish an interest rate regime like those used by the Fed and European Central Bank. One possibility, according to analysts, is an "interest rate corridor" with the floor and ceiling determined by the PBOC, while allowing the market to set rates within that band.

But that's still a work-in-progress for the PBOC.

What else does the PBOC do?

One of the PBOC's key responsibilities is to maintain the stability of the Chinese yuan. In addition to managing money supply and interest rates, the central bank guides movements of the yuan against a basket of currencies that include the U.S. dollar, the euro, the Japanese yen and the South Korean won.

As part of that mission, the PBOC manages the country's foreign currency assets, which it buys and sells to keep the yuan stable within the intended exchange rate range.

Source: https://www.cnbc.com/2018/08/06/china-monetary-policy-how-pboc-controls-money-supply-interest-rate.html.

The Transformation of China's Monetary Control Mode in the Stage of High-Quality Economic Development

Chinese economy has become the high-quality development stage from the high growth period, which means the financial policy should de-emphasize the quality targets and measures to fully play the role of the price leverage in financial resources allocation. With the interest rate liberalization reform was preliminary accomplished, due to financial innovation and disintermediation as well as the more sophisticated financial market and products, it is urgent to transform China's monetary policy from the quantity-based mode to the price-based mode, which is also the necessary step to achieve the high quality economic development.

We first elaborately review the theory of monetary policy and practices in the advanced economies. We find out that the quantity and price are the two sides of one coin and it is equivalent of the quantity based monetary policy and the price based monetary policy in theory. The quantity policy takes effects directly but is prone to contort the price mechanism and individual behaviors. The price policy takes effects with the adjustment of the individuals which needs a good financial market and interest policy transmission. The development of financial market and monetary policy channel play an important role for the monetary policy mode. The retrospect of monetary policy in China shows that the necessary conditions for monetary policy transformation have been satisfied, but we also point out that the practice of monetary policy in modern sense lasts for only around twenty years, after abandoning the direct controls on credit behavior and turning to the quantity indirect policy with the money supply as the intermediate target in 1998. Central bank in China is always confronting the impetus of investment and credit expansion due the traditional growth-led economic mode. Because of the governmental preference to a higher growth rate, there are soft budget constraint sectors such as the local government vehicles, stated owned firms and housing industry enterprises. The supervisory affaires of the central bank in China were separated. While, due to the industry development dominance of the supervisory ideology, there are race to the bottom in the financial supervision, which promote the rapid growth of the shadow banking in recent years and financial risks are accumulated heavily. Although there is enough market breadth of the financial market, there are still too strict regulations and the market depth is relatively low. The monetary markets and bond markets are still separated, the admittance of the market, esp. the derivative markets are still strictly controlled, the financial products are immature and there are still implicit dual interest track. The exchange rate is still lack of edacity.

So, with the problems above, monetary policy in China still needs quantity measures and we should do lots of preparations to fulfill the sufficient conditions for the monetary policy transformation. The crucial point is the development of the financial market system, including mature financial micro foundations, good guards of financial institutions and well functional financial product markets. Financial markets developments also promote the interest policy transmission and will ensure the success of the monetary policy transformation. With the deepening of the supply-side reform and reform in the difficult areas of hedge risks, esp. the improvements of the governmental debts and supervisory systems, we should vigorously promote price-based monetary policy transformation, with which to enhance economic and financial high-quality development.

Source: http://www.pbc.gov.cn/yanjiuju/124427/133100/3487653/3559889/index.html.

Terms and Concepts

· **Monetary policy**: The actions the Federal Reserve takes to manage the money supply and interest rates to achieve macroeconomic policy goals.

· **Contractionary monetary policy**: Contractionary monetary policy is the Federal Reserve's policy of increasing interest rates to reduce inflation.

· **Expansionary monetary policy**: Expansionary monetary policy is the Federal Reserve's policy of decreasing interest rates to increase real GDP.

Problems and Applications

Ⅰ. True or False

1. Monetary policy is conducted by the U.S. Treasury Department.

2. The Fed can directly lower the inflation rate.

3. Rising nominal GDP will increase the demand for money and short-term interest rates.

4. Expansionary monetary policy refers to the Fed's increasing the money supply and increasing interest rates to increase real GDP.

5. Changes in interest rates affect all four components of aggregate demand.

6. When the Federal Reserve increases the money supply, people spend more

because interest rates fall.

7. When the Federal Reserve increases the money supply, people spend more because they now have more money.

8. Contractionary monetary policy refers to the Fed's decreasing the money supply and decreasing interest rates to decrease real GDP.

II. Choice

1. The goals of monetary policy tend to be interrelated. For example, when the Fed pursues the goal of _____, it also can achieve the goal of _____ simultaneously.

   A. high employment; economic growth

   B. high employment; lowering government spending

   C. economic growth; a low current account deficit

   D. stability of financial markets; a low current account deficit

2. Which of the following would cause the money demand curve to shift to the left? _____.

   A. An open market purchase of Treasury securities by the Federal Reserve

   B. An increase in the interest rate

   C. An increase in the price level

   D. A decrease in real GDP

3. Using the money demand and money supply model, an open market purchase of Treasury securities by the Federal Reserve would cause the equilibrium interest rate to _____.

   A. increase

   B. decrease

   C. not change

   D. increase if the economy is in a recession

4. The Fed can increase the federal funds rate by _____.

   A. selling Treasury bills, which increases bank reserves

   B. buying Treasury bills, which increases bank reserves

   C. selling Treasury bills, which decreases bank reserves

   D. buying Treasury bills, which decreases bank reserves

5. The Fed's two main monetary policy targets are _____.

A. the money supply and the inflation rate

B. the money supply and the interest rate

C. the interest rate and real GDP

D. the inflation rate and real GDP

6. A decrease in interest rates can _____ the demand for stocks as stocks become relatively _____ attractive investments as compared to bonds.

A. increase; more

B. decrease; less

C. decrease; more

D. increase; less

III. Short Answer

1. If one central bank is going to take active stabilization policies, how will they change the money supply for the following events?

i) A wave of optimism boosts business investment and household consumption.

ii) Government increases taxes and reduces expenditures to balance the budget.

iii) Price of crude oil is raised.

iv) Foreigners reduce their expenditure for our automobiles.

v) The stock market falls.

2. If central bank took active stabilization policies, how would they change the interest rates to the same events listed in 1?

i) A wave of optimism boosts business investment and household consumption.

ii) Government increases taxes and reduces expenditures to balance the budget.

ii) Price of crude oil is raised.

iv) Foreigners reduce their expenditure for our automobiles.

v) The stock market falls.

vi) Explain the relationship between the policy of money supply and interest rate.

3. Today, interest rate is increased by a quarter of a percent to cope with future inflation according to News Report. Economists argue, "CPI has not increased, but the central bank is restricting economy growth, supposedly to fight inflation…"

i) What interest rate did the central bank increase?

ii) Explain the central bank's policy from the money supply.

ⅲ) Why might the central bank increase interest rates before CPI rising?

Answers to Problems and Applications

Ⅰ. True or False

1	2	3	4	5	6	7	8
F	F	T	F	F	T	F	F

Ⅱ. Choice

1	2	3	4	5	6
A	D	B	C	B	A

Ⅲ. Short Answer

1. Answer:

ⅰ) Decrease the money supply.

ⅱ) Increase the money supply.

ⅲ) Increase the money supply.

ⅳ) Increase the money supply.

ⅴ) Increase the money supply.

2. Answer:

ⅰ) Increase interest rates.

ⅱ) Decrease interest rates.

ⅲ) Decrease interest rates.

ⅳ) Decrease interest rates.

ⅴ) Decrease interest rates.

ⅵ) In the short run, with prices sticky or fixed, an increase in the money supply implies a reduction in interest rates and a decrease in the money supply implies an increase in interest rates.

3. Answer:

ⅰ) Funds rate.

ⅱ) Money supply is decreased (or lowered its growth rate).

ⅲ) Because there exists a lag for monetary policy functioning on the economy. If the central bank has no action until inflation has arrived, the impact of the policy may come too late. So, the central bank just wishes to respond to relative forecast of inflation.

10 Fiscal Policy

Learning Objective

By the end of this chapter, students should understand:
- definition of fiscal policy.
- how fiscal policy Influences aggregate demand.
- changes in Government Purchases.
- the Multiplier Effect.
- the Crowding-Out Effect.
- how the government can use fiscal policy to stabilize the economy.
- definitions of budget deficit, budget surplus and government debt.
- how the federal budget can serve as an automatic stabilizer.

Key Points and Exercises

10.1 What is fiscal policy?

Fiscal policy refers to the government's choices of the levels of government purchases and taxes that are intended to achieve macroeconomic policy goals.

- Some government changes on tax and spending, which are aimed at affecting national economy are not fiscal policy, such as environmental policy action, homeland security policy.

- Government revenues come from taxes on individual employment, corporate profits, excise taxes and so on. Government expenditure includes government purchases and transfer payment. Transfer payment refer to social security, medicare, unemployment insurance and so on. Government purchases usually consist of defense spending, public facilities maintenance, funding scientific research and etc.

· Automatic stabilizers mean that government spending and taxes changes automatically along with the business cycle. These kinds of changes in spending or taxes do not need any government actions, such as government pays for unemployment insurance decreasing during an expansion.

10. 2　The effects of fiscal policy on aggregate demand

Fiscal Policy is used by the government to stabilize the economy. For example, government can increase purchases or decrease taxes to raise aggregate demand in recession period, or decrease purchases or increase taxes to slow the growth of aggregate demand during inflation period.

10.2.1　Expansionary fiscal policy

Expansionary fiscal policies include increasing government purchases or decreasing taxes. An increase in government purchases will directly increase aggregate demand. Cutting taxes indirectly increases aggregate demand by increasing disposable income, and hence consumption spending. Decreasing taxes on business income can raise aggregate demand by enhancing business investment. Expansionary Fiscal Policy shifts AD curve to the right, from AD_1 to AD_2, increasing the price level and real GDP, and to restore long-run equilibrium, as shown in Figure 10-1.

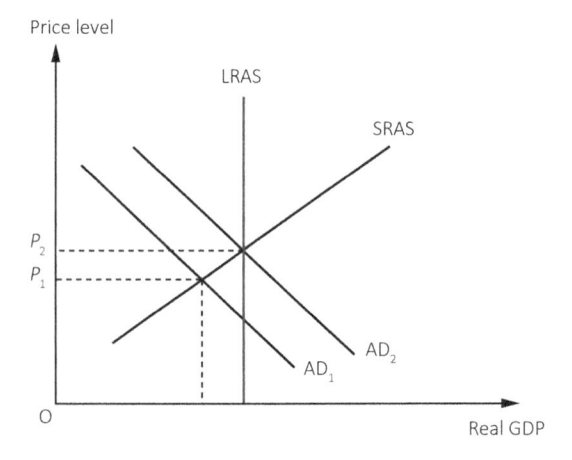

Figure 10-1

10.2.2 Contractionary fiscal policy

Contractionary fiscal policies include decreasing government purchases or increasing taxes. Contractionary fiscal policy is used to reduce aggregate demand in inflation period. Contractionary fiscal policy moves AD curve to the left, from AD_1 to AD_2, decreasing the price level and real GDP, as shown in Figure 10-2.

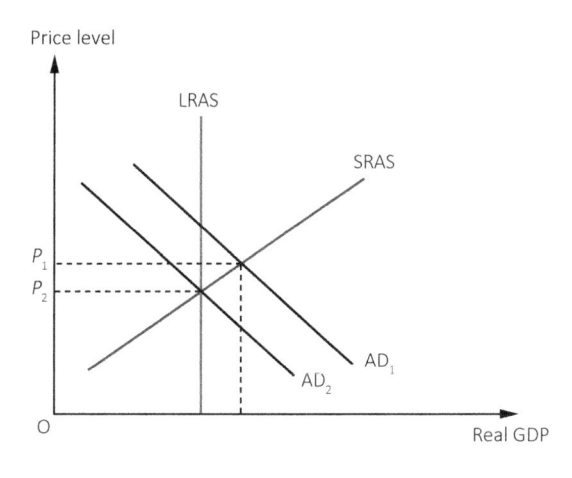

Figure 10-2

Keep in mind that:

· The above analysis is based on an assumption that everything else including monetary policy, is unchanged.

· Contractionary fiscal policy is not really leading a fall in prices. It causes inflation to be lower than it would have been.

10.3 Multiplier effect

10.3.1 The definition of multiplier effect

When the government decides to increase government purchase to increase aggregate demand such as spending ￥10 billion on infrastructure. The initial ￥10 billion in AD will lead to additional increase in income and spending on consumer goods, which will raise people's incomes in relative industry, and raise their spending and so on for many rounds. So aggregate demand will be increased much more than the ￥10 billion increase in government purchases. This is the multiplier effect on aggregate demand of government purchases. The initial ￥10 billion increase in government purchases is autonomous. The following increases in consumption spending from the initial ￥10 billion increase in autonomous expenditures are induced.

The multiplier effect is the series of induced increases in consumption spending that results from an initial increase in autonomous expenditures. Changes in equilibrium real GDP divided by Changes in government purchases is the government purchases multiplier. Therefore, the AD curve shifts by more than the change in government purchases.

$$\text{Government purchases multiplier} = \frac{\text{Changes in equilibrium real GDP}}{\text{Changes in government purchases}}$$

$$\text{Taxes multiplier} = \frac{\text{Changes in equilibrium real GDP}}{\text{Changes in taxes}}$$

The tax multiplier is negative number because changes in taxes and changes in real GDP move in opposite directions.

10.3.2 A Formula for the spending multiplier

From previous chapters, we have learnt that marginal propensity to consume (MPC), and it is the fraction of extra income that a household consumes rather than saves.

We assume that the government uses fiscal policy to control macroeconomy and spends ¥10 more billion on infrastructure. MPC is 3/4.

So, for the first round, incomes will increase by ¥10 more billion and consumption will increase by $MPC \times$ ¥10 billion. The second round, consumption will increase by $MPC \times (MPC \times$ ¥10 billion$) = MPC^2 \times$ ¥10 billion. In order to get the total increase of the consumption, we add up all of these data from each round. We get,

Changes in government purchases = ¥10 billion.

First change in consumption = $MPC \times$ ¥10 billion.

Second change in consumption = $MPC^2 \times$ ¥10 billion.

Third change in consumption = $MPC^3 \times$ ¥10 billion.

$\vdots$

Total Change in consumption = $(1 + MPC + MPC^2 + MPC^3 + \cdots) \times$ ¥10 billion.

We can find that $(1 + MPC + MPC^2 + MPC^3 + \cdots)$ is the multiplier. It is an infinite geometric series. It can be written as follows.

Here,

$$\text{Multiplier} = \frac{1}{1 - MPC}$$

In this case,

$$\text{Multiplier} = \frac{1}{1-3/4} = 4.$$

Total change in expenditure = Multiplier × ¥10 billion = 4 × ¥10 billion = ¥40 billion, which means that ¥1 of government purchases increase aggregate demand by a total of ¥4.

Besides government purchases, the multiplier logic can be applied to other changes in spending such as consumption, investment, and net exports.

10.3.3 The multipliers work in both directions

Increasing government purchases and cutting taxes have a positive multiplier effect on equilibrium real GDP. Reducing government purchases and raising taxes also have a multiplier effect on equilibrium real GDP, but the effect is negative.

10.4 Crowding out effect

Government purchases increase can raise aggregate demand, but this causes another problem. A temporary increase in government purchases will cause the need for money (raise incomes, which shifts the demand for money to the right), and so the interest rate (r) will rise, too. The higher interest rate enhances the borrowing cost and the return to saving. This prevents households from spending their incomes in new consumption or investing in new housing. Firms will also reduce investment, and not to purchase new production line or build new factories. As the interest rate gets higher, consumption, investment, and net exports will fall, as Figure 10-3 shows.

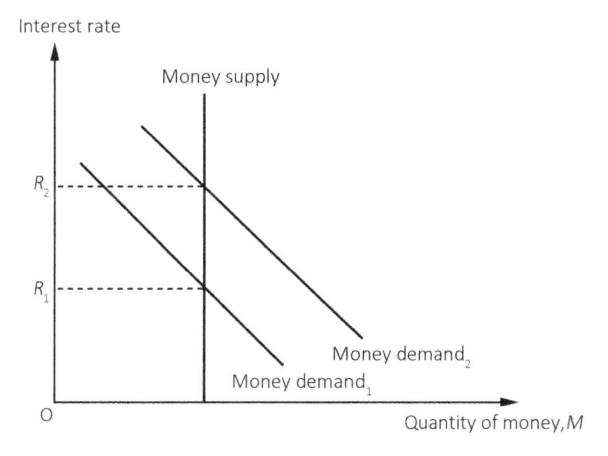

Figure 10-3

So, increasing government purchases will increase interest rates and reduce, or crowd out private investment. This fall in consumption and investment will pull aggregate demand back toward the left. Because of crowding out, the increase of AD may be less than the increase in government purchases.

Crowding out is a decline in private expenditures as a result of an increase in government purchases. It is the offset in aggregate demand that results when expansionary fiscal policy raises the interest rate and thereby reduces investment spending, as Figure 10-4 shows.

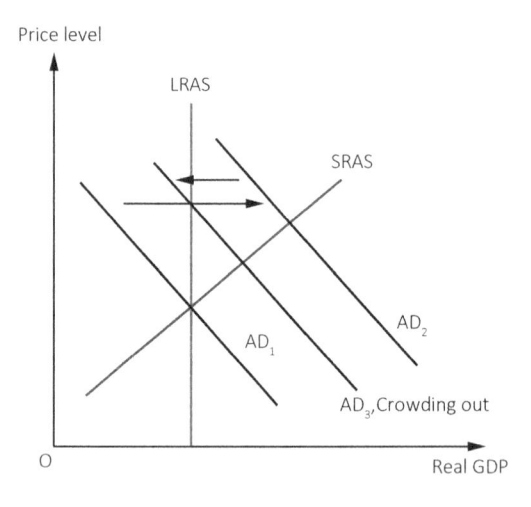

Figure 10-4

Expansionary fiscal policy causes AD_1 shift to AD_2. Because of crowding out, there is a decrease in AD. Actually, AD shift to AD_3.

Thus, when the government increases its purchases by ¥X, the aggregate demand for goods and services may increase by more or less than ¥X, depending on whether the multiplier effect or the crowding-out effect is larger.

If the multiplier effect is greater than the crowding-out effect, aggregate demand will increase by more than ¥X.

If the crowding-out effect is greater than the multiplier effect, aggregate demand will rise by less than ¥X.

· In the short run, with the higher interest rate, consumption, investment, and net exports all fall. The initial increase in spending is partially offset by the crowding out or an increase in government spending results in partial crowding out.

· In the long run, the increase in government purchases will have no impact on real GDP, and the reduction in consumption, investment, and net exports will offset the increase in government purchases totally and AD remains unchanged because the economy returns to potential GDP, even without the government's intervention. But keep in mind that it could be many years in the long run, so the intermediate increase in real GDP may be worth it.

· How large are the multipliers for government purchases and for taxes?

This question is very difficult to answer, and different economists produce different estimates. Several factors can cause the AD curve to shift, leading to a change in equilibrium real GDP. To isolate the effect of a change in government purchases on the equilibrium is very difficult. It also indicates the difficulty that economists have a consistent estimate of the effects of fiscal policy.

10.5 Budget deficits and budget surpluses

To control or stabilize the overall economy, it is useful to control budget surplus or budget deficit.

· A budget deficit is the situation in which the government's expenditures are greater than its tax revenue.

· A budget surplus is the situation in which the government's expenditures are less than its tax revenue.

Many economists believe it is good the government has a balanced budget when real GDP is at potential GDP. Few economists believe that the government should try to balance its budget every year.

During recessions, as government spending increases and tax revenues fall, the budget deficit increases. If the government wants to bring the budget to balance, it would increase tax revenues or decrease the government spending, which would reduce AD, thereby making the recession worse.

Similarly, during expansions, as tax revenues raise and government spending decrease, the budget surplus increases. If the government tries to bring budget back to balance, the government would increase government spending or reduce taxes. These actions would shift the AD curve to the right, thereby pushing GDP further beyond potential GDP and the price higher.

10.5.1 Government budget serve as automatic stabilizer

Deficits occur automatically during recession without any action by government.

· Tax system is a very important automatic stabilizer. When the economy moves into a recession, incomes and profits fall. Thus, both personal income tax and corporate income tax fall. This implies government's tax revenue falls accordingly. But this may stimulate aggregate demand.

· Government spending is also an automatic stabilizer. The government increases its transfer payments automatically when the economy falls into recession. Because More individuals are eligible for transfer payments in this period. These transfer payments provide additional income to them to reduce the stress and pain in the recession period, and may stimulate spending. During expansions, budget deficits decrease automatically. Just as the tax system, transfer payments help to reduce the size of short-run economic fluctuations.

Both automatic budget surpluses and deficits can help to stabilize the economy.

10.5.2 The government debt

When the government runs a budget deficit, the relative department need to borrow from investors by selling Treasury securities. When the government is in a surplus, the relative department will pay off some existing bonds. It is common for countries to have sizable government debt. A more meaningful measure of the government debt relates it to an economy's GDP. Figure 10-5 shows the yearly relative sizes of China government debt. In 2019, the percentage was 52.6%.

In 2015, the government debt as a percentage of real GDP in China is 41.5%. This number is neither high nor low relative to such debt percentage in other countries of G20 as Figure 10-6 shows.

10.5.3 Is government debt a problem?

· The central government is in no danger of defaulting on its debt. Governments can raise the funds needed by taxing households and firms to pay interest on its debt. But if debt is very large, the government may have to increase taxes greatly or decrease spending to get interest on the debt. You may wonder if a large public debt might bankrupt a nation or at least place a tremendous burden on younger generation. Fortunately, the answer is no. For most advanced economies, a large public debt does not threaten to bankrupt the national government, leave it unable to meet its financial obligations.

(% of GDP)

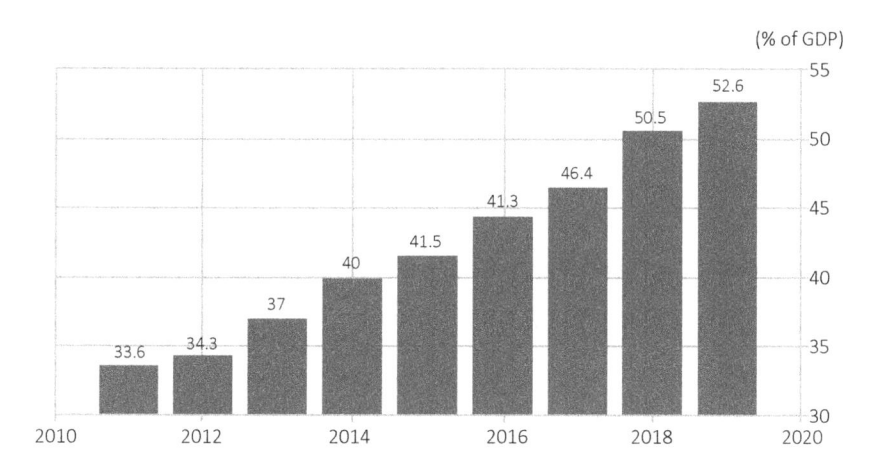

Bar chart showing values by year:
- 2011: 33.6
- 2012: 34.3
- 2013: 37
- 2014: 40
- 2015: 41.5
- 2016: 41.3
- 2017: 46.4
- 2018: 50.5
- 2019: 52.6

Source: Trading Economics.com | IMF.

Figure 10-5

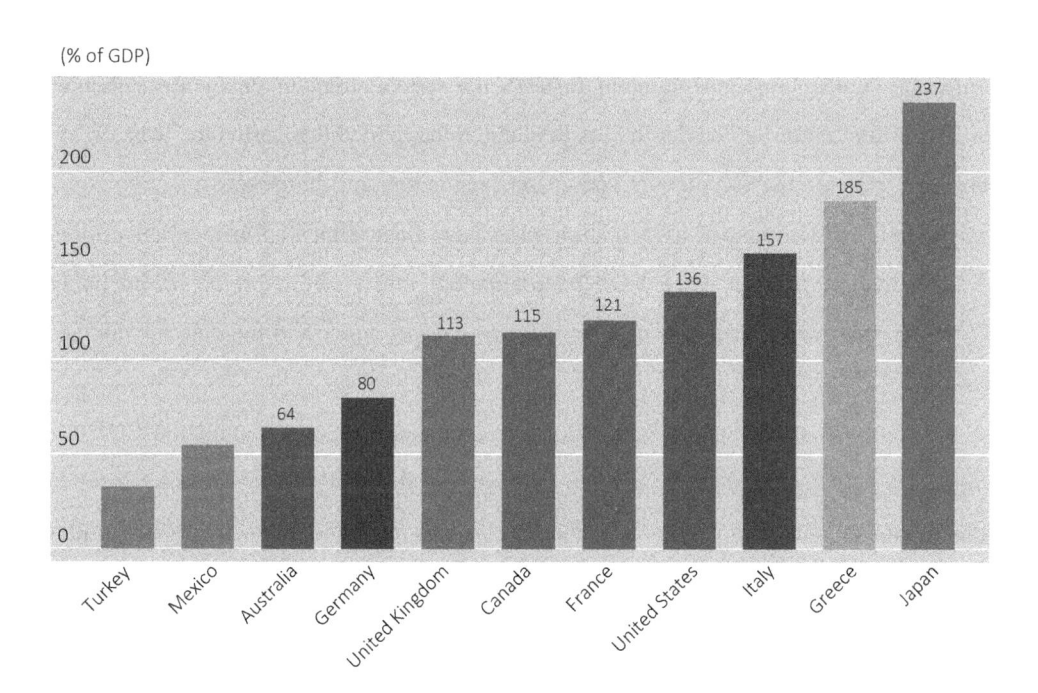

(% of GDP)

Bar chart by country:
- Turkey
- Mexico
- Australia: 64
- Germany: 80
- United Kingdom: 113
- Canada: 115
- France: 121
- United States: 136
- Italy: 157
- Greece: 185
- Japan: 237

Source: Organization for Economic Cooperation and Development, OECD.

Figure 10-6

· However, in the long run, a debt increasing in size relative to GDP may cause crowding out of investment spending if an increasing debt drives up interest rates.

Case Study

Fiscal Fund Transfers Stimulate Economy

China has nearly completed the special transfer payment of 2 trillion yuan ($ 289.72 billion) to local governments to support the economy, Vice-Finance Minister Xu Hongcai said on Aug 26.

It took less than a month from making the policies to implementing the fiscal fund transactions, said Xu. He called the special transfer payment mechanism, a channel that was established this year to directly transfer funds from the central government to the grassroots units, as "a great achievement" of fiscal system reform and innovation.

The central government said in May that funds would be made available to the prefecture-and county-level governments, through the special transfer payment mechanism, as a part of the nation's fiscal stimulus package to support the government's basic operations and mitigate the COVID-19 impact on businesses and households.

Of the 2 trillion yuan, 1.675 trillion yuan have been allocated to local governments and 1.45 trillion yuan of these have been injected into specific projects. The balance 300 billion yuan will be used to support the government's tax and fee cuts for this year, Xu said.

The purpose of the special fund transfer mechanism, designed amid the COVID-19 outbreak, is to ensure that the funds can be transferred directly to the primary-level governments and injected into projects immediately, and not allow provincial-level authorities to retain any money for their own use, said analysts.

The fund allocation process has been faster than scheduled and more efficient than the other fund transfers between the central and local governments. This has guaranteed the use of the funds and boosted investment, consumption and exports, said Xu.

A part of the funds was used for long-term COVID-19 epidemic prevention and control measures and for construction of public health systems, according to officials from the finance ministry. Wuhan in Hubei province, a hard-hit city, has set aside 4.73 billion yuan to support the reconstruction of hospitals in 11 central urban areas and for beefing up the city's primary medical and health service system.

Nearly 50 percent of the so-called "direct funds" was raised through bonds for COVID-19 control. The 1 trillion-yuan quota for the purpose was completed by the end of last month, and the finance ministry has asked local governments to complete their annual quota for local government special bond issuances by the end of October.

The average issuance interest rate of the COVID-19 treasuries was 2.77 percent, 10 basis points lower than the average yields of general treasuries trading in the secondary market, the ministry said.

"The funds raised by the special treasuries have been sent to the local governments in advance, and the local governments are injecting the funds into specific projects, helping boost the real fiscal expenditure," said Wang Xiaolong, head of the national treasury department at the Ministry of Finance.

"The ministry will further strengthen the management of issuing general treasuries and local government bonds, to smoothly complete the government bond issuance task throughout the year," said Wang.

To ensure that all the funds can be used effectively, the ministry recently clarified that local governments can transfer some of the "direct funds", which cannot be spent this year, to other qualified projects, said Li Jinghui, head of the budget department at the Ministry of Finance.

The central government has reiterated that fiscal funds should be used to ensure focus remains on the "six priorities" of employment, people's livelihoods, development of market entities, food and energy security, stable operation of industrial and supply chains, and smooth functioning at the community level, and to ensure stability in the six areas of employment, finance, foreign trade, foreign investment, domestic investment and market expectations.

Source: http://english.www.gov.cn/news/pressbriefings/202008/27/content_WS5f46eab5c6d0f72 57693b1d9.html.

Terms and Concepts

· **Fiscal policy**: The government's choices of the levels of government purchases and taxes that are intended to achieve macroeconomic policy goals.

· **Automatic stabilizers**: Government spending and taxes changes automatically along with the business cycle.

· **Budget deficit**: The situation in which the government's expenditures are greater than its tax revenue.

· **Budget surplus**: The situation in which the government's expenditures are less than its tax revenue.

· **Crowding out**: A decline in private expenditures as a result of an increase in government purchases.

· **Multiplier effect**: The series of induced increases in consumption spending that results from an initial increase in autonomous expenditures.

Problems and Applications

Ⅰ. True or False

1. A decrease in the marginal income tax rate is a fiscal policy which will increase aggregate demand.

2. An increase in the money supply is a discretionary fiscal policy which will increase aggregate demand.

3. Expansionary fiscal policy involves increasing government purchases or increasing taxes.

4. Contractionary fiscal policy is used to decrease aggregate demand in an attempt to fight rising inflation.

5. An appropriate fiscal policy response when aggregate demand is growing at a slower rate than aggregate supply is to cut taxes.

6. The multiplier effect following an increase in expenditure is generated by induced increases in consumption expenditure as income rises.

Ⅱ. Choice

1. Which of the following would be classified as fiscal policy? _____.

A. The federal government passes tax cuts to encourage firms to reduce air pollution

B. The Federal Reserve cuts interest rates to stimulate the economy

C. States increase taxes to fund education

D. The federal government cuts taxes to stimulate the economy

2. The increase in the amount that the government collects in taxes when the economy expands and the decrease in the amount that the government collects in taxes when the economy goes into a recession is an example of _____.

A. automatic stabilizers

B. discretionary fiscal policy

C. discretionary monetary policy

D. automatic monetary policy

3. Fiscal policy is defined as changes in federal _____ and _____ to achieve macroeconomic objectives such as price stability, high rates of economic growth, and high employment.

A. taxes; interest rates

B. taxes; the money supply

C. interest rates; money supply

D. taxes; expenditures

4. An increase in government purchases will increase aggregate demand because _____.

A. government expenditures are a component of aggregate demand

B. consumption expenditures are a component of aggregate demand

C. the decline in the price level will increase demand

D. the decline in the interest rate will increase demand

5. Using the static AD-AS model in Figure 10-7, an increase in taxes would be depicted as a movement from _____.

A. E to B

B. B to C

C. A to B

D. B to A

6. Suppose the economy is in a recession and expansionary fiscal policy is pursued. Using the static AD-AS model in Figure 10-7, this would be depicted as a movement from _____.

A. A to B

B. B to C

Price level

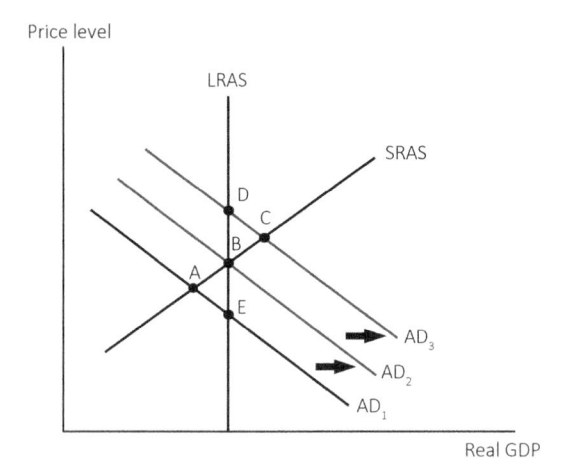

Figure 10-7

C. C to B

D. B to A

7. Suppose the economy is in short-run equilibrium below potential GDP and Congress and the president lower taxes to move the economy back to long-run equilibrium. Using the static AD-AS model in Figure 10-7, this would be depicted as a movement from _____.

A. A to B

B. B to C

C. C to B

D. B to A

8. Suppose the economy is in short-run equilibrium below potential GDP and no fiscal or monetary policy is pursued. Using the static AD-AS model in Figure 10-7, this would be depicted as a movement from _____.

A. A to B

B. A to E

C. C to B

D. B to A

III. Short Answer

1. If policymakers want to use fiscal policy to stabilize the economy, how should they change government spending and taxes?

i) A wave of pessimism reduces business investment and household consumption.

ii) Expectation of price increase causes people to demand higher wages.

iii) Foreigners increase their consumption for domestically produced Volkswagen automobiles.

2. Suppose the economy is in a recession. Governments estimate that aggregate demand is ¥10 billion below the amount necessary for the long-run natural rate of output. That is, if AD curve can shift to the right by ¥10 billion, the economy would be in long-run equilibrium.

i) If government need to use fiscal policy to actively stabilize the economy, how much should the government increase his spending? (MPC is 0.75 and suppose there is no crowding out.)

ii) If government need to use fiscal policy to actively stabilize the economy, how much should the government increase his spending? (MPC is 0.8 and suppose there is no crowding out.)

iii) If there is crowding out, will the government need to spend more or less than the amounts you found in a and b above? What are the reasons?

iv) If investment is sensitive to changes in the interest rate greatly, is crowding out more of a problem or less of a problem? What are the reasons?

v) If governments discover that fiscal policy lags behind by about 2.5 years, should this make governments more likely to use fiscal policy as a stabilization tool or more likely to allow the economy to adjust on its own? What are the reasons?

Answers to Problems and Applications

I. True or False

1	2	3	4	5	6
T	F	F	T	T	T

II. Choice

1	2	3	4	5	6	7	8
D	A	D	A	D	A	A	B

III. Short Answer

1. Answer:

i) Increase spending, decrease taxes.

ii) Increase spending, decrease taxes.

iii) Decrease spending, increase taxes.

2. Answer:

i) Multiplier $= 1/(1-0.75) = 4$;

$10/4 = $ ¥2.5 billion.

ii) Multiplier $= 1/(1-0.80) = 5$;

$10/5 = $ ¥2 billion.

iii) More.

Crowding out is a decline in private expenditures as a result of an increase in government purchases. As the government spends more, households and investors spend less so aggregate demand won't increase by as much as the multiplier suggests.

iv) More of a problem.

Government spending will raise interest rates. The more sensitive investment is to the interest rate, the more it is reduced or crowded out by government spending.

v) More likely to allow the economy to adjust on its own.

Because fiscal policy may function after 2.5 years. It is a little bit longer. If the economy adjusts on its own before fiscal policy woks, the fiscal policy may be destabilizing.